Michael
All the best
Julie Hill
November 2003

A Promise
to Keep

A Promise
to Keep

From Athens to Afghanistan

ARTHUR & JULIE HILL

To order additional copies of this book, contact:
Xlibris Corporation
1-888-795-4274
www.Xlibris.com
Orders@Xlibris.com
19169

Contents

THE TRAVEL DIARIES
OF
ARTHUR HILL

Foreword

by Jaime C. Laya

Globalization was a reality in the lives of Arthur and Julie Hill long before it became a household word. Their life together was a fusion of cultures — Greek and Australian. Work took them to faraway places with names that began to enter international consciousness (each time with a bang, too) only decades later — Afghanistan, Iraq, even the Philippines. They had "been there, done that," at times that many can only look back to with nostalgia. Their network of friends crossed countries and cultures, linked more tightly than ever before with e-mail.

The Hills were in the Philippines beginning in the late 1960s, before the Marcos martial law regime. He was with the Ford Foundation and I was on the University of Philippines business faculty. Responsibilities brought us together, but the vibes were right and we all became friends — Arthur and Julie, my late wife Alice and I. We were all young (and slim), had many interests in common and many of life's adventures were yet to come. We got together often. We took trips together, first in and around Manila, then farther afield, most memorably to the old towns and churches of the Philippines' north, and the relaxed coconut plantations and folk celebrations south of Manila. I introduced them to my artist friends and to my favorite (and secret) antiques sources. When our son Juan Claudio was born, Arthur agreed to be godfather.

Visitors see more of a country than do residents and the Hills were no exception. They were frequently in Mindanao, terra incognita to me, and their adventures (many in places that have long since been on lists of "places to avoid") were sources of unending fascination and amusement. On one small island, Arthur related once, there was only one road and only two jeepneys (passenger vehicle used by humans and cargo, both flora and fauna). One day, there was a big accident . . .

I remained homebound in the Philippines and went on to a career in academe, government, management consulting, and the accounting profession. The Hills went on to lead expatriate lives — Arthur to the international civil and diplomatic service and ultimately, both Arthur and Julie to multinational corporate careers. Our paths crossed from time to time, more frequently when Julie the expat executive would visit Manila as part of her work.

Julie's book, including the parts that Arthur wrote, relives not only sights and sounds of long ago, not only vanished lifestyles, but also the life of an expatriate executive, of whom there are more and more with the liberalization of trade and investments. The engrossing story that Julie and Arthur tell is of the personal and professional adjustments of expatriate life— of arriving in a new country and a new organization, of coping with fresh challenges and with different cultures and lifestyles. And when the peripatetic life ends, of at last laying down roots and adjusting yet again to new challenges, all the more confidently for the rich life and experience in many lands and among many peoples.

Jaime C. Laya is Chairman, KPMG/Laya Mananghaya & Co., certified public accountants and management consultants. He was Minister of the Budget, Minister of Education, Culture and Sports,

Chairman of the Monetary Board and Governor of the Central Bank of the Philippines, and Dean of the College of Business Administration of the University of the Philippines.

Acknowledgement

I never thought I would be writing a book, especially one dealing with my life.

Jose Dalisay has helped me create A Promise to Keep. Of his many contributions, polishing my English was only the most obvious. Through our collaboration, he forced me into a greater clarification of both the stories and my thoughts. I felt safe under his masterly pen, meticulous scrutiny, and his sound judgment.

The enthusiastic interest of my friends has been a perpetual source of encouragement. To all of them I am most grateful. I have received particular help from Maria Faur, Beverly Kimball, Kati Suominen and Kathy Waller.

Much of the book is the story of my husband. I hope I have done him justice.

Introduction

What am I doing? Roving around the house, staring with puzzlement at a fragile-looking bowl, touching and feeling the patina of an old silver candlestick, tangible objects collected through the years of our overseas assignments.

Every object has a tale, reflecting an event in our lives: the search for a rare coin in Afghanistan; the bargaining for a carpet in the bazaar of Kabul; the acquisition in Thailand of a Buddha head from Cambodia; a *tapa* cloth with a stunning geometric design, the gift of a Samoan chief; a Turkoman necklace bartered with nomads for a couple of gold coins; the discovery of a *santo* under cobwebs in an antique shop in Manila; a stunning impressionistic painting from a Filipino artist commissioned over 30 years ago.

Inanimate objects — do they have a soul that clings to our own through the force of love?

For whatever reason it has become more important than ever to set down their story, which we have been carrying around for so long. I see now that it is not their story but Arthur's and mine as well.

I met Arthur when we were both graduate students at the University of Minnesota. Arthur was from Perth, Western Australia. At first approach he was so formal, but what a wonderful grin he had! On getting to know him, the formality gave way to warmth, and he displayed his intellect — always used constructively — with a keen sense of humor.

I was an Alexandrian Greek full of vitality and passion, with echoes of Greek tragedy still reverberating in me. We fell in love, two young people from such diverse backgrounds, foreign students still in school, getting together, making our wedding vows on that great American holiday, the 4th of July. It was the year Hawaii entered the Union. I was certain that the fireworks display was intended for us.

After graduation, we returned to Australia, where Arthur had to fulfill his Fulbright requirements. We were fortunate to get the chance to travel around the world on the way to our new home. It was our first glimpse of Europe; we were able to visit my parents still stranded in Egypt, to explore the Indian subcontinent, and to encounter Southeast Asia. We were captivated by Bangkok, an exotic city, a helter-skelter of palaces, temples, and bazaars, interwoven with rivers and canals, the Thai capital of 40 years ago. Arthur vowed to return, to find a job there, and to make it our home.

A few years later, he achieved his ambition. He called me from New York to say that he was being sent to Bangkok to advise Thailand's Ministry of Education under the sponsorship of the Ford Foundation. You cannot imagine how delighted I was when I learned we would be able to live in Asia. My career was set aside and I never regretted it. For Arthur it was a gamble to be leaving a tenured position for a contract assignment in Thailand. We shared an enigmatic desire that could only be quenched with travels. I accepted the move, the challenge, the opportunity with alacrity; and an adventurous life began.

A couple of years later, the Foundation sent us to the Philippines, this time in a representational capacity. The country was so Western, surprisingly sophisticated, and at the same time easygoing. Manila was alive and vibrant. The Philippine economy was expanding at that time, a shining example among its neighbors with a revolution in rice cultivation, rising middle class, a burgeoning cultural consciousness, and a growing market for art. We met wonderful Filipino families. Lifelong friendships were formed around similar interests — old churches, old towns, paintings, antiques, and, of course, travel.

After nearly five years, it was time to move again. We both must have inherited a maverick gene that endowed us with a yearning to explore beyond the horizon.

The United Nations Development Program, Arthur's new employer, brought us to Western Samoa in the South Pacific — a new territory to discover, new rules to live by, new customs to learn, new sensibilities to absorb. We immersed ourselves in the history of the Pacific islands, in Margaret Mead's anthropological treatises; we learned the legends of the Polynesian people. Although a tropical paradise in the South Seas, Western Samoa was very isolated, and it proved to be a difficult assignment.

But it did not take long before we were on the move again, this time to land-locked Afghanistan, a harsh and beautiful country, a crossroads of the ages. We found new parameters in the diplomatic life; we traveled in search of a special kind of adventure, so rare in contemporary travel — to slip away for a few days from the protection of Western culture and assume the lifestyle and customs, the fears and hopes, of Afghans. It was an engaging experience, the most memorable trip of our lifetime.

The Russian invasion was imminent. It was time to put down roots, and we returned to America. It was a new adjustment, a new set of careers, this time with the corporate world. Arthur joined the Business Development team at AT&T's World Headquarters. I was hired by what a few years later became Lucent Technologies, a giant telecom manufacturer at that time.

New York, only 20 miles from home, provided us with the excitement that only this great metropolis could offer. We loved the theater, the opera, the restaurants. There were baseball games to attend, fishing expeditions off Long Island, memorable 4th of July celebrations. But our hearts remained in Asia. Our positions brought us back countless of times, to the great corporations of Japan, to burgeoning China, to the manufacturing entities of Korea and Taiwan. Our overseas experiences stood us in good stead. We made countless presentations, negotiated many deals and partnerships, and uncovered opportunities, but mostly we created jobs. We continued to vacation in Asia, and whenever we had the opportunity we visited our friends in the Philippines. Paths and careers had diverged but not the friendships developed during our stay. Nothing in the world had taken their place.

Suddenly, the years had gone by. It was time to retire. Not that it had not been expected; there was even an element of anticipation but never of dreariness. We did not draw back in retirement; we moved to the balmy climate of Southern California. We resumed the road to life at a different pace. There was the *New York Times* puzzle to complete every day. We continued to travel, making a nostalgic return to Thailand's almost-lost paradise, to the golden land of Myanmar, to the ravaged land of Cambodia. We followed Marco Polo's footsteps across the Taklamakan desert in China, and we were awed by the changes that had taken place over the years. We were inspired by the spiritual devotion of the Tibetan people. Arthur had time now to write a journal of his travels and distribute it to our friends.

He reveled in telling his stories, his anecdotes, his encounters not only with the rich and famous but also with ordinary people who crossed our lives. He wanted to write his memoirs. He started many times, sketched a chapter or two, and penned a few bullet points — but when he got serious, it was too late. Could you go through with these memoirs, he asked me, sounding skeptical and distant. I promised I would do it, but it took me a few months. We had not kept a log or a diary when we lived overseas. I found scrapbooks, photographs, clippings, carbon copies of letters written years ago, papers on development that lingered in some forgotten file, papers so dated, reflecting the thinking and action of the time — achievements so mundane today but applauded for their success at that time.

I was starting to become a writer. Now I needed someone to help me to pull the stories together, to weave them, to smooth out the prose. I found it again among friends in the Philippines. What evolved is an enumeration, a list of events, a selected collection of memories, an accumulation of images, dots of colors in an impressionistic painting. The picture shifts and changes much as life does, fleeting revelations as when the sunlight shines through the fog.

And so this is our story, and the first voice you will hear is Arthur's, in the brief opening chapter, after which — like Arthur — you will have to trust me with the telling.

Marriage and Minnesota

(by Arthur Hill)

I begin with my marriage; what came before is prelude. It was on July 4th, 1959. Julie, my bride, was Greek — but no ordinary Greek. She was in flight from Alexandria, Egypt, that great Hellenic city at the eastern end of the Mediterranean, now that President Nasser had essentially decreed that all half a million foreigners, 60 percent of them Greek, could no longer stay. So, in 1956, she came to America to pursue graduate studies in chemistry at the University of Minnesota, having refused an offer at MIT in favor of the chance to work with a Nobel Prize winner.

Alexandria was a highly cosmopolitan, polyglot city and its citizens generally reflected this ethos. Julie spoke Greek, French, Italian, Arabic, and English in about that order of proficiency. She was educated from kindergarten through high school by native French teachers in the local Lycée Français, and topped the country in her baccalaureate exam. In other words, she was brilliant — and I was smart enough to know what a prize I had captured. Myself, I was an Australian graduate student, working as fast as I could toward a PhD.

As an Australian, I had been raised in a stiff-upper-lip environment, learning never to express emotions or to wear my heart on my sleeve. Julie, by contrast, was a well of emotions, and happily I quickly learned to adapt to her ways, which became the source of so much happiness throughout our lives together.

We were married in the Twin Cities literally, at an Episcopal ceremony in Minneapolis, followed by a Greek Orthodox blessing in St. Paul that same afternoon. It was exhausting, but oh so worthwhile. Julie's wonderful American host family, John and Louise Diracles, generously gave a reception for our 14 guests, including only one relative, her brother. They told us they would serve punch at the reception, and knowing the strong ingredients they used in their punch, we asked them to prepare a bowl of punch without alcohol for our Muslim and Hindu friends. No one touched the non-alcoholic punch!

We spent another uneventful year and a half in Minnesota while I completed my degree. By then Julie was working as part of a University Medical School research team on new techniques for open-heart surgery. As both of us came from temperate climates, snow was a new experience. Glued to a window, it was magic to see the flakes coming down. With others foreign students, we found ourselves invited to many rural communities of Minnesota and became unofficial ambassadors of our countries. The YMCA or the Minneapolis Rotary Club sponsored those outings. There was always bewilderment with Julie. Did she represent Greece or Egypt? She had two miniature flags on her lapel. Diplomatically she represented both.

We have many happy memories of our first year-and-a-half together, but it is our honeymoon that stands out. One of my graduate student friends lent me his fiancée's 1956 Chevrolet, as there was little chance that my own 1949 Chevy had the stamina for a trip to the Black Hills of South Dakota, which was our destination. On our first day out, we found that our friend had thoughtfully provided a bottle of retsina, the Greek resinated wine, for our nourishment. Its taste was new to me, but I discovered that I could down a glassful if it was mixed with Coca-Cola. Along the way across western Minnesota and eastern South Dakota, we laughed at the Burma Shave signs and looked forward to visiting the widely advertised Wall Drug Store, where coffee for honeymooners was free. It was huge and memorable in a tiny town in the prairie.

The interstate was not yet built; everyone drove the odd two-lane roads. Burma shaves were posted all over the countryside in farmer's fields. There were small red signs with white letters — five signs about 100 feet apart, each containing one line of a four-line couple, and the obligatory fifth sign advertising Burma Shave, a popular shaving cream.

The Black Hills was a worthwhile destination for a couple in love and on a very tight budget. We still remember the quaint little towns and the lovely Sylvan Lake where we rented a cabin, but most of all we remember the grandeur of Mt. Rushmore, which met and exceeded all our expectations. This was our first visit to a National Park, a system that did not exist in Australia. It was another eye-opener to America — a park system to conserve the scenic and historic heritage of the country for the benefit and inspiration of its people.

We returned to Minneapolis with just 89 cents in our pockets, our total worldly fortune. Fortunately there was an assistantship check coming.

In all our married life the only dissonant note came during our honeymoon. Who was taking better pictures? I had an expensive Leica; Julie had a little brownie Kodak. My pictures were sharper, her pictures more artistic. We compromised, and years later she proved to be the winner.

Upon completion of my degree I was offered two teaching jobs in Australia, and chose the University of Melbourne. My Fulbright grant covered my return trip to Australia, and the university was willing to pay our fares. After a little negotiation each institution agreed to pay its share of our return trip via Europe. And so we set off on our great adventure, the first time we would see both Europe and Asia!

A Prelude
to Asian Adventures

T hat trip turned out to be the first of many. We saw the highlights of Europe, visited my parents still stranded in the increasingly Arab city of Alexandria, then traveled on through Asia to visit Arthur's parents in Perth, Western Australia, before taking the final leg to Melbourne. Our most memorable stop was Bangkok, Thailand, then an exotic old Oriental city. Arthur was enchanted and vowed that someday he would return to live and work there — little knowing that it would come true.

Life in Australia was not easy. Arthur's starting annual salary was only $4,600, and we had spent all our savings on our grand tour. But we managed, made good friends, and settled in. Unfortunately, this was a period when most Greeks in Australia were recent migrants, most with little education, and hence at the bottom of the social ladder. For all the wrong reasons, I met with many slurs, and it was not a happy episode. I felt an outsider; I felt I did not belong. Women in Australia were not given opportunities, and salaries for women were 25 percent lower than those for men. It still has not changed.

But there were good times as well. I got a good job with the Commonwealth Scientific and Industrial Research Organization (CSIRO), and we began to save money. Our best friend was a Belgian post-doctoral fellow, Robert de Deurwaerder, whose fiancée Michelle soon joined and married him. A three-month-premature daughter, Dominique, arrived and made up the family. We did so many things together, packing all in our old Volkswagen Beetle; we visited Phillip Island to see the fairy penguins coming in from their day's fishing and waddling up the beach to feed their young. But the most memorable day of that trip by far was the morning that we arrived to pick up our friends at 5:30 a.m. for a long day's outing to the beautiful beaches of Lorne and Apollo Bay. As we drove to our friends' home we heard on the radio that President Kennedy had been assassinated. We were shocked and devastated. All sorts of essentials were forgotten.

Among the trips we took within Australia was a visit to the beautiful Great Barrier Reef, including a cruise among the islands, and a stay for a few days on Orpheus Island. Orpheus was the legendary poet and musician whose enchanting lyre playing had the vitality to charm the gods, mortals, and animals, and to move rivers, earth, and trees. In reality, Orpheus was indeed an enchanted island afloat on the kaleidoscope of the Great Barrier Reef and evidence of the magical works of the legendary lyre player abound. It was a family-owned resort; to reach it we had to charter a seaplane, and its isolation provided the ultimate in tranquility and seclusion. Fish was abundant in the sheltered bays and Arthur catching a red striped bass was a high light. At that time the resort did not have a liquor license, but there was no restriction to buy a whole bottle of whatever liquor one wanted! Everyone was coddling a bottle, entering the resort's dining room.

We visited Cairns up in Northern Queensland, and what we remembered most from that experience was going out on the river behind Cairns and seeing an 18-foot crocodile on the riverbank.

Crossing the Nullabor

Arthur wanted me to feel the immensity of Australia, something air travel alone could not communicate. He suggested, when visiting his parents in Western Australia, to take the train, a three-day journey. Years before, he had driven across the continent on the unpaved dusty road linking the two coasts. We would cover the 4,350 kilometers by train, a transcontinental journey approximating the distance from New York to Los Angeles.

We boarded the train in Melbourne for the 12-hour overnight service to Adelaide; we had to change trains in South Australia. In the '60s every state had a different gauge railway, to protect their state trade and commercial rights and keep the federal government from capturing this lucrative sector. It took years before standard gauge was implemented from east to west and trains could go the whole way.

As the train continued west, the golden sunlight intensified the red soil; we were entering the outback. Just before the Nullabor, we stopped at Cooks, in the middle of nowhere; passengers stepped off, we bought an ice cream, and the train refilled its water tanks. In previous years, before the arrival of diesel trains, aborigines sold their wares at this stop and entertained the passengers; none were to be found now, and the stop over was very short.

Finally we entered the Nullabor plain, a seemingly featureless, dry, and infinite flat region — a desert so different from the Sahara or the Gobi, with no sand dunes, but a dry red earth. It stretches for 1000 kilometers across the base of Australia, and for all that distance the train did not hit a single bend.

I woke Arthur very early the following morning; there was a flock of emus running parallel to the track. I was so excited; I did not want him to miss the sight. But soon it got boring, as the emus ran along the track all daylong. We also saw camels, bands of which still roamed the outback; camels had been brought in from Arabia more than a century earlier. We did not spot any kangaroos but the wedge-tailed eagle and various hawks spiraled in the hot air off the desert looking for some prey, a rabbit perhaps.

Continuing across the desert, the train occasionally paused at homesteads for passengers, or goods and mail drop-offs. By the second evening we reached Kalgoorlie — another leg stretching opportunity, another train change, another gauge, meeting now Western Australia's requirements. Some passengers rushed to one of the workmen's pubs, but we dined on the train, on mediocre fare. Kalgoorlie is a mining town, known for being home of President Hoover, who worked there as a mining engineer.

When the long gleaming train finally pulled into Perth's terminal, it was all covered with dust. We were ready to abandon our tiny headquarters and breath fresh air again. It was a lifetime experience.

After three years teaching at the University of Melbourne, Arthur's Fulbright commitment was complete and we decided to try our hand again in the US. He obtained a position at the University of Texas in Austin and we went back on the road.

Oil wells and blue bonnets

On the way to Texas we traveled via Thailand, Cambodia (where we spent Christmas of 1964 at Angkor Wat), Vietnam, and Hong Kong, including our first stay in the wonderful old Peninsula Hotel. Arthur's desire for a chance to live and work in Bangkok remained.

Upon arrival in Austin, we immediately began the process of settling in; we got a new car, and our first house — a lovely modern home in the Westlake Hills with a view down to the city, bracketed by the State Capitol and the University Tower. We enjoyed our lives, traveling down to San Antonio, and to Dallas and Houston. Best of all, my parents finally made it out of Egypt, and came to visit with us for ten months.

And here I come to an important aside. In the 1920s there was an exchange of people between Turkey and Greece upon the breakup of the old Ottoman Empire. My parents were forced to leave with only the possessions they could carry. And now it had happened again, only this time my father was relieved of his prized gold watch by an Egyptian official, as he was about to board the boat for Greece! This history colored my need for security, and added to the need I had for protection.

For Arthur, my mother was by far the most outstanding person he ever met. She had a wonderful sense of humor. She spoke Greek, Turkish, and Arabic, but not a word of English. Arthur set to work to remedy this through his own crash course in Greek. They communicated splendidly. We remember her most vividly from a great picture of her sitting in our garden and eating a huge slice of watermelon.

We explored Texas with my parents, who loved the dry climate, the wildflowers, and the fields of blue bonnets, scattered for miles in the countryside. They were intrigued by the oil wells and more than bewildered to see oil pumped in the middle of a cemetery.

During our two-and-a-half years in Austin, the highlight was the summer of 1965 that Arthur spent in a post-doctoral program at Stanford University. We drove out to California via the southern route, getting our first look at San Diego, then up the coast to Palo Alto. The program was first-class, and one of his colleagues was a Japanese, Hiroshi Azuma, who will reappear in this story. On the return trip we visited Yosemite, Bryce, Zion, and the Grand Canyon, all memorable in their own unique ways.

But now his ambition was about to be fulfilled. In the spring of 1966 he was offered a position to lead a research program in Bangkok, which he accepted with alacrity, calling me after the fact to announce the decision; fortunately, I was as happy as he was. So we put our house on the market, sold it, and packed our possessions for our next adventure.

Sacred Adventures
in Greece

Like all contracts involving commitments from Third World governments, Arthur's took some time to come to fruition. We left Texas in the spring of 1966, but it would be fall before we were actually to arrive in Bangkok to begin work. In the interlude, we took a few more trips to help Arthur prepare for his new job and occupy himself.

The government of Liberia, on the west coast of Africa, asked him to come over for a six-week consulting stint. This poor country gave him a new baseline for odious comparisons, especially as far as inefficiency and corruption were concerned. When the bulb in his room at the Intercontinental gave out, he made repeated requests for its replacement but drew a blank, and Arthur ended up paying a hotel staff member to go out and get the bulb. His assignment was to develop entrance tests for the higher educational institutes of the country. It took barely two hours, after the tests were typed, before finding them on sale in the streets of Monrovia for 25 cents!

During his Liberian sojourn, I stayed with my parents, who were now established in a suburb of Athens. There was no way to communicate with Arthur except by cable. No telephone circuit existed between the two countries; as for the post office in Greece, it did not recognize the existence of Liberia! One had to wonder, as so many of our ship owners, were flying the Liberian flag. Liberia was a choice tax haven.

While Arthur was in Liberia the Festival of Athens was on and Aeschylus trilogy was presented in the ancient theater of Epidaurus. The festival of Athens in the '60s did not extend the whole summer season as it is today, but was limited to couple of weeks. Tickets were hard to come by and accommodations for an overnight stay at a premium. Friends were able to assist. I would stay in a village home, but had to sleep on the floor. To me that was more convenient than face the three-hour night drive to Athens.

The theater of Epidaurus is built in a peaceful and impressive rural setting and is one of the very few theaters that retain its original circular orchestra; the aesthetics and acoustics are breathtaking. I sat on an ancient limestone seat way up and thought of all the generations that shared that seat with me. At dusk the performance began. The audience fell silent, the nightingales continued their cheerful twittering; the chorus arrived and a thrilling performance was underway.

I was among the very few staying at the village and was invited to the dinner reserved for the performers. The villagers, as it was custom those days, had prepared a feast. When the last car and bus departed, tables were rapidly assembled on the main street; white sheets served as tablecloths; the actors, leading artists of the National Theater, were ready for their dinner. What was striking for me was the villagers' familiarity with the play; while carrying platters of food, they emerged as discerning critics. They talked to the actors on a first-name basis; they knew every theatrical trick, the intonation of every verse, the choreography of movements. "You were more spontaneous at rehearsal, not enough passion tonight," shouted the baker to the leading actor. For those villagers, theater was in their blood; they have witnessed performances countless of times.

A foreigner, a *xenos*, was sitting in my table; he did not speak Greek, nor English. He was a tall young man, with a black crop of hair, but so thin, so emaciated. He was charming, courteous, seemed to buzz with vitality. I noticed his shoes, the most odd pointed shoes I have ever seen. He spoke some French. No one was paying much attention to him; after all it was nearly midnight, we were all hungry. Who was he? Did he miss his transport to Athens? Was he staying also overnight in Epidaurus? I greeted him with a "*Bonsoir.*" He turned and pronounced one word: "*Magnifique.*" He was the great Rudolf Nureyev, who recently had defected from the Soviet Union and had moved to Paris. I never had the opportunity to see Nureyev dance, but I shall always remember that enchanted evening, with nightingales keeping us company. The great dancer was acknowledging his debt to the performing arts; he was paying with his presence a fitting tribute to the Greek theater.

Back to Europe via Nigeria

After completing his stint in Monrovia, Arthur traveled to Lagos, Nigeria, for a few days to visit the international project there that was being initiated in several other countries, including Thailand, Brazil, and Korea.

The team's assignment was to develop entrance tests for vocational and technical institutes. A pilot study was underway. The US-based tests were irrelevant and could not be applied in developing economies. They had to be adapted, modified, but mostly generated from scratch. Technical manpower was needed, but training was expensive, and so a selection process had to be developed. Whom were they to admit? What criteria were to be applied to applicants? How could they keep the attrition rate at a minimum? It became a priority of the ministries of education. In evaluating the results of the pilot study and coordinating the results, Arthur's background in mathematical statistics proved relevant.

The project managers gathered in Lagos. Arthur thought Liberia was corrupt, but he had never been to Nigeria. As he left, he swore never to return — an oath he would repeat on two subsequent visits. Finally, he left for Rome and Athens to join me for several weeks while waiting out the "go ahead" for Bangkok. What he only learned much later was that there was a coup in Lagos on the afternoon of his departure, and his colleagues had to wait a week before they could leave.

What a joy it was for Arthur to be back in Europe. His main memory of his one night in Rome was finding a small café on a back street and having a wonderful meal, capped by the largest, juiciest peach!

He joined me in Greece, where he was so pleased to see the old folks established in a Greek environment and they were overjoyed to see him again. We had a great time visiting the many sites and sights of Athens — the Parthenon, the archaeological museum, the temple of Poseidon at Cape Sounion.

One evening we were sitting at the terrace of the St. George Hotel with friends. The Parthenon was illuminated, endowed with splendid new lights. Arthur decided that if we ever came to live in Greece he would Hellenize his name. "Hill" would never do. Hill is "Lofos" in Greek, but that has no ring to it. What about "Lofidis"? And then again, why stop there? "Lofidopoulos" sounded better. Many Greeks have Pappas preceding their name, accounting their heritage as descendants of a priest (Orthodox priests are allowed to marry) so Arthur was ready to settle for "Papalofidopoulos," but he would lose his initials, so he experimented some more and came up with "Hadjipapalofidopoulos." The "Arthur" became "Aristotle," the "Henry" became "Haralambos." Even the waiters were laughing.

Our visits to the sites of Athens were all significant but one had to get to the country and visit the temples of Delphi, Agamemnon's Palace of Mycenae, the amphitheater of Epidaurus, the Byzantine monasteries, the Venetian castles to get the feeling and pulse of Greece.

On the trail of Lord Byron

We had, of course, been to Greece earlier. Part of our first grand tour in 1960 was a visit to Greece and our first sightseeing trip to Delphi. We did not have much money to rent a car, so we took a local bus. The conductor read the names of the passengers as they boarded. They were all Greeks. When he reached our name, he blinked and said "Xenos," foreigner. We sat in the back of the bus and enjoyed observing our fellow passengers; their plastic bundles were full of provisions, gifts from Athens to relatives in the remote village mountains. Halfway through the trip, at the village of Arahova, our driver decided to stop — for a cigarette, perhaps? An hour passed, then another. There was no particular schedule of the time we were supposed to arrive. Some of the passengers were getting edgy; others were accustomed to the ritual. A girlfriend in town? The driver appeared after a couple of hours. He treated us with dried figs. No questions were asked. No one wanted a fistfight.

The driver continued his route; the road etched in the mountains was terrifyingly narrow. At every hairpin, a small, shrine with a faded icon, some flowers, some biscuits, a half-empty bottle of olive oil, seemed placed to ensure our safe passage. Suddenly, we reached the main road of the village of Delphi. A few men were sitting in the *kafeneion*, the coffee shop, smoking and fingering their knotted worry beads.

It did not take us long to start exploring the ruins, the *stoa* of the Athenians, the treasury, and in the valley below we were rewarded with the wonderful view of three Doric columns, part of the sanctuary of Athena. It must have been an important building, judging from its position, and we walked towards the sanctuary, to admire the fine workmanship. There was a feeling of eeriness and I was half expecting, at any moment to encounter some ancient shade walking among the broken columns. If you listened, you could hear the oracle. It was magic. In that misty winter weather it was not surprising that Delphi seemed haunted.

The oracle at Delphi spoke on behalf of the gods, advising

rulers, citizens, and philosophers on everything from their sex lives to affairs of state. The oracles were delivered by the pithea, a priestess of Apollo who sat on a tripod, her divine utterances made in response to petitioners' requests. In a trance, at times of frenzy, she would answer questions, give orders, and make prophecies.

We roamed freely though the ruins, shrouded in mist. There was not a single tourist; the whole area was empty of people, and Delphi was all our own. We climbed to the amphitheater and sat on its stone benches. I could relive in my memory few verses of the immortal plays of the Greek dramatists; they reverberated in my mind:

> O master of my soul,
> I float on air, the sweet
> Music of flutes would win me now
> And twining ivy-tendrils whirl me round
> In Bacchanalian dance
>
> (Sophocles, Women of Trachis)

We found a path to the top leading us to the stadium, a free open space. We stood there engulfed by sky, with the sacred Mt. Parnassus going right up. I felt the gods were looking upon us. One does not leave Delphi without stopping at the Castalia spring, quenching one's thirst with the crystal pure clear water sprouting from a ravine.

From Delphi, we proceeded to the fishing village of Itea. It was wintertime, and every eating-place was closed. We stopped at the police station to seek advice. "Knock on the door of the last house on the waterfront," responded the police officer. "Nikos is a fisherman, he goes fishing even with *meltemi*," he added, referring to the windy days when the swells are high. It helped to be speaking Greek when we knocked at Nikos's modest home. It did not take long before a table was placed on the water's edge; a paper tablecloth was anchored with clothespins, and chairs were found. Yes, Nikos had caught a sea bass that morning and his wife was grilling it now for us. Winter tomatoes were still available. "What about some cheese? Any local wine?" A feast was produced, for just few dollars.

We would visit Delphi again in the '70s and '80s, but were disappointed to find that we could no longer roam freely through the ancient ruins. An entrance fee was required, the coffee shops gave way to a modern tourist hotel, souvenir shops crowded the village street, the path to the stadium was well marked, and a large boulder was strategically placed for the photographers, with the Olympic rings carved on it. Mass tourism required protective measures. Delphi was still remarkable, but not the same. The theater has been reconstructed, receiving busloads of tourists; the chorus of the ancient tragedies did not reverberate anymore in my mind. Itea had now a number of flourishing restaurants, and prices had gone up, but the fish remained fresh as always.

In the shadow of Byzantium

Our good friends from the Philippines, Amit and Neepa Chowdhury, joined us in 1972 on a journey to Northern Greece. We aimed to explore among others the Byzantine heritage of the country. Ioannina, a historic small town up north, was our headquarters. The city offered its treasures: a mosque, a palace, the ancient Turkish quarters, historic sites including the very house or merely the site of the house, depending on which guide book you read — where Byron lived. We drove to the quay and the lake of Ioannina suddenly appeared like a magical mirage — shallow, dark as polished onyx reflecting minarets and towers. It had a dreamlike quality, unruffled by scullers in training, by fisherman in low narrow boats and by the motorized little launch that took us for a ride towards a small island in the middle. The lake teemed with eels, trout, crayfish, and frogs, and every taverna displayed a tank of live seafood. We were invited to choose what we wanted for the chef to cook.

With the aid of a guidebook, we viewed the 16th century monastery of Panteleimon, the house where Ali Pasha the Turkish leader took refuge, the ceiling through which he was shot dead by the Turks, and the jeweled dress of his young wife a Greek who may or may not have betrayed him.

We visited numerous monasteries in this trip. So many of them were dramatically situated, perched on cliff tops or hidden in remote valleys, a characteristic of rural Greece. Church architecture was less important than the symbolism of the internal layout; the icons hanging on the iconostasis, the elaborate silk embroideries and of course the paintings on the walls.

From the frescoes we learned some of the more exotic tortures Christians endured and laughed with delight at an Adam and Eve in a painted paradise teeming with animals. We visited Meteora, where the monasteries are built on one of the largest flat-top rock formations; we admired the colorful frescoes, the elaborately carved wood, and the inlaid pedestal of the bishop. Greek communists disfigured many icons in 1945, in one of the saddest periods of our history, at the end of the German occupation in World War II.

We stayed at village homes, well-kept modest dwellings. We shared the living room with the families and we were welcome to join family and friends. Amit, a journalist with an inquisitive mind, would ask questions. "Do you have a mistress?" was an opening gambit of his when talking to the gasoline attendant. I served as the interpreter and it was hard to keep a straight face. Neepa traveled with a small carry-on bag, but managed to pack a number of her silk saris. As we walked though the villages, we could discern curious eyes behind the wooden shutters, looking at a foreign woman in her resplendent silks. Not many Indians traveled to these mountain areas.

Summer in the Peloponnese

On many weekends, we explored the Peloponnese, often on overnight trips. We headed south towards the great theater of Epidaurus to the fishing village of Agios Nicolaos, and watched the caiques come in, trailing kerosene lanterns and laden with the morning's catch of fish. The serenity was only occasionally punctured by cries of ubiquitous salesmen who advertised their wares — whether watermelons or plastic containers — from megaphones mounted on the roofs of their trucks.

It was early summer when we visited the Peloponnese. The hillsides suddenly flowered. The fields were filled with larkspur, anemones, poppies, and asphodel, with stalks of giant fennel in whose slow-burning pith Prometheus brought fire to the earth. Pink and white oleanders hemmed the roads, house fronts were decorated with shocks of bougainvilleas, but even with the abundance of flowers, the Peloponnese retained a kind of severity year around. The barren mountain peaks were always present. The occasional monasteries built into sheer cliff faces reminded us of the isolation of the place.

We aimed to visit Sparta, the archrival of Athens, and a sedate city that stands on a vast lush plain below the jagged peaks of the Taygetos Mountains. This was where the ancient Spartans left their weaker infants to die.

We settled down in the town square once to have a *granita* and enjoy the view. Something set off laughter, which we just could not stop. Soon all the old men in the café were laughing with us. For years the word "granita" brought laughter in our home.

Sprawling up a hill three miles from the modern Sparta is a ghost town: Mistra, once a jewel of the Byzantine Empire. It was once called the Florence of the East, but is deserted now by all but a few nuns, although its Byzantine churches earned three stars in the Michelin guide to Greece. There is so much realism in the golden-brown shells of its mansions and churches with their extraordinary murals.

The Aegean Islands

We visited Greece through the years many times. The islands were our favorite destination. One year it was the island of Samos, one of the lushest green islands of the Aegean, and we stayed in the port village of Pythagoreon, the ancestral home of the great Pythagoras. We marveled at what must have been in the air of what was now a very small town. Two thousand five hundred years ago, it must have been an even smaller village that led to such fertile mathematical creativity. There is a very fine modern memorial statue of Pythagoras standing with one hand extended straight up, pointing to the end of a tilted bar, thus forming a large right-angle triangle. It is extremely effective.

Statue of Pythagoras in Samos

Samos, at its closest point, is less than a mile from the Turkish mainland. We took a local ferry to reach it; halfway through the crossing the Greek flag was lowered, and the Turkish hoisted — the reverse of procedure on our return. It was a one-day outing to visit Ephesus, the home of St. Paul's chronic

Ephesians. It has been, and continues to be, significantly re-constructed by the Turkish government, and is really a very impressive site. In 1993, we were told there were four million visitors. Fortunately, we were there early enough in the tour-ist season that the crowds were relatively sparse.

Another favorite island was Myteline, the island of Sappho. We rented a dilapidated car and headed, like most tourists, for Molyvos. The village was a wonderful place to soak up Greek atmosphere. The men lived in the cafés sipping their strong syrupy coffee or studying their ouzo. The women were al-ways working and occupied a special place in the island. Bright colorful geraniums decorated balconies and sills. The layout of the streets, alleyways, and passages was as unfathomable as it was interesting.

One day we strolled to a small taverna on the hilltop and immediately looked into the kitchen. All the appetizers, warm stews, and fresh fish were on display. There were a few scat-tered chairs and small table. The grape vines covering the pergola afforded enough shade in that hot noon sun. We spent that entire afternoon eating a sumptuous lunch and consum-ing two bottles of cold Santa Helena. As if this was not enough, we ordered rice pudding, which had just from the oven bub-bling, permeating the air with the divine aroma of freshly grated cinnamon. The proprietor looked at us and exclaimed the high-est compliment that a Greek can give: "You ate well!"

We made many visits to Chios, my ancestral island. Chios has an exciting history, and as early as the 7th century BC was an independent naval power. Homeric rhapsodies flourished on Chios and many believe that the great epic poet was born there. Not far from town, on the coastal road, is a huge boul-der on which legend says Homer sat teaching. We sat on Homer's rock while plane trees sheltered us from the hot ray sun.

Chios is considered the shipowners' island. Many distin-guished shipowning families like the Livanos and the Chandries trace their roots to Chios, where they owned summer homes.

My grandparents came from the village of Elata on the western part of the island. Michael Peratikos, a ship owner friend, considers Kardamyla his ancestral village; he always teased me by saying that "In Elata, people are of a different race." Our ancestral villages are just 30 kilometers apart!

Chios is famous for the monastery of Nea Moni. It is in the island's woody center, a monastery that dates from the 11th century and remains one of the finest examples of Byzantine art and architecture. We marveled at the solemn yet human mosaics of angels and saints, and, especially, the vast fresco of the Second Coming. Nea Moni was a monastery for men, but because of lack of monks it was changed to a convent. My uncle was the chief medical doctor of the island; for years he took care of the monks and nuns of the island's monasteries. During our visits we were escorted by the abbess, admired hidden treasures, illuminated bibles. We enjoyed listening to the nuns tell some of the less well-known legends that surround their convent. On departure marvelous embroideries or hand woven bedspreads were presented to us, precious gifts for the doctor's niece. Needless to say that later on, our contributions were very generous.

We met many Greeks during our travels, but the two who stood out in our memories are Alexis Mardas and Michael Peratikos.

Alexis Mardas

Arthur met Alexis Madras in 1989 when AT&T was bidding for a wireless license in Greece. Alexis made his name and his millions as the head of Apple Electronics, a division of the Beatles' recording company. Inventor and gadget freak, "Magic Alex" — as he was known to the Beatles and their fans — went on to perfect the design for a bullet — and bomb resistant car which has been adopted by numerous heads of state including King Juan Carlos of Spain, King Hussein of Jordan, Sultan Qabouz of Oman.

Over dinner he pulled out his Sharp Wizard organizer (this was in 1989, before those gadgets were widely available) and punched a few keys to show the Rolodex listing of King Juan Carlos II along with personal direct numbers, explaining that for 25 seconds this would produce a "system busy" signal before reverting to a ringing tone. Thus a wrong number caller would simply hung up before the call went through. In his pocket he also carried such items as a portable cellular phone and a wristwatch-sized device for use in accessing a computer from a telephone without touch-tone capability, but only with pulse dialing.

On our way from Athens to dinner at Microlimano, he explained the secret of the remarkable series of green lights. Greek traffic lights are equipped with a radio receiver, which enables emergency vehicles (police, fire ambulance) to change the light green ahead of them. Alex checked the law and found no prohibition against his taking advantage of this availability, so he analyzed the spectrum, built a transmitter, and simply drove on through.

Over dinner, he told the story of a Greek scam that had just been resolved. For the past year, ads had run for lottery winners (up to $15 million) to turn in their tickets for face value plus 5% in cash, no questions asked. It was an attractive proposition for most lottery winners, who were poor and did not want to have their names publicized, pay 53% in tax, and be descended upon by all their poor relatives near and far. On the buying side, the purchaser could sell the ticket for up to 40% above face value to rich Greeks who needed to establish to the government's tax authorities the source of the money with which they bought yachts, real estate, and expensive cars. In the absence of such proof, the government assessed substantial taxes based on a formula; Greeks notoriously underreport their income.

Sultan Qabouz sent a Hercules transport to London for Alex to bring his secure vehicles and other high security equipment to Oman for demonstration to himself and his senior aides. Alex refused a separate jet aircraft ride, and elected to take the 14-hour flight in the Hercules along with the vehicles, equipment, and 14 of his staff, four of them females. The plane was completely without compartments, up to including the pilot's area. Some two hours out, the women asked where was a toilet. Enquiries of the pilot led to four pipes, which led straight out into the ether. The women ended up using a military helmet as their chamber pot!

For Alexis Mardas, who was based in London, Hydra was what Bavaria was for King Ludwig II — a place in which to build, listen to Wagner, and dream. He restored the main house, purchased additional property around him, filled them with simple but expensive furniture, and entertained his international guests, who included Joan Collins and Michael Jackson, among others. From the verandah of the main house he would fly two flags: the blue and white flag of Greece and one with a cross, an anchor, a dove of peace, and spear arrayed on a red and blue back ground — the flag of Hydra.

Alex had a collection of 1,100 Swatches. When they were first introduced, everyone he knew who went to Switzerland brought one back; pretty soon he had 50 and he just went on from there.

Michael Peratikos

Several years back we were houseguests in Eastern Long Island. Another houseguest was a Greek who turned out to be one of the wealthiest but least ostentatious of the major Greek ship owners. We had long conversations with him, and he followed up the next week by calling and inviting us both to have dinner with him in New York City, which we did.

Since then we saw him a couple of times a year, either in London where he has his main home or in New York. His apartment in London was adorned with few minor Impressionists, a Braque, and a precious collection of worry beads. We visited him in his London home; after drinks and before proceeding to a local restaurant, he suggested to his first-time guests that I should select an item from his étagère, a small remembrance of our meeting. I selected a lovely blue flask from the Isle of Wight, which we filled later with cologne or perfume. There was a white Bentley parked on the street and we all proceeded to a modest Indian restaurant. As the conversation centered on opera, he told to us to keep a particular evening clear because he had tickets for the opera in Covent Garden, with Luciano Pavarotti and Kathleen Battle on the program. I innocently asked him: "Michael, how did you get them in such a short notice?" and was suitably put in my place when he quietly replied that he was a patron of the Royal Opera. Needless to say the evening improved when he picked us up in another of his Bentleys. We started wondering if he had a different-color Bentley for every day of the week.

Michel was a wonderful man, in his mid-70s who told us his problems about the family and running his business of 40-plus major vessels as well as what was then a very large shipyard in Eleusis, Greece.

We had Easter that year in his home in Portoheli, a small village in the Peloponnese. It was a four-hour drive from Athens but it could also be reached by hydrofoil from Piraeus. High above the bluff, almost buried in an orange grove and masses of geraniums, was his lovely retreat. From the outside it was a traditional village home. It was filled with simple furniture and electrified oil lamps; the walls were filled with mosaics, the work of the leading artists of Greece. The murals all shared the motif of the sea-fishing, bathing, sailing. From the verandah the view was unsurpassed: the blue Aegean, a small island emerging here and there. Figaro, Michael's golden retriever, was always walking a pace in front of him. Water, a precious commodity, was imported weekly, and the sand in his cove was refreshed yearly.

A few years later Michael invited us to spend Greek Easter with him again. Four years earlier he was between yachts, having sold the previous one and still waiting for the new 78-foot catamaran under construction on the Isle of Wight. When we saw him the cat was now three years old and sailed magnificently.

Michael Peratikos and Julie at the helm of the catamaran

Arthur admittedly felt a lot of irony in being there in this setting with all this old wealth, including such other guests as the wife of the chairman of Lloyds of London, the daughter of the Mexican ambassador to France, herself an archeologist. It was quite a ways from Arthur's humble start in Australia. Nevertheless we had a wonderful time. They were remarkably decent people, but some of the hangers-on were real name-droppers. It made for very interesting listening.

We sailed among the islands and along the coast of the Peloponnese every day, and had an exhilarating experience as the wind was picking up. The mast was 120 feet high, but with the push of button the sails unfolded. The latest technology had been applied to this magnificent vessel.

There was swimming in secluded coves, there were evenings of poetry reading, others filled with music, mostly opera. Michael introduced us to the work of a new generation of Greek poets making their mark in Greek literature alongside Seferis and Elytis, the recent Nobel Prize winners. The readings were in Greek. Some times an English translation was available. One evening we saw a video, the first performance of the Three Tenors before the commercialization of these artists. Dinner always stretched past the early hours of the morning.

Easter was a joyous celebration. We attended the midnight resurrection service at the monastery, where the octogenarian nuns did their best to carry the hymns. The abbot was resplendent in his new robes and hypnotized all of us with his incense. Easter was marked with all the traditional festive dishes. An array of *mezethes* or appetizers flowed from the kitchen, as the cooks were busy preparing the traditional feasts. Three spit-roasted lambs and a roasted goat were cooked for hours. The guests came and went in their private yachts.

Arthur loved rice pudding so he asked Michael if it was possible to have it prepared. He thought it was a very simple request. A day passed, and then a second day, but still no rice pudding. He did not dare to ask. Finally, on the third day, the rice pudding arrived. It seems that the three chefs — one from London, one from Athens, and the chef of the catamaran — had been arguing which recipe to follow and what kind of rice to use. They had to call Athens to have the right variety brought in. Knowing now all the turmoil that he had caused, Arthur decided to stoke the fire, with Michael's concurrence. When the steaming cinnamon-scented rice pudding arrived, he said, "This is not really what I had in mind, but that other Greek desert *galaktobouriko*, the semolina custard pie." I do not think the cooks took kindly to his joke.

It is sad to note that Michael's son Costis was assassinated by the November 17, a group of ultra-radical terrorists. It took six years after the assassination, in 2002, for the culprits to be arrested. With all his power and wealth, Michael was helpless.

Greece's continuing appeal

And if we had our favorite Greeks, what was our favorite island? That changed many times. A few years ago it would have been Skiathos — a barren, typically Greek island, where we rented a room and where a man with a donkey brought us water each day. It was the first island we ever visited. Crete was wonderful but we did not stay long, Rhodes had too much of a Venetian influence, and was not Greek enough. Some how we plighted our troth to Chios with its mountains and verdant valleys, its pretty villages, its Byzantine churches, its late medieval mansions and twisting lanes. Perhaps it was the fountain in the middle of the square in Elata, erected by Michael Nyhas, my medical doctor uncle, that made Chios so special.

What was the continuing appeal of Greece, visited so many times? First, it was home; my parents lived now in Halandri, a suburb of Athens. For years we spent our holidays in that country. Cost also played a part. Prices in Greece were cheaper than many places in Western Europe. Where else could you find, in the mid-'90s, a room in a hotel, with a balcony facing the ocean, for $18?

Was the appeal the sun? The blue waters of the Aegean? The wild flowers? The butterflies? The catching of fresh fish for our dinners? The warm hospitality of a newly found friend such as Michael Peratikos?

Greece is a country where you can stretch your imagination. For ancient Greeks, a tree might be a dryad and a spring a water nymph. The sacred and miraculous are everywhere. One feels the pull of legends when clambering in Delphi. Serendipity abounds; you can drive through a modern dull city or a flinty landscape and suddenly the place pulsates with history. We loved the tiny Byzantine churches, the Greek or Roman columns unpredictably sprouting amid the concrete anonymity of central Athens.

There is also Greece's texture, by which I mean its horizontal richness, the layer on layer of history. A new subway line was completed in Athens in 2000. This major undertaking was postponed many times as archaeologists unearthed another find. An underground garage was to be built; the archeologists prevented it, as it was the site of Turkish, Byzantine, Roman and Hellenistic civilizations. Ancient churches became mosques, mosques reverted to churches, ottoman baths became flower markets; beneath all natural complexity, all those remnants of invaders, who knows what mythical beings once moved?

Most importantly, as in so many other parts of the world, it is the people that make a difference in Greece. Greeks have belied their dour looks and abrupt manner with countless kindnesses: grapes thrust into our hands by a smiling farmer in Samos, the gift of apples from a market vendor in Chios, the offer of a loukoumi, a special sweet, from the nuns in a remote monastery, the local liqueur shared with a woman tending a miraculous icon, the unsolicited extras in so many tavernas.

Starting Over in Thailand

When we first stopped in Thailand in 1960, tourist information was hard to find; Cooks & Wagon Lits, a major world travel agency at that time, did not have a single promotional brochure in their New York office.

We knew so little about the country; our exposure was limited to the film *The King and I.* In our misguided high school education, Asia's history revolved around and was limited to "the colonies" — whether British, French, or Dutch. Thailand was never colonized; it was not included in any curriculum. We were naïve and ignorant. But Bangkok was one of Pan American Airlines' destinations, and we had heard there was an Australian professor living there. Why don't we stop?

The Bangkok that captured our imagination was a very different place from the booming, modern, highly Westernized metropolis it is today. It was an enchanting world of golden pagodas, endless rice paddies, saffron clad monks and gentle people. We had expected a city more in keeping with the traditional Western ideal of orderly streets and quadrants. But Bangkok was nothing of the sort, a helter-skelter of palaces, temples, and bazaars; life took place in the tracery of canals and rivers. There was the incredible temple of the Emerald Buddha, the most sacred of the capital's innumerable temples. Devout Thais sat cross-legged for hours on the temple floor.

Devotion to Buddha was elevated into an art form that encompassed every aspect of life. We were awestruck.

There were spirit houses of graceful Thai architecture, strategically placed outside homes, government buildings and the two or three proper hotels.

The most popular form of transportation was the jaunty little pedicab or *samloh*, the memory of which still inspires nostalgia. They were equipped with jingling bells, which the drivers sounded at the slightest provocation. They were banished to the provinces that year, so we must have been their last customers.

The city was still small, with no shortage of living space and therefore few apartment houses. Tourists were few, arriving mostly on cruise ships. The famous Oriental Hotel had just been renovated; it was a popular meeting place as well as a semi-permanent home for a number of Western residents.

Many people still lived along the canals, their houses floating on the muddy waters. The more prosperous residents lived in vast rambling houses with spacious verandahs that overlooked tropical gardens and numerous servants. Such was the compound of Hugh Philp, the Australian professor we met. He was then the UNESCO representative.

We were casual visitors, but this stop in Southeast Asia opened our curiosity, holding a place in our memory as a kind of semi-mythical golden age, and proved a history lesson to apprise; it brought us face to face with our own destiny. We felt a passion for Asian history, art, and culture that brought an extra dimension to our lives. The landscapes of Thailand were never to leave us.

Bangkok once more

And so it was that in 1966, we landed once more in Bangkok, this time to make it our home.

Arthur and I had been in search of such a "home." In Australia, as Greek migrant, I was not accepted. Different challenges faced us in the academic setting of Texas. Arthur did not particularly like teaching; lectures on mathematical statistics were not very exciting. His publications were well received, and he was rewarded with a tenure-track position, but felt that his contribution was insignificant, beyond impressing his chairman or another faculty committee.

For some deeply private or inexplicable reason, Arthur wanted to desert the ordinary, the secure and familiar world, and start a new life amid totally different surroundings in the Third World. As a student, during summer vacation, he ran a camp for aboriginal children. He treasured a certificate presented to him, citing him "a kindly father to 80 aboriginal children, a tower of strength to the Camp Director and a thoroughly unselfish hard worker at all times." He gave unselfishly of his time, channeling his energy and intellect to making a difference to young people in the developing world.

For me, an Alexandrian Greek, where was home? I felt nostalgia for a home I did not know. Perhaps I was in search of something permanent to which I wanted to attach myself, perhaps in a strange place. There was a country, visited few years back, that left us with an indelible impression; a position was found there and the Ford Foundation was a most prestigious and generous employer. I was not hung up on a career; Arthur's happiness was the most important aim in my life. I was willing to follow him, with alacrity. When he expressed his wish to move to Bangkok, I could only agree.

Bangkok's canals were now filled, giving way to paved roads. The samloh had been replaced by motorized vehicles. Cars and buses crowded the few roads. The Vietnam War was in full swing and American civilian dependents were flocking to the city. Housing was at a premium. For three months we stayed at the lovely old Erawan Hotel while we waited for our apartment building to be completed. The air-conditioning didn't always work, but the windows were left slightly ajar so that our hotel room was redolent with tropical aromas and night-blooming orchids.

For Arthur, getting started on his project was a major activity. Thailand's educational system was very weak. A single curriculum was mandatory across the country. Admission tests for entry at universities and at technical and vocational institutes did not exist. A process had to be devised, just as they had been in Africa, and this was where Arthur came in with his experience and expertise.

Still we found ample time to visit the many spectacular wonders of Bangkok. The Royal Palace was once again one of our destinations with its truly incredible Temple of the Emerald Buddha; we remained awestruck by the beauty of the temples, a gaily-colored confusion of halls and pagodas. It was still not crowded then! The Marble Temple with its gallery of Buddha images was another cherished destination. We marveled at these Buddhas from different eras and countries and in different styles, all cast in bronze, all the same size, giving an odd symmetry to the gallery. A gaunt, emaciated Buddha was our favorite. The original stands in the Museum in Lahore, and we made a point to see it years later.

There were spectacular fairs, and important ceremonies like royal cremations and the Ploughing Ceremony, which insured a bountiful crop each year. Another favorite destination was the Sunday market, with stalls selling all sorts of practical goods. We were delighted by the plethora of tropical fruit, especially the mangoes and durian. Years earlier, the government had imposed a tax on the number of fruit trees a farmer could grow. The farmers subsequently cut down all but the most productive trees, those with the sweetest fruit, a selection process that ensured the survival of the best and most prolific trees.

Making the best of it

Finally we were able to move into our new apartment, Pricha Court, just down the road or *soi* from Arthur's office.

There were inconveniences to face for anyone used to Western comforts. Adjustments had to be made. Electricity was highly erratic; we kept candles within easy reach for the almost nightly failures; drinking water had to be boiled, bottled water to be delivered. Air-conditioning, which has made life in the tropics bearable today, was still unknown. Imported foods were rare and expensive. We still carried Australian citizenships and did not enjoy the many privileges of our American counterparts. Thailand began to teach me that it was possible to whittle down my list of necessities. This lesson traced a curious freedom in its path; I did not panic with the cessations of utilities.

There were no malls, no shopping centers. The only stores carrying Western food items were on Sukhumvit Road, labeled the "underground stores." Products from the American military exchange found their way into their shelves. There was only one department store, Japan's Daimaru, which had installed the first escalator in the country in 1967.

Yet for all those discomforts, there was clearly a tremendous charm. There were lectures at the Siam Society that opened our minds and exposed us to Buddhist culture and art. Celadon, the finest high-fired stoneware to come out in the Orient in 600 years, was now manufactured in Thailand. The process intrigued me, coming from a chemistry background. We had fascinating and insightful political discussions with Mr. Bunthin Attagara, the director general of education. He compared the Thais to "a rice field bending with the wind." It was the peak of the Vietnam War; the Thais were supporting the American effort — was it reluctantly?

I had a facility with languages, and so learning a tonal language was a pursuit I assumed seriously.

Our maid, Rheam, was attuned to the different sounds of the itinerant merchants on the soi below, and would hurry off to buy her *ooliang* (iced coffee) or some exotic fruit juice, sold in little plastic bags with a straw. Her daughter Daeng stayed in the maid's quarters. She was a very shy child and attended school only sporadically. We interceded and enrolled her in a school nearby, bought her books, uniforms, encouraged her, and provided for her education through the years. Daeng became a primary school teacher, an achievement of which we were very proud.

We often entertained Thai officials. Upon entering our apartment they would congratulate us, as they could smell "new" rice. We did not know the difference, but luckily, Rheam had purchased the right type of rice.

Pricha and Yu: a prosperous Chinese family

Our landlord, Pricha, was Chinese. He represented the pharmaceutical company Merck, but his major occupation was 18 holes of golf daily at the Royal Bangkok Sports Club, of which we became members. Arthur also played golf there, but more often he joined his Thai friends who patronized the Thai military golf course at the Bangkok airport, where it was not unusual to see snakes on the fairways or cobras head popping up in the rough.

Pricha also took care of his stable of fine racehorses. Nearly every weekend we were invited to join him at the Club to watch the races. As many as three of his thoroughbreds might be running in a single race, so he was often the winner. From time to time I was privileged to parade his winner and receive a trophy!

After the races we went out for Chinese dinner. Pricha invited a number of his tenants, but I believe we were the favorites. He always followed the cook, and our knowledge of Chinese cuisine expanded. We never again experienced such great Chinese food anywhere – even, as it turned out, in the same place.

Once, we had visitors from the States and wanted to treat them to one of Pricha's exquisite Chinese dinners. We asked him to write down, in Chinese, the memorable menu we had sampled just the week before. We took our visitors to the same restaurant, with all the detailed instructions in hand. Dinner was served — but it was hardly what we had savored

Arthur and Julie leading Pricha's winning horse

with our landlord. Worse, when the bill came, it was three times Pricha's statement. We were foreigners. Why should the restaurant waste their good Chinese wine to simmer their asparagus for us? We left very disappointed.

Pricha's wife Mom Yu had a fabulous collection of jewelry, sets of earrings, bracelets, rings, pins, necklaces. Gold was for the morning, precious stones for the evening. Her sapphires matched the blue dress, emeralds the green outfit, diamonds any costume, any time. Once she took me to the vault of her bank, opened her safety box and poured out diamonds, rubies, star sapphires, emeralds — all unmounted stones. "We are

Chinese," she explained. "Not always welcome, we cannot take real estate or our stable if we have to leave the country in hurry, but precious stones are easy to smuggle."

Mom Yu was particularly keen to show me an emerald. It was the size of an almond, and its brilliance and clarity were unsurpassed. It was a magnificent stone, and I asked where it came from. "A minor wife of King Chulalongkorn's (the young son in The King and I) was selling it," she answered. It must have been worth a fortune. What a gem! How many events it must have witnessed, how many celebrations and intrigues it could recount! Now it lay in a safety vault, an insurance item for a wealthy Chinese family.

But I was able to indulge my own taste for art and history, albeit much more modestly. A weekend favorite was browsing the antique shops in search of silver place card holders, of which we accumulated quite a collection of different designs. There were antique Laotian drums, Buddha heads, ceramics, and all manner of wonders. The art galleries were also treasure houses because of the thriving Thai art scene.

Teaching at Prasan Mitr

We had been in Thailand for few months and although I found the country exotic beyond my expectations, something was missing. I contemplated getting a job. I had a graduate degree in chemistry; I had worked in Australia and the United States. I wanted the opportunity to meet Thais outside the professional circle of my husband.

I had worked in the most prestigious scientific laboratory in Australia, CSIRO. I was a member of a team of scientists investigating protein configurations. In science, you have to dream a little . . . Could I apply my experience in Thailand? Thais were extracting starch from mung beans to make noodles but were throwing away the residual protein. Could we use that protein and make a fortified drink? How could we enhance the flavor? It became one of my assignments at a scientific institute in Thailand associated with Kasetsart University.

I had to resign from that job, however, when I needed to join Arthur in Japan and Malaysia. Thankfully, I found an opportunity to teach.

I had earlier met Dr. Sarot, the President of Prasan Mitr Teacher's Training College, which has since become a full-fledged university. The college was located on the same street as our apartment, just a 15-minute walk away. Lessons were taught by rote; students were drilled in regurgitating facts and teachers neither asked nor encouraged the asking of more substantive questions aimed at independent thinking. I went to meet Dr. Sarot and proposed to give a series of lectures in analytical chemistry. My command of Thai was limited, but the students had already ten years of English and the subject involved was mostly mathematical. Why not expose them to a different thinking and approach?

Dr. Sarot was very gracious and referred me to the chairman of the chemistry department. Dr. Chawan was a sour old man, wearing a white suit and smoking a pipe. He did not ask about my credentials nor my experience. If I wanted to teach at the college on a Thai salary that was fine by him. I was hired on the spot for the grand sum of $75 a month; it did not cover our housemaid's pay.

I was hired as an *acharn*, a professor. For many Thais, working for the government was prestigious enough, even if the salary was meager, while their wives joined lucrative business enterprises. For a foreigner, a *farang*, being an acharn was a distinct honor. They had never had a farang teaching at the college before. This was not Chulalongkorn University, Thailand's premier university, where numerous British and American distinguished scholars were teaching.

I was surprised at the number of students who registered for my class. I had 40 students, all seniors, taking analytical chemistry. In class they all wore their Prasan Mitr uniform of white shirts and blue trousers or skirts. They all had raven-black hair and brown eyes: they all looked alike, and they all were richly endowed with long flowing names. With desperate zeal I forced myself to recognize them. From the first day they would rush to me and ask excitedly, "What is the exam like? Is it difficult? Could we answer the exam in Thai?" My interest was to meet students and faculty, and develop a practical curriculum that could prove beneficial to their education and teacher training. I never thought of exams, of grading papers, of passing or failing marks.

The students were always punctual; they never missed a class, they were so eager to learn. They materialized out of nowhere in my office, in the corridors, sometimes with peculiar requests, and I tried to deal with them.

Once, a student cornered me and said, "Please, sir!" (They loved to call me "Sir", then be corrected "Madame.") It was a boy named Sawat, "I implore you to write a recommendation for me, I applied for a SEATO scholarship." (SEATO was the Southeast Asian Treaty Organization, the regional equivalent of NATO.) I peered hopefully at those dazzling brown eyes; I knew Sawat only as a presence in my lecture class but I could not bear to dim that happy countenance. With a woeful lack of integrity, I wrote that Sawat was an exemplary student, deserving a scholarship, needing perhaps some remedy in the English language. He got the scholarship.

One morning, as I sat at my desk in the office, an attractive young girl with wavy black hair and intense brown eyes named Needa appeared, pleading, "Could I borrow your book?" There was no assigned book for my class, so I distributed my mimeographed notes. I gave her my book most willingly. I doubted that she could comprehend much as it was more advanced than the material we were covering in class. The next week I was summoned to the chairman's office: "Why did you give your book to your students? Now they will know as much as you do!" I was flabbergasted. I remained silent; I was not planning to rock the culture.

One of the nicer aspects of teaching at Prasan Mitr was that I often received invitations from other acharns to accompany them on trips outside Bangkok. These trips were part of the Director of Education's program in teacher training. One of the invitations was to spend a week in the country in the small town of Pimai. I was reluctant to accept it at first, but Arthur encouraged me to go.

I traveled up country by third-class rail to participate in the program. With my crew of student teachers we searched for plants, nuts, flowers in the fields and in the jungle. We collected leaves, needles, and spores as the basis of a simplified botanical classification: leaves with parallel veins, leaves formed from one seedling, leaves stemming alternately from a stalk. What about the gender of ferns? We could differentiate them from spores that adhered in the back, and when we were not certain, we labeled them "hermaphrodite"! It was an elementary but practical botanical investigation. They called me the professor "in charge of nature."

Julie in "charge of nature"

My Thai was passable and the teachers' English not much better. But somehow we communicated, we smiled a lot, we took walks in the jungle. The best part was in the evening when my students were determined to instruct me in Thai dancing. I was so clumsy; I understand now the expression of a white elephant. I spent a week with them, living on soupy rice three times a day. A jar of Nescafe was produced one day; I must have complained, missing my coffee. Pimai boasted some of the best-preserved ruins, and we explored these remnants of the Khmer civilization within Thailand with the students.

We occasionally had staff meetings. They were carried out in Thai, but I always went to observe the proceedings and to talk with the faculty. I recall asking to be excused on Christmas Day, a working day in Buddhist Thailand. My request was granted.

During the holidays I invited my entire class to our apartment. We had a plastic tree with a few ornaments from around the world. My students were so eager and excited to be invited to a farang home. They sampled with gusto the delicacies I had prepared. After a while one student could not resist: "Do you have some pepper sauce? Some red chili?" I unearthed a small bottle of Tabasco, which went around very fast.

Although it was impossible not to have a few favorites among them, I was fond of them as an entity, all of them — the bright, the dull, even those who were bored in my class. My love for Thailand ran deep because it was the country of my students.

There was a young boy in my class who came from North Eastern Thailand, an area devastated by poverty and drought. The boy was tall and attractive, his eyes bright and alert. His presence at the College must have involved a struggle of massive proportions. At night he slept in at a temple and begged food from the monks.

He identified passionately with his small village. He told me he missed his family, whom he had not seen for three years; his village was very poor, with no paved roads and no electricity. Unlike a majority of country boys who elected after graduation to remain in Bangkok and promote their own fortunes, he was determined to return to his village and teach, "I want to help my people," he said, "because their civilization is so low."

I gave him my books, my entire library. Before our departure from Thailand he presented me with a piece of silk of a deep green shade "like your Christmas tree." Thirty-five years later I still use that piece of green silk as the skirt of our Christmas tree.

Youth is the wonderful and timeless glory of every country; even the most corrupt will find it hard to withstand the idealism of the young.

The Loy Krathong festival

Thais love festivals. It is hard to decide which is the more popular — Song Kran, the Thai New Year, or Loy Krathong, the festival of lights. Both have water in common.

Loy Krathong is held in the 12th lunar month, generally in November. It is an old festival dating back to the times when the royal capital of what was called then Siam was in the northern city of Sukothai. During the two years we lived in Bangkok, we went to the Oriental Hotel for dinner and to witness this festival, a major tourist attraction.

Thousands of *krathongs*, beautiful floats decorated with flowers, begin their journey from the banks where they are launched. They are made in various fanciful shapes, such as lotus blossoms, adorned with flowers and twinkling candles. The krathong is not complete without a few joss ticks. A candle that burns for long implies longevity and is a signal that wishes will be granted. For lovers it is a test of their togetherness. Krathongs that float together signify a long relationship, but if they drift apart . . . well, you do not want that to happen. The incense is wafted on the breeze. It was such a pleasure to see all those krathongs rushing down, glistening into the night.

We were also fortunate to witness the plowing festival, another ancient ceremony. This originated in India, and is a traditional occasion that marks the beginning of the rice-planting season. The rice grains to be scattered were grown on the Palace grounds. The lord of the festival, wearing state robes and a conical hat, presided over a procession that included Hindu deities and Buddha images. A Brahman high priest presented him with three *panungs* — colorful silk flags — of different lengths. If he selected a long panung, the rainfall would be plentiful, but if the panung was short there would be a drought. We held our breath, hoping he would be fortunate in his choice.

Three beautiful Thai girls walked in the procession behind a red and gold plow. They carried from their shoulder pole gold and silver baskets of rice grains. The lord of the festival took the plow in hand, which was yoked to a magnificent pair of oxen who pulled it in three concentric furrows. He then scattered the seeds as he ploughed the three furrows. He sprinkled lustral water on the earth as an offering to the Goddess Earth. The oxen were unyoked and offered a selection of grain. Whichever they chose would be plentiful in the growing season. This ended the ceremony, and the crowd rushed into the field to gather up the hallowed rice grains. Not a single grain of the coveted rice was found after everyone had left.

A royal pageant

Every 12 years the royal barges are gilded and paraded down the river with the King sitting under a nine-tier umbrella. We were privileged to witness one such parade, which coincided with our stay in Thailand. It was a grand spectacle we viewed from the verandah of the Oriental Hotel.

In the beginning the river was silent. All normal traffic was stopped. The only sound was the faint rumble of Bangkok's road traffic, with an occasional strident horn breaking vaguely through the background. Suddenly, a number of craft appeared round the distant river bend. Fairytale-like, with a gliding motion, indistinct, and still with no sound, more and more barges appeared behind them. The river at that point of the bend became dark with river craft. Still no sound.

The barges were symmetrically spaced out. In the silence, they looked like some unearthly procession from an ancient Egyptian folk tale. Then the barges approached and suddenly the procession was upon us. A cacophony of sound erupted: the thumping of long poles on the decks of the front barges, and from still far away, the chanting of the crewmen of the rear barges, the main barges. All at once, there was a mass of color, the bright colors of traditional signaling flags and ancient uniforms. The chanting grew in volume as the brown-hulled escort barges in front of the procession passed. Then the three main barges, freshly painted in gold, were in front of us. Their crewmen's chant filled the river, their uniforms a brilliant red; the golden paddles were lifted into the air in unison after each stroke. You were left feeling as if you had awakened from some incredible dream, not a modern dream, but the kind ancients used to imagine for gods and not men.

It was a display of majesty and splendor. The King was to present ceremonial robes to the monks at the Temple of Dawn, the procession destination. His barge, the largest, had a golden mythical bird not quite equivalent to the phoenix.

People could see the procession for only few baht from any public landing — standing room only, though. We did not stay for the return of the procession. I understand the return is more impressive than the downstream run, for the men are paddling against the tide, the procession moves more slowly, but there is no chanting. After the presentation of the robes His Majesty returned for the short upstream run in front of the Royal Palace.

Allegiance to the King

As a monarch King Bhumibol was and still is highly esteemed, even revered as a demigod. Protocol was strictly adhered.

We were invited to Prasan Mitr for a graduation ceremony. It was held in an open-air auditorium, built and used only once a year. Lovely little sparrows or tiny rice-birds were flying in and out twittering gaily. In the modern age of air conditioning one forgot their presence, but in this open structure they were already exploring new sites for their nests.

A temporary altar was built where a golden Buddha image, on loan from the Palace, was placed. It was surrounded by yellow chrysanthemums and artistically arranged white and purple flowers. Monks sat on a wooden bench, their chanting continuous and monotonous. It was hot.

Dressed in flowing academic robes, Their Majesties arrived. The students, in their rented gowns, curtsied or bowed seven times as they came down the aisle and marched onstage. His Majesty conferred the degrees. As the students retreated, they seemed to be entranced, gazing in the air. Photographers immortalized the scene.

Unconceivable as it seemed, mechanical, 1059 students received their degrees in a medieval setting from the monarch's hand. In chorus the students proclaimed their allegiance to the King.

While we were in Bangkok, President Lyndon B. Johnson paid a visit and signed the International Education Act in a big ceremony, which we watched on TV. The President, although warned, in the heat and the droning of Thai speeches, crossed his leg, pointing his shoe directly at the King. We all groaned as the TV camera zoomed in and out to record this *faux pas.*

Joining in the laughter

We had many visitors, made new friends, and got to know a number of business associates and acquaintances. One of them who stood out was Henry Scholte. A Dutchman, he was not only a promoter for the Dutch airline KLM, but also a Greek scholar, invited to Thailand by the Royal Court for private tutoring of the Majesty's children. Being Greek, I decided to invite him over to hear his lectures and enjoy his slides. They were magnificent; helicopters had hovered for hours above the Parthenon in order to catch the last rays of the sun cast on the ancient monument. Humbled by his collection, we decided to stop taking slides. We met Henry many times in Bangkok; on a visit to Amsterdam, I was privileged to join him for a private tour of some of the most special gems of the city.

There were always exchanges among the staff of our building. When you were invited by a neighbor it was not at all unusual to find yourself being served with your own serving pieces!

One of our neighbors had an unusual experience. He was having dinner and was expecting to carve a duck at the table. At the appropriate time, the maid appeared with the duck, but tripped as she entered and shot the duck onto the floor. As she gathered it up, the family decided to wait and see how she would handle the situation. After quite an interval, she reappeared with a piece of roast beef. Recounting the story to his car pool the next morning, a neighbor commented, "I was expecting beef last night, and instead we had duck!"

A resident of our apartment building was engaged in a research project funded by the Department of Defense. When he learned that Arthur had a solid background in statistics, he told Arthur on more than one occasion that he needed his advice on methodology. But then he began hedging to exclude classified material (Arthur was an Australian citizen at the time), and they always ended up talking about innocuous topics like sailing on the Gulf of Siam. One night we invited him to dinner, along with other guests, and persuaded him to stay after the others had gone. Arthur plied him with cognac, and some time after midnight he spilled the beans — fascinating stuff that was almost certainly never published.

When we had to eat at local restaurants, you could be sure

that the level of hygiene was low and any non-bottled water was dangerous. Indeed, we carried with us a supply of 3.2% alcohol beer to quench our thirst and to clean our teeth when we traveled. Before eating, the standard practice was to take a napkin or piece of paper and thoroughly wipe plates and utensils. On one occasion reported to us by a neighbor, Rolf Krafft, a WHO malaria engineer, he was visiting their headquarters in Geneva when he absentmindedly cleaned up his utensils at a Swiss restaurant, only to be informed by the maitre-d' that he would not be served if he thought that the restaurant was not clean, so he had better go elsewhere — which he had to do.

Our apartment building had only one phone, and an operator who really spoke no English. One morning at about 2:30 a.m. the phone rang in Krafft's apartment. It was Graham Martin, the US ambassador, who was trying to reach another neighbor, a man named Carr, a CIA Air America pilot! It was a rude reminder of the war in Vietnam.

We were in Bangkok when Jim Thompson, an American businessman and the founder of the modern Thai silk industry, disappeared while supposedly on a stroll in the jungle-clad Cameron Highlands in central Malaysia. The circumstances were unusual, and led to a massive search operation. We visited the Cameron Highlands for a short holiday after his disappearance while the investigation was going on, and ran into a teeming rumor mill. Questions ranged from "Do tigers eat shoes?" to "What was his role in the CIA?"

Neither Jim Thompson nor his body has ever been found; the case is a true life-mystery of international proportions. Many books have been written about his disappearance; he remains a legend in Southeast Asia. With his fortune he built a house and an art collection, which are among Bangkok's top tourist attractions. His home, now a museum, draws thousands of visitors every year.

First visit to Japan

Arthur had many international trips from Bangkok, involving project conferences and coordination with the teams in Nigeria and Korea. I joined him in Korea and from there we went on to take our first holiday in Japan. His friend from Stanford, Hiroshi Azuma, was informed of our visit and on our arrival at the hotel we found a message from him to invite us to a dinner that the Stanford Alumni Association was giving that very evening in honor of a professor they had worked with.

During the course of the evening, Hiroshi told us that he had mentioned to one of his senior colleagues that Arthur was visiting, and that we had been invited the following evening to dine at the professor's home, a signal honor. The next day Hiroshi picked us up at the hotel and we traveled by two subways and train to the professor's home. It became apparent that Arthur was the guest of honor, so he asked his host, "Professor Okatsu, I am flattered and honored to be invited. I am also very puzzled why you wanted to meet me." He laughed and replied that he often wrote articles for academic journals. Sometimes he wanted to reach a wider audience, and so he wrote letters to the newspaper. Occasionally he wanted to be seen as an outsider, so he had signed his letters Arthur Hill. He wanted to meet the real Arthur Hill. How did he arrive at this name? Simple: "Hill" in Japanese is Okat, and the "at" gave him the Arthur! The Japanese have very great difficulty in pronouncing the letter "r." Since "Art" is the diminutive of Arthur, for the Japanese it sounds like "at."

Years later when Arthur was a guest of the Japanese government in a program for Cultural Understanding, he paid a courtesy call to the president of the University of Tokyo. He told him about Professor Okatsu. The president took the phone and who joined them now, but Dean Okatsu!

Crossing the mighty Mekong

Before leaving Bangkok, Arthur had the opportunity to visit northern Thailand with Tom Wilson, a friend from USAID. Arthur applied for and was issued a visa to visit Laos. With Tom he arrived at the Thai town of Nonghkai, on the Mekong

River opposite Vientiane, the Lao capital. At that point the river was more than half-a-mile wide, and the riverbank was a steep cliff. At the landing, wooden steps led down from the road to the river, a descent of about 100 feet. A boat took them across the river to Laos, where they hired a taxi to see the city. It was very much a Third-World rural town, even though the French influence showed in the cuisine, a delicious *lapin* (rabbit) stew.

By the time Tom and Arthur headed back for Thailand it was late and very dark. The taxi deposited them at the riverbank and they scrambled down the stairs in the dark, only to find no boats at the dock. Tom flashed his cigarette lighter a couple of times. A boat engine started up on the Thai side. The boat arrived and carried them across the river. At the other dock they felt their way up the steps and went across the road to the Thai immigration post. Tom was stamped back into Thailand officially, but when the official looked at Arthur's passport, he announced firmly that Arthur could not be admitted as the visa he had was only good for entry at Bangkok airport. "You must return to Vientiane tomorrow morning," he said, "and get the correct visa from the Thai Embassy." Arthur protested that he had already used his single-entry visa for Laos and would not be readmitted to do this. "No problem," the immigration official stated, "I will give you a letter to the Lao officials that will serve to admit you to get the visa." As they walked out of the immigration office to head back to their hotel, they discussed the matter and decided to forget it.

Arthur kept this passport and decided not to risk entering Laos again. Obviously he had the wrong entry visa for Thailand. He would let the people back in Bangkok sort it out upon his return. The next morning, as they headed south deeper into Thailand, Arthur was disconcerted to spot an immigration check mainly designed to prevented Lao refugees straying from the border area. When the officials saw that Arthur and Tom were Westerners they waved them through with no document review. South and west of Nonghkai they again reached the Mekong River at the town of Mukdahan, opposite the Lao town of Savanaket. The Thai officials they visited suggested they cross the river with them, but Arthur said that was not possible, as he did not have his passport with him. "No problem," they assured him. "We know the Lao officials and they will let you pass." Tom was enthusiastic as he had AID colleagues in Savanaket, so off they went.

Here the Mekong was more like a mile wide, and Savanaket was somewhat upstream from Mukdahan. About halfway across the boat ran out of gasoline and they began floating downriver towards Cambodia. The boatmen were not fazed — most probably this was not the first time this had happened to them — but simply pulled up a couple of the seats and used them to paddle ashore on the Lao side. They scrambled up the steep riverbank and hiked the mile or so into town, along with one of the boatmen who then returned with fuel to bring the boat up to the dock. In the market in Savanaket — remember the French influence — Arthur found something that to this day he regrets not to have bought: a bottle of Gilbey's gin inscribed "Bottled in France under British supervision." Tom found his friends, who insisted that he stay overnight.

Arthur was also asked to stay, but he demurred, saying that he would return with the Thai officials — which he did, without difficulty. During the night he could see tracer bullets across the river and hear the noise of explosions. The Vietnam War was closer than was comfortable. Next morning, he went down to the dock to wait for Tom's return. When he had not appeared by 10:00 a.m., he became concerned. However, a little later a boat showed up and there was Tom. He had arrived quite early to cross. The boatman asked him, "Do you have a passport?" Tom did not want to divulge he had a passport. He said he did not, and the boatman charged him the local fare of five baht (about 25 cents). Tom asked in his passable Thai "How much would it be if I had a passport?" "Twenty baht" was the reply. The boatman waited for more passengers, but none showed up. Tom asked him how long he would wait, and he said until he had twenty passengers. He then offered him a 100 baht for departing at once, but this was not acceptable. They waited until the passengers arrived — mostly market women with melons to sell in Thailand. Tom recounted that there had been a Viet Minh attack during the night and that the USAID officials had been on alert status for possible evacuation by air to Phnom Penh. Arthur did not know what he would have done if his friend had disappeared this way, but I suspect that he would have found a way back to Bangkok.

Tom had access to the US air bases supporting the war in Vietnam, and they ate at the officers' mess at several of them. He would point out the insignia of the flyers and describe the kinds and the capabilities of the aircraft they flew. Once when they were almost done eating, a pilot stopped to chat with a group of officers at the next table. He did not sit down, but he placed a device he was carrying on Arthur's and Tom's table as they talked. Tom looked at it, then said, "Let's go." When they were out of earshot he said, "I don't know what that was, but I was not going to talk into it."

Mission completed

Arthur's two-year assignment contract in Thailand was coming to an end. The pilot study had been completed, and the Thai government took over the implementation. Tests had been devised, applicable to students in the developing world; data had been gathered and results coordinated with findings from other countries; meaningful patterns emerged. A book was written to provide insights on testing for vocational and technical careers.

Arthur's administrative skills were brought to the attention of the Ford Foundation in New York. He was offered the position of Deputy Representative in the Philippines. He would be heading that office three years later.

With the Ford Foundation in the Philippines

*A*fter a brief orientation at the Ford Foundation's New York headquarters, we flew to Manila; it was 1968, and it was our first time in the Philippines.

The reports we had of the Philippines suggested a land and society ruled by anarchic violence, political patronage, corruption, administrative inefficiency, and economic hardship. We found this to be sadly true. But we also realized that all these negative things were but one aspect of Philippine national life — and were not the truly significant aspect to con sider. They were merely symptoms of a deeper ferment, the diseases of growing up.

The Philippines was perhaps the least fortunate of colonies in its "choice" of colonial masters — first, the Spanish, who were determined to convert the people to Spanish Catholicism, and second, the Americans who were determined to provide universal education in English. Each succeeded in leaving deep marks through out the social and cultural fabric of the Philippines, whereas other colonial powers soon suppressed whatever missionary impulses they had, and settled down to exploiting the commercial possibilities of their Asian Empires. An awareness of the tensions produced by the dichotomy of living in two civilizations — one traditional Malay, the other Western-educated Christian — goes to the heart of growing up Filipino. This experience colors the decision-making of every Filipino leader. Not surprisingly, decisions at each extreme of the spectrum are loudly proclaimed and vehemently argued.

In 1968, with the possible exception of Vietnam, social change was occurring in the Philippines at a faster rate than anywhere else in Southeast Asia, this was key to understanding the Philippines. Because the props and structures of traditional Philippine life are being broken faster than new ones were set, Philippine society appeared a great deal more chaotic than its neighbors, where customs still largely prevailed.

Because of its situation and its needs as a developing country, the Philippines has sought and received help from a number of international agencies and institutions — among them, the Ford Foundation, for which Arthur worked initially as Deputy Representative.

Making a difference

Arthur believed that international philanthropy served more than the ends of economic development. He saw that external assistance had an impact on nation building, including social and cultural variables, in ways that were not always measurable. He believed that the Foundation should help countries define their own criteria for development, and to think in terms of generations, instead of merely grant periods. Crisis to him was essential for change. Without a crisis, significant change was unlikely, and without change, development was unlikely. From this view, the Philippines was ripe for rapid development.

The major thrust of the Ford Foundation's program in the Philippines was what was called "institution building," in the jargon of the time. Arthur was pleased to see how well the Filipinos used Ford funds in building on their strengths. Ford helped set up many centers of excellence in many units of the

University of the Philippines, as well as bridges between these centers and related activities around them — especially in the countryside, where most poor Filipinos lived. These Ford-supported centers included internationally respectable colleges of agriculture, engineering, business administration, public administration, and economics, as well as a science education center and a demographic institute.

The Science Education Center was instrumental in upgrading national science teaching, while the College of Agriculture helped strengthen agricultural education throughout the country and provided support to the Department of Agriculture and National Resources. The College of Public Administration and the School of Economics each had something to offer in increasing the level of sophistication in public management and economic development.

The Foundation also co-sponsored the International Rice Research Institute (IRRI) in Los Baños with the Rockefeller Foundation. Innovative, interdisciplinary teamwork by Asian and Western scientists achieved radical advances in rice culture at IRRI.

In addition to his Foundation work, Arthur served at the invitation of Ambassador Henry Byroade as a member of the board of directors of the Philippine-American Educational Foundation and the Eisenhower fellowship selection committee. As the relationship of the US government with the Philippines was undergoing a mutual re-examination, the ties that the educational exchange program was promoting were increasingly important.

In Manila, the Foundation's focus was not limited to the University of the Philippines, but encompassed development programs at De La Salle College (now a university); library projects and development of the Center of Educational Television at the Ateneo de Manila University; language research at the Philippine Normal College (also now a university); and graduate business administration at the Asian Institute of Management.

Arthur's work brought him all over the islands visiting educational institutions: library and educational administration development at Xavier University in Cagayan de Oro; assistance to Mindanao State University in Marawi; improvement of pre-service and in-service training at Notre Dame Educational Association in Cotabato, Marbel, and Jolo; development of financial resources and undergraduate programs at Silliman University in Dumaguete. He completed what the Ford Foundation started: establishing Notre Dame College of Jolo as a center for the social sciences, Notre Dame Marbel College as a center for Science and Mathematics, and Notre Dame University of Cotabato as a center for language and teacher training.

Although education was the major focus, substantial resources were earmarked for agricultural development, agriculture extension, and the accreditation of colleges of agriculture. In addition there were projects in population and human reproduction at the University of the Philippines and the University of Santo Tomas. Arthur had a team of distinguished advisers whose guidance he respected.

During his entire tour of duty, he rendered educational institutions a most friendly and sympathetic assistance; he guided them smoothly through the completion of major grants. He assisted librarians in observing computerized library models abroad. He encouraged people with good ideas; he had a genuine concern and personal interest for the people who were part of the Foundation's projects. Conferences, discussions on development, and public events were not for him cold transactions but pleasant meetings of human warmth and good humor. He felt comfortable in any situation, whether in the glittering city of Manila or in the backwaters of Cotabato and Sulu. He is still remembered as a model of depth, precision, and brevity of speech.

Many discussions were held in the Manila office with the Foundation's Southeast Asian representative on the role of the Foundation in the years ahead. The talks included the University of the Philippines and educational planning at the national level; assistance to a regional educational association to develop as a resource for socio-economic planning; and research in agricultural marketing in the Department of Agriculture and Natural Resources; and a new approaches to rural development. Two criteria that Arthur imposed were, first, that the Foundation should build on strengths they had helped to develop, and second, the Foundation should reserve a small percentage of its funds for higher-risk, innovative programs more directly related to social development. As an example of the latter he thought of possible support to some imaginative, well-led programs being developed for squatter resettlement.

An emphasis on agriculture

As a considerable majority of Filipinos relied on agriculture as their means of livelihood, a special emphasis was placed on agriculture and it became one of Arthur's priorities. This was a program close to his heart. He traveled all over the country to learn about the existing institutions and I was privileged to join him on many of those trips. There were so many different kinds of institutions, with so many different forms of control that they were unresponsive to any simple approach to improvement or change. There were too many degree-granting institutions for the resources available. There was continuous political pressure to introduce college departments into high schools, to upgrade Bureau of Vocational Education schools into state colleges, and to convert state colleges into state universities.

What could be done? This proliferation had to be stopped, and standards had to be raised. Arthur and his team felt that the most urgent need was for a moratorium on the creation of new degree-granting institutions in agriculture and a sharp reduction in the number of existing ones. Along with this it would be desirable to simplify the state institutions so that they were all similarly organized.

He recognized that downgrading many institutions would not be a popular move politically, and there would have to be a quid pro to make it acceptable. Arthur did not present a solution but came up with a few suggestions for consideration. The most important was the establishment of an accredited body with procedures, a body empowered to accredit specified programs. Only accredited programs would continue to be recognized by the government for new employees with a waiting period of, say, two or three years to enable present programs to adjust or to phase out if necessary. New programs would be recognized only if they met the accrediting body's criteria. Those schools not accredited would revert to high schools offering extension services. Opportunities would be provided for faculty members with graduate degrees to transfer to the accredited institutions if they wished and special scholarships were to be provided to enable students from areas with no college to attend one of the accredited colleges. It may have been necessary to channel some of the scholarships through the local congressman to serve as a counter to the loss of the college.

Little savings were expected in state institutions, as their budget was barely adequate. Within individual schools quality needs set out under the problem of "Improvement of Standards" required attention whether or not accreditation was adopted.

The accreditation program was put to motion, the system was rationalized, and support was sought from bilateral and multilateral agencies.

The Education Task Force

Among Arthur's various assignments, the one that stood out was heading an Education Task Force. Its goal was to review educational priorities, recommend changes, and assert guidelines for accreditations, focusing on graduate education. His team embraced leading educators from the Philippines and expert consultants from Australia. It was a monumental task. Arthur felt that strengthening and equipping a college was not enough. Continued and strong support by the government was required to enable a college to fully realize its potential contribution to national development. At the end of his tour he was pleased to learn that "a government bill had a second reading in both houses of Congress providing for a ten-year development program. Specifically the bill was seeking to ensure that the output of the educational system is geared to or consistent with the requirements of national development" (from a letter of Executive Secretary Alejandro Melchor.) Again progress was being made.

The Education Task Force report was not another study shelved and covered with dust. It became a blueprint for improving Philippine tertiary education. Millions of dollars of grant money were received from the World Bank. Years later, the recommendations were still in effect, the foundation of many improvements in the country's educational landscape. Three decades later, Arthur was still remembered for this important contribution.

Settling Down in Manila

With diplomatic privileges extended to the Foundation representational staff, we did not have to go through the chaos of a developing nation's airport when we arrived in Manila in 1968, although our passports and belongings were delivered couple of hours late. We were whisked to our new fully furnished house in one of the gated communities of Makati, a posh suburb of Manila and also its central business district. It was to be our home for nearly five years.

An informal get-together party was arranged for the next day, to meet key members of the University of the Philippines faculty, recipients of major foundation grants. They were a bubbly and fun-loving group. One person stood out among them; a quite, reserved, and humble academic; he was dean of the School of Business Administration, Cesar Virata. He was to serve the nation for a long time in greater capacities, first as Secretary of Finance, and later as the Prime Minister.

CPR: a towering figure

Within days of our arrival, it was essential for Arthur to meet the president of the University of the Philippines and to discuss the future directions of Foundation assistance. The president at that time was Carlos P. Romulo. He had a great regard for Arthur's predecessor, so this first meeting was important to both for sizing up each other.

The diminutive but urbane Romulo was well known for his credentials as an international figure. He had been the first Asian president of the United Nations General Assembly, and was one of the original signers of the UN Charter. He addressed the founding session of the UN with the words, "Let us make this floor the last battlefield."

Arthur asked his office to make an appointment, a courtesy call, to meet Romulo. I was delighted to be included. A luncheon was to follow. We drove to Diliman, the wooded University of the Philippines campus in Quezon City north of Manila, and immediately found ourselves surrounded by people. "What is going on?" I asked Arthur. "Who is coming? Why are there photographers?" At that time I was not aware of the Filipino compulsion of immortalizing events, meetings, celebrations, and even ordinary occasions.

We were ushered into an impressive, heavily paneled office. Romulo was sitting behind an ornate wooden desk, and got up to greet us. I immediately noticed how small he stood, at just a little over five feet tall.

In this first meeting with him, I discovered what a delightful and charming host we had, what a great raconteur. He loved to regale his guests with stories, and we quickly fell under his spell. Romulo told us that he came in the '20s to the United States as a graduate student, taking the long voyage by steamboat over the Pacific, and landing in Vancouver. He knew that both Arthur and I were not American-born and asked "What about you? Did you arrive by plane? Or enjoyed, like me, the long sea voyage?"

Arthur responded that he traveled from Australia by Super Constellation — one of the most highly regarded propeller-driven planes of its time — although it still had to make many stops, as planes in the '50s were not equipped to fly all the way from Australia to the West Coast.

"I stopped in Fiji, my first trip outside the US," Arthur recalled, "then we were to stop in Honolulu, but the winds were against us and we landed for refueling in Canton Island [in what is now known as Kiribati, in the South Pacific]. I found a washroom with hot water and clean towels, my first experience on American soil. We did not have that back home in Australia."

I, on the other hand, told President Romulo my story — how I came by steamboat "on the *Queen Frederika*, named after our then Greek queen. We docked in New York. It was exactly one day after the *Andrea Doria* sank in the fog, off the Canadian shore."

"What was the cutlery like?" asked Romulo. I was dumbfounded. Why did he take an interest in cutlery? He proceeded to tell us that he crossed the continent from Vancouver to New York on the Canadian Pacific Railway. During his journey, he systematically "acquired" a set of cutlery. "What a better way to regale my professors at Columbia University than with cutlery embossed with my own initials: CPR!"

The conversation shifted to more serious matters. However, we kept wondering about all the pictures taken during our meeting. Next day, they were delivered at the Ford Foundation office, autographed. This set of pictures was the first of many that we would receive over the years.

Romulo's tenure at the University of the Philippines was followed by his nomination as Foreign Secretary. We were privileged to be invited often to join lavish entertainment in his lovely compound in Forbes Park, one of the most exclusive enclaves of Manila. We mingled with dignitaries from around the world. Romulo had quickly taken a liking to me. While at the UN, he had had a Greek secretary, from whom he learned a few naughty Greek words. The moment he saw me, there was a warm embrace and an abundance of Greek sweet words. Once, as I moved through a receiving line, getting introduced and shaking hands, I heard his endearing Greek words. I got so confused and embarrassed that I found myself shaking hands with a Thai monk, and breaking a taboo thereby.

The waiters were attentive; drinks and an assortment of Filipino appetizers were passed around. The delicious *lumpia* — a kind of spring roll — in its tangy sweet and sour sauce was very tempting, but I declined. Romulo was behind me. It did not take long before I heard his voice, "if it was *keftedakia, tiropitakia*" — Greek appetizers — you would have sampled them."

He reveled in the company of intelligent, charming women. At his receptions, especially when men were bunched together, he went over to the women. "I see men all day," he explained with a twinkle in his eye. "I want to be entertained."

He made fun of himself. When in New York, "I always stay at the Waldorf Towers between the 35th and 53rd floor," he told me. Why those floors? "I cannot reach any higher button on the elevator." On another occasion, when India appointed a new ambassador to the Philippines, he staged a reception in his honor. The new ambassador was also a short man. Romulo seized the moment and thanked the Indian government for sending "a man of my stature" to represent his country.

He recalled that in New York, Henry Kissinger, the German-born US Secretary of State, gave a toast and said, "Don't you find it odd that the Minister of Foreign Affairs of the Philippines speaks clearer English than the US Secretary of State?"

Romulo was a gallant, impish, and humorous personality. This trait, added to his brilliant intellect, made him a successful diplomat and highly respected representative of his country in many world forums.

In the golden ghetto

The rhythm of life in the Philippines was very different from anything we had experienced before. Our home in Urdaneta Village, one of the gated communities, could be described as the golden ghetto of foreign expatriates. Visitors came and went. It was all official entertaining. Breakfasts, lunches, and dinners sometimes generated up to a hundred guests a month. They held a variety of professions, representing the arts, academic, and business communities. We had to bring together our overseas visitors with the right mix of expatriate advisors and distinguished Filipinos, leading members of the government, academia, and the business community. Entertaining always took place at home, where we had an able staff of four to help me. They took care of the details of maintaining the household and caring for the visitors. To be sure, there were a host of more or less amusing entertaining incidents.

Siri had been running the Foundation's guesthouse. In the late '60s, the Intercontinental Hotel had opened and, our visitors had a place to stay close by; the guesthouse was closed, a substantial saving for the Foundation. This was how Siri joined our household as a cook. She was from Leyte, one of the Visayan islands, and before long our whole household fared from Leyte.

Siri, Filomena, part of our household staff in Manila

She was a very capable and hard-working woman who started baking early in the morning. She always put the newspaper neatly on its place on our breakfast table. It was common to start breakfast with a large wedge of papaya with half a *calamansi* or native lime to squeeze over it, or a huge mango split in thirds with a knife that pierced the large seed so that every bit of this king of fruit could be enjoyed.

Our overseas visitors were not ready to tackle the mango, but preferred the deep orange-fleshed papaya. We had to persuade them to taste a mango, and they subsequently teased us for not having insisted in offering this delicious fruit earlier.

Siri produced a *pan de sal* (a soft fist-sized morning bread), an *empanada* (a meat pie), or a fluffy Spanish roll, but most often it was her famous freshly baked sour-cream coffee cake that was on the table. The delicacies were washed down with strong Batangas coffee. Whenever the fruit of a certain season was ripe, it was out on the table. Generally the fruit in the Philippines was spectacular and different from anything we had before. Papayas and mangoes were our favorites. They were much larger and sweeter than the Mexican and Hawaiian varieties that one finds in the US. There were many varieties of bananas, ranging from tiny ones no larger than a man's finger to the large ones weighing a pound or more and at least ten or twelve inches long. There were red bananas, green bananas, cooking plantains.

Our driver Ponciano and our gardener Ernesto decided it was time for us to have our own banana tree. But which variety? We left the decision to their able hands and here they came from the market with a six-foot tree. Next decision was the time to plant it. Our instinct was to proceed early in the morning before the hot sun descended on us. We were wrong. You plant the banana tree at noon, after a good lunch. "Stomach has to be full, so that the fruit will be big and heavy." It was a wise decision. Our banana tree the following year was heavy with those glorious bunches.

Ponciano, Ernesto, Arthur and Julie planting a banana tree

There were so many other wonderful fruits in the Philippines: star apples, chicos, rambutans, a variety of lychees, oranges, custard apples, and huge pomelos, which resemble giant red grapefruit.

The wonderful fruit of SE Asia

They were all unfamiliar to us. The calamansi was used much like we use lemons — to sharpen the flavor of papayas and melons, or to squeeze over fish or anything that required tart flavor. Calamansi juice was always available. Years later, we still missed it.

Mindanao produced jackfruit and durian with their infamous odor. Foreigners in South East Asia would recall the odor with a shudder, but would also remember eating durian and enjoying its beguiling flavor. The foul-smelling spiky exterior of these fruits encloses large seeds covered with a buttery flesh that tastes to the initiated like heaven. Durian could not be carried in a plane from the Southern islands. The regulations pertained to the passengers — but who would stop the pilot and the crew from carrying the fruit? Mangosteens were shipped carefully from the Southern Philippines to Manila. They are delicate fruits that bruise very easily. Their stiff magenta-colored leathery skin covers a translucent white flesh, with a perfect balance of sweetness and acidity, and it was one of our favorites.

I planned the menu the day before. After breakfast, Siri took a bus to the local market, where she purchased fresh vegetables, fish — usually *lapu-lapu* (a sea bass variety) — and meat. Loaded with supplies, she returned by taxi. Basic staples were available at the supermarket, and nothing was lacking in Manila. I enjoyed arranging the flower centerpieces, especially since we had access to so many glorious tropical flowers. Filomina, the house girl, had the tablecloths neatly pressed. Did we need extra help for the evening?" I called the office to ask about the latest number of guests who accepted our invitation. If the number of guests was large, I would call the Polo Club and ask for Pedro, our favorite waiter, to come and help. An extra pair of hands would ensure smooth entertaining. For a festive occasion we would hire a musician to play the violin.

Siri was able to make a variety of superb desserts based on our local fruits. Mangoes were sprinkled with brown sugar, anise seeds, and perhaps a drop of Pernod, and slightly sautéed in butter. It was a remarkable dessert well remembered years later. Often she prepared *suman*, a marvelous concoction of sticky rice and coconut milk baked in banana leaves and served with a generous slice of mango. The calamansi meringue pie was a staple. It was always refreshing, and always available in our household.

Visitors and some surprises

Our own visitors represented a diverse spectrum of the academic, government, and business world. Dinner parties were always sit-down affairs. Invitations to single people were addressed to "Mr." and "friend." Place cards had to be written at the last moment in order to correspond to the friend.

We had a few surprises. In one occasion, a Dutch priest, who was also a teacher in one of the colleges, appeared with a KLM airhostess. We got accustomed to the variety of companions. Our experience in Thailand served us well. It was not unusual to have the minor wife replacing the senior one in our dinner parties.

We once entertained a population-planning expert and gathered the right entourage of Filipinos. One of them was married to Aurora, who at that time was a leading actress. There was much excitement in the household for having the leading actress at home. The buzz reached the neighborhood. Every maid on our street volunteered to come, help, serve, and just to be there. No pay! We had had the Prime Minister of the Philippines in our home. Once we hosted Robert McNamara, the US Defense Secretary and a Ford Foundation board member. Our staff could not care less for these personages, but Aurora was something else. She was petite, with a very round face, almond eyes, and a magnificent smile. But when the flash of the smile was gone, the face was no more attractive than those of many other beautiful Filipino ladies.

With the Foundation having an interest in agricultural projects, professors from Cornell University and the University of California in Davis were frequent visitors. One of our most frequent guests was Dean Dioscoro Umali of the UP College of Agriculture. I still recall the story he told of traveling from Manila to Bangkok, when at the airport lounge he met a young mother with her two children. He was a friendly type, liked children, and chatted with them for a while. After boarding the plane, the young lady just dumped the two youngsters to sit next to him. Here was a kind soul, she must have thought, who could take care of my children during the flight. Umali wanted to work, so he asked the airhostess if she could bring two glasses of milk and drink of Scotch. He took the Scotch, poured it in the milk, and gave it to the kids. They slept all the way to Bangkok.

There were many functions to attend from simple family dinners to prestigious formal affairs. Men often wore their glorious embroidered *barong tagalog*, and the ladies, some of them heavy with jewelry, displayed their mestiza *terno* dresses with butterfly sleeves embroidered and beaded in elaborate designs. Once there was a performance by the Vienna Boy's Choir in the lush garden of the home of Washington Sycip, senior partner of the major consulting and accounting firm of the country and the honorary consul of Austria. It was not uncommon for business people to acquire diplomatic credentials. The honorary consul of Costa Rica was another case. The honorary consul of Finland was a Miss Universe married to a Filipino millionaire. They all made the sought-after list of the diplomatic corps.

An Adamson from Arta

The honorary consul of Greece was Alex Adamson, a businessman in the paper industry and founder of the private Adamson University. He hailed from Arta, a village near Delphi. He often gathered the Greek community and anyone remotely connected with Greece. The Sunday dinners Alex hosted were always a treat, and the aperitifs alone reached a staggering variety. Lillian, his wife, taught her cook well to prepare traditional dishes.

Alex devoted handsome amounts of time for his honorary duties. Greek ship owners favored Filipino sailors, so there were plenty of visas to issue and backgrounds to check.

Alex was willing to issue a Greek passport for Arthur. "Just make the Sign of the Cross and I'll issue a Greek passport. After all, you're married to a Greek." We didn't know how serious he was, but we regretted not taking Alex up on his offer. With Greece becoming part of the European Union, it would have been a useful document for crisscrossing the European borders.

After a Sunday dinner at the Adamsons, we took advantage of the chance to attend an occasional polo game. The Manila Polo Club had an attractive Olympic-size swimming pool, a bowling alley, and numerous tennis courts. It was a meeting place for diplomats, Filipinos, and expatriate businessmen. The polo players came from the elite of the country, and each player used up to six horses during a game. This was a game for the super-rich.

Days of good deeds

Life was not confined to entertaining dignitaries or traveling in the islands. I got invited to join a dozen of warm-hearted, compassionate Filipino ladies. We ran a thrift shop in a very depressed area of Manila. A Catholic shelter run by nuns had provided us with two spacious rooms.

We collected donations each month from relatives, friends, and neighbors; I tapped the wives of the Ford Foundation consultants for clothing and household items. I still recall the generosity of an Australian lady who offered every month a case of soap for the thrift shop, where we sold our donations. We strongly believed that items purchased were better appreciated than given away. They cost only a few pesos, perhaps even a few centavos. With our proceeds we hired a couple of manicurists who taught their skills to low-income young girls. We hired a radio repairman who daily instructed young boys how to repair radios. His class was very well attended; his workshop was well furnished with tools and gadgets, the generous donation of a Filipino banker. The nuns taught the process of papermaking from cogon grass and rice straw. Lovely notes were made, decorated with pressed flowers and leaves. For years we used these handcrafted notes for our Christmas greetings.

It was a minimal contribution of my time and we found great satisfaction when we were able to place our graduates with plush shops in Ermita or Makati. Just our presence sparked those students' hope in an otherwise bleak place.

The Manila art scene

The art scene was vibrant. Manila, a centuries-old entrepot, was rich in art and culture, and we were privileged to visit many private art collections. The National Philharmonic under the baton of Redentor Romero was world-class. Most importantly, the whole orchestra was an ensemble of Filipino musicians. When one traveled in Asia, it appeared that every band and every musician came from the Philippines.

Art galleries flourished. A self-exiled painter stormed into town and set new price ceilings. The audience increased. So did the column inches devoted to art in the newspapers and magazines. It cannot be denied that the catalyst was Mrs. Imelda Marcos, the famous wife of the President of the Philippines.

Imelda Marcos at an art exhibit with Phyllis Harvey and Julie

She bolstered the arts to new heights. She was always there at the opening of the exhibits and induced a great number of people to take an interest in the arts. She sparked an art fever among the members of the social register. Art patronage began to rise.

The Luz Gallery in Makati was run by Arturo Luz, a leading painter, known for his high standards of professionalism. His gallery gained the trust of the public and the artists. The Solidaridad gallery and bookshop was located in Ermita, run by novelist Frankie Sionil Jose. He had been the editor of the widely circulated *Sunday Times Magazine* and was a prolific novelist. Solidaridad was to be the middle ground between the established artists exhibiting at Luz and smaller galleries where new talent was championed. You could find superb examples of prints, drawings, miniatures, relief metal sculptures, collage, photographs, and paintings all over Manila.

We were interested in meeting the artists and visiting their studios, but were reluctant to pay the gallery prices. If we liked the work of a particular artist, why not buy directly from him or her? This was how we searched for and found the home of Hernando Ocampo.

Hernando Ocampo was a pure abstract expressionist with a daring originality in his paintings. His work was unmistakably Filipino, ascribing this national character to his unique, tropical colors. A typical Ocampo painting is not unlike a honeycomb, a complex weave of color and tone with each individual cell suggesting a large, more real life form. His work is tropical and warm and suggestive of symmetry. The colors and shapes seem to dance before the eyes. His home in Maypajo was a mecca for friends, admirers, and collectors. He had an open house on Sundays. Good food and hard and soft drinks were ready for guests. Visiting Ocampo, we felt welcomed not only by the artist but also by his family. We commissioned a painting. Sketches were drawn;

Arthur, Julie with Hernando Ocampo

we followed the progress of our painting with our weekly Sunday visits, and sampled the wonderful *pancit*, that ubiquitous Filipino noodle dish, that was offered. We photographed the progress of his work. He completed the "Song of Summer", a mastery of color in 17 different shades of red. It would hang proudly in our home in California, and continue to provide intense, pleasurable excitement, another reminder of our times in the Philippines.

Hidden treasures in Ermita

It was difficult not to be interested in antiques when you were in the Philippines, given its rich Spanish and Chinese heritage. Leandro Locsin, a noted architect who designed the Cultural Center, had a fabulous collection of ceramics. (Interestingly, Luz, Jose, Ocampo, and Locsin would all later be named National Artists, the highest artistic honor conferred by the Philippine government.) Indeed, his house was built around the collection. In architectural terms, it was the most stunning house we visited in Manila. Jaime Laya had collected *santos* or antique religious figurines through the years. With a keen eye, a deep historical perspective, lots of bargaining, and a network of trader's contacts, he managed to accumulate one of the most extensive collections of santos in the Philippines. He was always avidly looking for new purchases, and we often joined him on in his acquisitional sorties. There were weekly visits to the antique shops in Ermita, to such places as those of Ms. Cortez, who owned an extensive compound. When traveling around the country, browsing antique shops became a priority. I asked Jimmy once about this hobby, about the pleasure his collection gave him. His answer was the satisfaction "of dusting and oiling my santos." I wonder if he still has time to do this.

A wave of church renovations and modernizations resulted in the appearance of many meticulous pieces of great craftsmanship in the market. Cash-strapped heirs of collections disposed of their possessions, which included santos, old hanging lamps, portraits, silver candelabras, and old colonial jewelry. As Jimmy was a good customer, newly arrived pieces were put aside for his inspection and potential purchase. We accompanied him many times. Our interest was sparked, a few pieces were purchased, and a modest collection was established.

The Press Foundation

Amitabha Chowdhury was the president of the Press Foundation of Asia. He was a renowned Bengali journalist and a winner of the prestigious Ramon Magsaysay Award — the equivalent of a Pulitzer Prize — and a good friend of ours. Evening at the Chowdhury's was a real treat. Neepa, his wife, was an artist — a painter and one of the best cooks I have ever known. Her repertoire was not limited to Bengali cooking; she experimented and excelled with various Asian and European recipes. Neepa introduced me to Bengali cooking, which involved the art of blending freshly pounded aromatic seeds, barks, and nuts.

News organizations employed only non-Asian foreign journalists at the time. Reuters and Agence France Press had their biases, and CNN had yet to be born. Amithaba questioned this prejudice, and asked why foreigners, and not Asians, disseminated Asian news. He became the catalyst in getting funds and establishing the Press Foundation of Asia with an initial grant from the Ford Foundation. It was the time when tiger economies and the Vietnam War placed Southeast Asia on global economic and political maps. Reporters from Asian capitals were hired, and every week a magazine called *Asian Finance*, founded by Amitabha, rolled out of Hong Kong. It specialized in in-depth coverage of political and economic news of the region from an Asian point of view. It was read by expatriates and Asians whose national media were often partisan or parochial.

Tarzie Vittachi was the editor of *Asian Finance*, and his humor pieces were a delight to read every week. Who can forget Tarzie's descriptions of filling out an immigration form in Singapore? He filled the "profession" category of the form with "smuggler." No one at immigration paid attention. On a

Japanese form, Tarzie replied to the question "Where did you spend the last fifteen nights?" by writing down "With my wife, with my mistress, with my mistress, with my wife, with my mistress, etc." Tarzie wrote under several pseudonyms, as there was not very much money to go around when the *Asian* was first launched. A few years later, the Press Foundation received the prestigious Magsaysay Award.

Neepa was able to create a fabulous atmosphere. She often placed a tent in the middle of her dining room. Her black marble dishes were encrusted with semi-precious stones, and the shiny silver bowls were full of aromatic chutneys. Indian ragas were always playing in the background. Leading journalists, editors, and cartoonists congregated at their table. It was at their home where we met Joaquin "Chino" Roces of the prestigious *Manila Times,* Geny Lopez of the *Chronicle*, and leading Asian and American journalists. Some of them became friends and it was a pleasure to visit them in their home countries years later. There were long insightful discussions of politics and the economy that covered the whole of Asia. A gathering at the Chowdhurys became one of the most stimulating evenings of our stay in the Philippines.

With Neepa, we decided to co-author a cookbook as a fundraiser for Bengali refugees. It was an ambitious project. Try melding Greek and Indian recipes! Did *samosas* originate in the island of Samos? What was the difference between Greeks using sour cream and Indians using yogurt? Was *paneer* close to feta cheese? Measurements had to be standardized to the Western ways. As so much of our cooking was inspirational, it took months to put our cookbook together. A leading journalist served as our editor. We had lined up a publisher, who unfortunately was put in jail, an anti-Marcos dissident as he was. By the time the cookbook was ready, our publisher remained in jail, and the book remained an unpublished manuscript. I still flip through its pages from time to time, recounting the treasured recipes.

In the Grip of a Typhoon

The weather in the Philippines was always hot and humid, with very little difference between summer and winter. We were, after all, in the tropics. Air conditioning was available only in the bedrooms, and there was just enough cooling to alleviate the humidity for a comfortable sleep. During the day, the overhead fans in our patio and dining room swiveled at full blast.

During the rainy season we had depressions, steady downpours with thunder and lightning. Before long, the eaves of the house had torrents running off them. The roads were flooded in rivers of water. But nothing prepared us for the arrival of the typhoon season.

Typhoons — also known as cyclones and hurricanes elsewhere in the world — originate somewhere in the Pacific Ocean and hit the islands with regularity. Mostly the pattern for a typhoon was to hit the Visayas, the string of islands in the middle of the archipelago. The year 1970 was one of typhoon damage, as three major typhoons devastated the country. The third, Typhoon Yoling in its Philippine name, and Patsy in the international naming system, went through Manila, with winds clocked at 125 miles per hour. This was the most powerful wind in any typhoon to hit the Philippines since 1883 and certainly the most destructive in memory. Makati where we lived is the business center of Manila, and the enclave of some of the exclusive gated villages, but it was not spared the full force of the storm. Fortunately it came and went in daylight, and we had no rain since it passed.

Our own damage was discouraging, but no one in our household was hurt. So many people suffered so much more. Arthur was in his office that morning, through the first and worse part of the storm. From his sixth-floor window it must have been spectacular and terrifying to see trees breaking, roofs lifting and peeling off construction site sheds nearby, and sheets of galvanizing iron being picked up and carried 50 to a hundred feet into the air and sailing along before being unceremoniously dropped again. Whole roofs were flying around, trailing chandeliers. At times the downpour came in horizontal sheets, bending and up rooting palm tress, flooding streets and pounding roofs. Some large plate glass windows popped both from the vacuum created by winds and from the sheer force of the wind. Fortunately they were either in corridors or in the visitors' office not in use that day.

The winds really began to pick up early morning. It was soon after that the electricity went off and our phone at home went out. The office phone survived throughout. Since Arthur was no longer in contact with me, he became concerned. By noon, he decided he would use the few minutes of calm when the eye of the storm was passing to come home. The wind had slightly dropped, the sky lightened, and he decided to leave. He ran down the stairs, jumped in his car, and set off. A number of cars had bumped into each other, blocking a nearby corner on his usual route, so he had to go around. At the entrance to the village where we lived he found the road blocked by a concrete light pole, complete with wires. He headed off in another direction and within a hundred yards of our house only to find a tree blocking the road.

He turned around the block. By now the eye of the storm had passed and the winds were picking up rapidly. To his horror, he found that more fallen electric poles blocked the other way. At that point he decided to bump right on over them. When he reached our gate, the wind was very high indeed. For a moment he pondered how he could get out of the car, unlock the gate and get into the house without being blown away or carved by flying sheets of metal. He looked at his rear view mirror and saw a whole roof advancing straight towards the back of the car. There was nothing he could do, so he decided to sit tight. The wind had strengthened, and the roof, tilted into a vertical position, was picked up by the wind. It flew right above the car without making a scratch, and came down in front of the car, erasing a piece of chrome upon landing, and then kept going down the street. Another sheet of galvanized iron flew by. Then the wind seemed to ease a bit, so he jumped out of the car, slammed the door, opened the gate and ran into the house. He could have been decapitated. He was soaked by the time he got inside.

In the house our staff were busy mopping up the water, which was blowing under the door and under the windows. We had louver-type windows in many of our rooms. The bedroom and one bathroom were on the stormy side. The wind broke the louvers and water was being blown in. The rugs were rolled and put on tables. We took books from a bookshelf and put them in a linen closet in the center of the house. By mid-afternoon the worst had passed and we were able to go outside and inspect the damage. It was devastating.

A roof in the garden

A large section of someone's roof was lying in our front garden complete with beams. It had broken a large section of a high stone fence, and snapped off two beautiful native palm trees. We had a projecting section of our roof, which the intruder had also broken down. Ten yards farther and undoubtedly it would have come right through our living room wall. Normally we had a row of flowerpots of beautiful bougainvilleas along the top of the front garden wall. We had lifted these down and put them on the ground. In spite of these precautions, most had blown away or broken.

The back of the garden was almost completely wiped out. Some of my most valuable orchids had disappeared, blown away by the winds. I managed to rescue my favorite one. Our mango tree was flat on the ground, although we tried later on to make it stand. Our big palm tree was completely uprooted, and a very large acacia tree was leaning crazily over the back fence with the major root sticking up into the air. The trees were striped of leaves and very few shrubs and flowering plants remained. The rain had been pounding for three hours.

Later that afternoon, the Foundation's administrative officer arrived. She climbed over the fallen tree to inform us that the roof of one of the Ford Foundation advisors had completely blown off. We drove over to superintend the operation of the rescue. The family concerned, Henry and Jane Feenstra, were Canadians with two children aged three and five. First we got the children shipped off to another family, ascertaining that none was hurt. Then we went to the rescue. Henry had been upstairs checking on how things were holding when he saw the roof start to lift. He headed for the stairs, and was about six feet from the top of the stairs when the roof went off and he was picked up bodily by the wind that pushed him over the stairs without touching a step and dumped him on the floor about six feet past the foot of the stairs. It was as if a vacuum sucked him downwards. Fortunately the stairs went straight down without a bend. His elbow was hit hard and had to be checked. No point in rushing for X-rays to a hospital, though, as they had some real emergencies to deal with. For the next few hours we packed Henry's things into one of our station wagons and moved them to a dry house. We then checked how the other families fared.

The Kimballs, our education advisor team, were on home leave. They were living in an apartment on Roxas Boulevard overlooking Manila Bay, and their roof was also lifted off. A student living with them found refuge with the dog in a bathroom, the only intact room. Arthur opted to let them know. They cut their holiday short and hurried back to deal with the awaiting disaster.

A democratic storm

Three days after the typhoon passed, many parts of Manila were still without water or electricity. In our area, electricity was cut out for three weeks thanks to the destruction of whole streets of power lines. The telephone took much longer to operate, as the telephone company was even less efficient than the Manila Electric Company. The airport was also just about wiped out. Water was being connected with an electric pump, and we had to buy water from a truck that was making daily rounds. We sweated without air-conditioning. We made good use of our two-burner gas cooker and bought ice shipped from areas where electricity has been restored. The price of a block of ice came down daily, and the slabs were getting bigger as the days passed and more electricity was generated. We were the last village to get connected. After the storm, invitations for "showers" were forthcoming and welcomed. Freezers and refrigerators were rapidly emptied; barbecues and candle light dinners became the norm. We survived.

If the plush Makati was hurt, Manila's roads were a disaster. In some sections of the town areas the only trace of roads was where the protruding power line poles and clustered abandoned vehicles that had piled up, with only their top showing. Hundreds of these vehicles — buses, trucks, trailers, and cargo delivery vans — were left there for as long as a week, some with their drivers still tenaciously guarding them and other laying abandoned after the waters threatened to swallow up the drivers. In some areas, portions of the highways had vanished and were now undistinguishable from the vast sea that they had spawned. Many towns were isolated from each other since no ordinary vehicle could negotiate the submerged roads leading to them. Even motorized bancas now hesitated to venture into what had become a vast sea for fear of floodwaters. The extent of nature's power was impressive.

In all the flooded areas, the only people who were dry were those who lived in two-story houses. Families remain imprisoned inside their houses waiting for the water to recede. But hundreds have to move in waist-deep water. The specter of starvation in the barrios was real. Months late there was still no accurate account of the number of deaths or injuries. In addition, the damage to property had to run into hundreds of millions of pesos. Just to cite two instances, the Intercontinental, which stood only 100 yards from our house, suffered approximately one million pesos worth of damage. The Adamsons, our friends, lost half a million pesos on their paper factory. Poor people who lived in shacks and shanties were wiped out. Ships had sunk in the bay or been driven up on the shore. Crops, including coconuts, which take years to replace, were destroyed.

The Philippines was beginning to recover from its economic mess, but was badly hurt by the two earlier typhoons, and now it had to absorb this one as well. Corrugated roofs were common in the less affluent section of the city; they were swept by the wind like flying saucers. It was a democratic typhoon: with the affluent people later repairing their homes, the less privileged could find enough corrugated material to reassemble and install roofs over their homes.

Traveling in the Philippines

The routine of life in Manila was happily broken by our travels within the country. The Philippines is a large archipelago of more than 7,000 islands, and it was always an adventure getting around them. Philippines Airlines (PAL) and Air Manila were the major carriers to the islands. The planes were small, with the DC-3 the most common aircraft. As electricity was unreliable in the provinces and navigational equipment virtually non-existent, planes departed early in the morning from Manila's domestic airport, hopped from island to island and returned in the evening back to base.

Arthur's first visit to the provinces was to Cotabato in the great southern Philippine island of Mindanao. Upon finishing his job and preparing to return home, he found that no plane had yet arrived, and there was no way to alert me. There were no phones, no telegraph. When he did not arrive at the expected time I called the airport to inquire and was told, "We don't know what happened to that flight." I had a stiff drink; fortunately Arthur's driver came by to reassure me that it was not uncommon for flights to be delayed, with the weather as the main culprit. Needless to say, Arthur later found his flight and his way home.

Another time, Lou Goodman, a Ford Foundation advisor, was delayed for an early morning departure from Manila to

Iligan, a major city in northern Mindanao. He approached the PAL counter to inquire what happened, and was told, "We don't have any equipment, we've lost so many planes lately." Not very reassuring.

No mangoes, please

On an Air Manila flight, we once heard the pilot announce from the cockpit, that "You cannot buy any mangoes in Cebu." The plane had left Davao in southern Mindanao. It was already overloaded, not an uncommon occurrence, and it had to land in Cebu in the center of the archipelago for refueling. No mangoes? The best mangoes grow in Cebu; baskets loaded with fruit were always available at the airport, the last purchase for many travelers heading back to Manila. Passengers were required to be weighed; we climbed on a rickety old scale and then proceeded for boarding. Did the portly 220-pound American pay the same fare as the skinny Filipino? We never learned. No passenger bought mangoes, the plane was already overloaded, the winds against us. We were all concerned if there was enough fuel for our return flight.

Ces Jesena was with the Association of Colleges of Agriculture of the Philippines (ACAP); he was always on the road and was labeled the "traveling VP." Arthur took many trips with Ces. One such journey took him from Roxas City to Iloilo in the Visayas. It was late in the afternoon and shadows were getting longer. The pilot informed them they could not land, as the local airport staff was refusing to turn on the lights on the runway for not having received their salary for two months. Another delay.

The next morning they chartered a small plane to reach their destination, as there were not many commercial flights from Roxas City. (Arthur used his American Express credit card at the local hotel, but they did not have any forms and presented him with a Diners' Club form instead. A year later, when checking in the same hotel, he was told they were never paid and would he please sign again another form. He asked why they did not contact him; they said they knew he would be back!) The rain was pounding, the clouds were low. They could hear the plane; it had come from Manila, and was circling above. But it could not land. There were no navigational instruments, the telegraph office was closed, and the telephone was not working.

Another eventful outing with Ces Jesena was a trip to Samar, a large and rough-hewn island in the eastern Visayas. The road, which winds along the coast to Catarman, had been washed out for the last 18 months; the airport was closed. To reach the town, Arthur and Ces hired a motorized banca from the coastal town of Calbayog. For the first two hours, in those tranquil waters, there was a perfect reflection of a banca, a mysterious beauty. Peaceful, timeless fishing villages, palms bending out over the blue sea, colorful fishing boats. When the banca turned towards the Pacific to reach Catarman, they were on the open Pacific and the reflection became blurred. Arthur recounted this trip many times. The reflection of the banca remained vivid through all his life.

Our travels brought us to the remote southwest island of Palawan. It stands as a narrow bridge — a long, narrow island — between Borneo and the central and northern Philippines. We were guided by the noted archeologist Robert Fox, who had done extensive excavations in the area and had come upon fossils from more 25,000 years ago, as well as sophisticated pottery of more recent vintage. They were beautiful, with pleasing forms, highly decorated with impressed and incised designs. These vessels had been used in elaborate rituals and not simply for household use.

Accompanied by Senator Jovito Salonga, we visited the Philippine Rural Reconstruction Movement (PRRM) in its national center in San Rafael, Nueva Ecija. The PRRM was a private organization that urged the barrio folk to help themselves. A welcome committee stood at the entrance of the center, framed by big banners. Trafalgar, Arthur's favorite driver, was behind the wheel that day. Raquedoto Pastores, the head of the center, came out to greet us. He threw his arms around Trafalgar, ignoring the honored guests. The two men had been together in prison camp in Mindanao during World War II. As they reminisced their times together, we seemed almost a disturbance.

We visited the island of Mactan in the Visayas. There is a monument there that commemorates the death of Ferdinand Magellan in battle with the native warriors of Mactan. There is a difference of accounts that appear on two sides of the obelisk monument. One side the monument records a noble European death: "Here on 27 April 1521, the great Portuguese navigator Hernando Magallanes, in the service of the King of Spain, was slain by native Filipinos . . ." On the other side is recorded an Asian triumph: "Here on this spot the great chieftain Lapu-Lapu repelled an attack by Ferdinand Magellan, killing him and sending his forces away."

We took day trips to explore the countryside, short excursions to get acquainted with wonderful and new experiences, people, and places. One of the trips we loved and took often our guests was a drive to Tagaytay. The drive was about 40 kilometers from home, running through extraordinary coconut groves and barrios. Nipa huts were festooned with brilliant tropical flowers, mainly bougainvilleas. Coconut trees towered over the papayas, with enormous yellow and green fruit clinging in their trunks in clusters. On the ground, pineapples grew in rows. A marvelous tropical fruit salad, one grove after the other.

Our destination was the Taal Vista Lodge Hotel, built on a high ridge on the north side of Lake Taal, a spectacular setting. In the center of an enormous lake was the island formed by the cone of an active volcano. In the crater was another lake. When an eruption was imminent, the lake bubbled and steam emitted great white clouds before the lava would eject a fiery blast. There was a major volcanic eruption during our stay, and we, like so many others from Manila, faced the traffic to see the emitting flames. The great sweep of sky over the entire panorama was a mighty stage for awesome displays of lightning and clouds — huge white and puffy clouds through which the most glorious sunsets were reflected.

Goats on the runway

There was no domestic flight landing in Jolo, one of the islands of the Sulu archipelago. The closest airport was in Zamboanga on the southwestern tip of Mindanao. We had to charter a small plane for the last leg of our trip. It was not a long flight. The view was spectacular as small islands and atolls emerged from the emerald sea. They were spread out along the horizon in a jagged and uncertain silhouette. You could visualize the birth of an island. A reef surrounded one atoll, another had some vegetation and low shrubs, and still another had trees taking roots. An island was forming. We were ready to land when the pilot made a sharp turn and started climbing towards the sky. There were goats on the runway. Father Gerard Rixhon, a Belgian missionary, appeared and chased goats off the runway. This was our welcome to Sulu.

We visited a local Catholic college, part of the Notre Dame educational institutions scattered around Southern Philippines. Bishop Frank McSorley, an Irish-American from Philadelphia and a missionary, was its president. He was a big man, with a crop of red hair, a friendly smile, and a quick sense of humor. He was rightfully proud of the beautiful cathedral that was built during his tenure. But this was a Muslim area, so why should the locals not have a mosque as splendid as the cathedral? He proceeded with a well-planned fund-raising drive, asked his Christian parishioners to contribute to the building of a mosque as beautiful as the cathedral, which rose during his lifetime. It was the kind of ecumenical gesture for which the bishop was loved and respected throughout the Sulu archipelago. Our admiration for his pastoral work never ceased.

While in Jolo, we were guests of the Carmelite monastery.

It offered such wonderful, sparkling accommodations in this remote part of the world that we named it the Jolo Hilton. The Carmelites are nuns of a contemplative order. Only one of them, Sister Mercedes, was allowed to communicate with the outside world. She was a charmer. Breakfast was served at the monastery, and what a delight were those eggs, freshly gathered early every morning. We could not refrain from smiling when we asked for water and Sister Mercedes arrived with a Haig pinch bottle — a contribution from the Fathers?

We spent unforgettable evenings sitting in the verandah of the bishop's residence, eating lanzones — another of those exotic, sweet-sour tropical fruits — and enjoying the beautiful views of the sea, the fantastic tropical cumulus clouds, the blazing sunsets, and at night the flickering lights of the fishing boats.

Jolo had a collection of villages on stilts perched over the sea, home to the Badjaos, the sea gypsies. For centuries the Badjaos were the expert divers of the region. The tropical waters of the area — the habitat of a rare breed of oysters — yielded superb specimens of South Sea pearls. We stopped to photograph these stilts houses and bargained for pearls, although we never bought any. Tausug Muslims in Jolo could be distinguished by their colorful clothing and elaborate turbans. On special occasions, the dressing became more elaborate with embroidered and appliqué costumes, embellished with tassels, shells, beads, and metal disks. The Tausugs wove interesting fabrics with geometric designs, in various shades of green, yellow, and purple. We always purchased a few pieces as gifts to friends in Manila and around the world. They made attractive tablecloths or stunning wall hangings when mounted. What a surprise it was when, years later, I found them at Bloomingdale's in New York — but the price was five-hundred-fold what we paid in Jolo.

A great joy was the plethora of uncrowned sandy beaches — the setting of many picnics — the beautiful coves, and the abundance of marine life. A visit to the mosques was part of our itinerary. I was asked to sign their guest book and add few comments in Arabic. Never did they expect that I would include a few verses of Persian poetry in the guest book. From then on we were always welcome.

The flying fathers

The bishop and the Oblate fathers in Jolo, members of the Notre Dame College, owned a four-passenger Cessna. It was made available to us, and Father Jim Holland, who loved to fly, was assigned as our pilot. Our destination was Sibutu, a remote island. Before departing, Father Holland used a hanging wire to measure the fuel, checked his instruments, and made the Sign of the Cross. How many pilots perform this ritual before departing? As we were climbing up, we could see the outlines of hills and bays separating themselves into a maze of islands. Among them were secret channels, narrows, inlets, and bays. Smugglers were common; their engines outran those of the local Coast Guard. This was the setting of many legends. It was here that pirates and buccaneers who preyed upon the trading ships in the straits used the islands as a refuge. Smugglers brought in cigarettes from nearby Borneo, and returned loaded with San Miguel beer.

Our first stop was Ungus Matata. The runway, carved on the coral reef, was just 400 feet long, and we used every single inch. An honor guard of schoolchildren welcomed us. We did not know the saluting protocol, but Father Holland quickly instructed us. After a while, the children grew curious to learn more about us, to be photographed, and to sell shells collected along the reefs. For ten cents you could purchase the most precious golden cowries, treasures of the Philippine seas. "Ungus Matata" sounded so romantic. What did it mean? "Long Island." What a disappointment! We should never have asked.

Sibutu was the last island of the Sulu archipelago. The mountains of Borneo emerged across the sea. Wild boars roamed freely and swam the straits (so some locals would tell visitors!) With the non-pork-eating Muslim population and without predators, the boars wandered freely around and then dove back into the sea. For the two Fathers living there, it was their main meat supply. We tasted the delicious sausages they prepared. Occasionally wealthy businessmen from Manila who loved to hunt would arrive in their private planes, and had field day in this heaven for hunting.

As we walked down the jetty one evening, a young Filipino with his guitar sang love songs. The sky was dark like black velvet; thousands of stars were twinkling, shining like diamonds. With no pollution, the stars appeared so close. You wanted to touch them, and surely you could reach them. The young man continued to sing, undisturbed by our presence. The songs were in English, and the insignia on his T-shirt was from the Harvard Glee Club — a T-shirt a long way from home.

Upon our return to Jolo, we hit a storm. The sky darkened, the tropical clouds burst, and the small Cessna bounced furiously in the air. Father Holland tried to go through an opening in the clouds, and then tried to go under the clouds. After three passes, he decided we could not make it. We were petrified. With all these maneuvers, we were running short of fuel. There was no choice but to search for a landing strip at the nearest island. It was such surprise for the local Father in Siasi to see the Notre Dame plane landing. He welcomed us, and we had a home for the evening; the storm continued through the night. By morning, the sky was clear and we were ready to continue our journey. But then we learned there was no aviation fuel on the island. There were bancas, local ferries that plow the islands. It would be a long trip to Jolo. Father Holland sent a telegram. He had to stay with the plane, until aviation fuel was shipped.

The banca was crowded with villagers going to the big town. The vessel sailed slowly towards Jolo, a five-hour trip instead of a 30-minute flight. All of a sudden the banca made a 180-degree turn. What happened? A fisherman was dynamiting the area, and a fish escaped and floated. The sailors could not leave such a prize. They jumped in the water, swam, and, with a net in hand, scooped the floating fish. They were prepared, as they had done that before. This was a good catch: a healthy meal for their extended families or a source of hard-earned cash in the Jolo market. Arthur took his camera to record the scene. Everyone turned toward him, a foreigner with a big camera taking pictures. Did he pay his fare? The fare was only ten pesos or fifty cents. I am sure he had paid, but perhaps there was an extra fee for the camera. It was all worth it. Arthur produced from his billfold the right change of crisp bank notes. This provided further excitement, as the fellow passengers had never seen clean bills. They were accustomed to the crumpled, dirty, filthy notes that filtered in this remote part of the country, they all wanted to examine the notes. Was this real money?

Doorbell nicknames

The most amazing thing was the nicknames used by Filipinos. It's very hard not to flinch when you hear an archbishop referring to his secretary as Baby, or when you get introduced to a government official with the name of Boy. Names like Bing, Ding, Ting, and Ming were common. Obviously Filipinos like names ending in "ing" and "ong" — "doorbell nicknames," as someone aptly described them. Sometimes the name is repeated, as in "Bongbong," the nickname of President Marcos's son.

Diminutives are used in many languages, but fade away when a child grows up. This was not the case in the Philippines. "Ito" is the diminutive in Brazil and "Aki" in Greece. Arthur becomes Arthurito in South America and Arthuraki in the Hellenic world. Christian first names such as Maria, Jose, Juan, and Jesus, were still widely popular in the Philippines when we were there, as they are in Mexico.

Glancing through the Manila telephone book, we found that the list of Reyeses or Santoses was very long, names of Spanish origin. Visitors would ask whether we knew a Mr.

Santos and provided very little additional information. It was as if one was seeking a Mr. Branco in Brazil. There must be a lot of confusion to maintain the relationships with all those Santoses. What a nightmare for any sort of administering of justice or conducting a financial investigation!

Holy Week with the Layas

The Philippines was our home now, and we wanted to learn whatever we could about the country, its history, its customs, its festivals, and the people among whom we were living. We enjoyed the laughter and the pleasures of the large families. Filipino families of academics, business leaders, and even of our Filipino medical doctor generously opened their doors. We found ourselves included in their picnics, excursions, and evenings of music, theater, and festivals. None of these precious ties endured longer than our relationship with the Laya family. We were introduced to Jimmy Laya then a professor of business administration, soon after our arrival.

Arthur, Julie, and Jimmy Laya with daughter MiAnn

He and his lovely wife Alice took upon themselves to introduce us to Philippine life through the eyes of Filipinos. This
was a rare and wonderful opportunity, and our relationship
endured through decades, until today.

We traveled with Jimmy, Alice, and their young daughter
MiAnn to the island province of Marinduque just south of Manila
at Easter time. As commercial flights were full, we chartered a
small Cessna to bring us to Gasan 12 kilometers from Boac, the
island's capital. Mrs. Sandoval, Alice's mother, was waiting to
greet us. She was a very charming lady, whose gray hair — a rare
sight in the Philippines — was neatly combed in a bun.

It was Holy Week and we came to witness the colorful
rites, highlighted by the dramatic presentation of the life of
Christ and the elaborate church ceremonies. Medieval rituals
mingled with local traditions in Marinduque, where a most
interesting tradition known as the Moriones was still practiced. There was an air of excitement in town; a television
network had a crew in place to film the pageantry.

We walked all over town to observe the festivities. Man-
size, ornately robed santos — carved saint images — were
prepared and balanced precariously on the freshly painted
carozzas, or wagons. They were brought up from churches or
from leading families. They represented Saint Peter with the
key and a rooster, St. John with a pen, St. Veronica, Magdalena,
the Virgin Mary, etc. The pious ensemble was decorated with
flowers and candles. On Holy Wednesday the Virgin Mary
was "dressed" in richly embroidered dark blue velvet, which
was changed to mourning black on Good Friday. The carozzas
were either on wheels or carried on the shoulders of the faith-
ful, some of them electrified by a noisy motor trailing behind
them.

We had a grand view of the festivities from an old house
in Gasan, one of those gentry homes with its gleaming wood
floors, carved doors, a display of antique furniture, heirlooms,
and two stunning paintings by the Filipino master Fernando
Amorsolo. The procession was very orderly, followed by

hundreds of children wearing their best clothes. A band played solemn tunes; Boy Scouts were interspersed, keeping a distance between each carozza. The carozzas gathered towards the center of the square, where vendors were doing brisk business selling sweets, flowers, and candles. After a while we followed the procession. We got tired and sunburnt. Jimmy's shoulders ached as he was carrying MiAnn — a very bright kid who had an ethereal look and talked continuously — all the way.

Starting as early as Holy Monday, men dressed as Roman soldiers and wearing grotesque masks roamed the streets of Boac in fulfillment of religious vows or as part of a family tradition. Costumes were made of bright shiny silks, braids, tassels, and pieces of leather. Some were decorated with hundreds of shells, which made the attire very heavy in that hot humid climate.

Easter in Marinduque, the Moriones

On Maundy Thursday, churches were elaborately decorated. The old Filipino tradition of visiting as many churches as possible on this day reminded me of a similar tradition in Greece, where the custom was to visit seven churches.

On Good Friday, the Holy Week drama of the 14 Stations of the Cross was re-enacted by local townspeople from early dawn to noon. At about mid-day a man dressed as Christ was crucified on a hill with a choir chanting the significance of the season. There were three crosses on the hill and costumed Roman soldiers crowded around the crosses with the spectators. Flagellants (bare-backed men who flog themselves with spiked whisks as a form of penance) converged on the cemetery in the capital town of Boac as a finale of a week of sacrifices. In the evening was the burial procession with the body of the "dead Christ" taken solemnly around town. Young men carried Christ wearing a blond wig on a bamboo pole stretcher.

Chased, judged, beheaded

We did not attend the Alleluia service. This is a beautiful dawn ritual to witness the procession where a child dressed as an angel amidst the singing of Alleluia by a choir removes the mourning veil of the blessed Mother. But we were there to witness the cinematic grand finale, the beheading. A man dressed as the Roman guard supposedly responsible for the death of Christ was chased by the Moriones. After a long chase, he was arrested across the river, in a coconut grove. He was brought to town, and judgment was passed. In a specially built area, a mock beheading was carried out. The whole sequence was so disorganized, but this was its charm — far from being commercial, it was a sincere representation by the people of their beliefs, their heritage, and their tradition. We felt fortunate to witness this colorful pageant.

Our memories were not only confined to the Moriones or to the refreshing swims we took at Hidalgo island, a few minutes away by motorized banca, in the emerald waters, but extended to the hospitality of the Layas. We stayed at the Laya family's traditional *nipa* or straw hut. The house was built on stilts off the ground; the columns of the house were tree trunks, the floor made from large bamboos. The furniture was all bamboo. An abaca mosquito net was available, just as a precaution. All amenities were there, and I still recall the brand-new colorful towels that Alice carried all the way from Manila for us. While relaxing in Marinduque, Arthur remarked how much prettier it was than Bali.

During the Holy Week, we sampled a number of exquisite delicacies, the fresh fish of the region. It was all delicious — the small fish, big fish, fried fish, fish simmered with tomatoes or fish with ginger, the shrimps cooked in coconut milk. Suman, the white or brown sticky rice wrapped in a coconut or banana leaf, was a favorite, as were the rice cakes, loaded with butter and some other confection with mounds of freshly grated coconut. On Easter Day carabao (water buffalo) meat appeared. It was a bit tough, but a break from the Lenten regimen. It reminded us of Greece, where Lent was broken with the traditional roast lamb, or roast goat and the cracking of the red Easter eggs.

Up to the Spanish North

Another unforgettable outing with the Layas was our journey to Ilocos Norte, up north on the main island of Luzon, for another Easter celebration and exploration of the glorious Spanish churches sprinkled all over that area. A detailed program for a reconnaissance of the Ilocos region was put in motion. Memories have faded from a trip taken so long ago, but who could forget those great churches in Masingal, Laoag, and Paoay, the glorious cathedral of Vigan and of course Santa Lucia? Santa Lucia, a saint who holds her eye on a plate. The Paoay Church in Ilocos Norte, Santa Maria in Ilocos Sur and later Vigan, the city, became UNESCO heritage sites.

We found some of the best examples of Spanish architecture in Vigan, a bit further south. Attractive Spanish colonial houses stood along narrow cobblestone streets and charming plazas surrounded by mango trees. Chinese mestizos built many of these old houses in the 19th century at the height of the indigo trade. The houses incorporated sliding *capiz* (sea shell) windows and many floral decorations. Every house had a tale, and every door had charm — admired, photographed, and incorporated into Philippine art books. Vigan had a genteel charm of a bygone era, the times when life was slow. Horse-drawn *calesas* or carriages clippity-clopped on the cobble streets.

The palace of the archbishop in Vigan was constructed in 1783; it served as an ecclesiastical center for a century. It changed hands through the years, occupied by revolutionaries and used as a garrison by the Americans. It was back in service as a church center, the residence of the Archbishop of Nueva Segovia, and home to a priceless collection of ecclesiastical artifacts, aside from breathtaking courtyard and gardens filled with bougainvilleas. The museum was a little gem with its many silver icons, altar ornaments, antique furniture, embroideries, ivory statues, paintings, and sculptures. There were many manuscripts, priceless records of Filipino history, a historian's treasure. Much still was to be done with the archives since there was neither an air conditioner nor a humidifier for the preservation of historical documents.

The hotel in Vigan was our headquarters. There was an old bird that ended up as fried chicken for our Vigan dinner and who fought till the very end, bending Jimmy's fork. It must have been the loser at the latest cockfight.

The Crisologos were the most prominent political family of the area and benefactors of the town. Their home was a museum exhibiting artifacts, documents, antique furniture, and items of a past that gave insights into Vigan's political and social life.

Santa Lucia was considered miraculous. I knew the Layas wanted to have another child. We prayed and as we were leaving, they were still in their pews praying. I conveyed, "I wish it is a boy." We left the Philippines few months later. When we were in Western Samoa a telegram arrived from the Layas. Jamesy was born, and we were to be the godparents.

Sand greens in Baguio

Baguio was our second home in the Philippines. Once a month on a weekend we took a break from business meetings and the social demands of Manila life and rode the DC-3 to Baguio, nestled up in the northern highlands. Baguio had been developed by the American colonial government as a summer resort. One of its main attractions was the Baguio Country Club — part hotel, part restaurant, and part golf course; a large verandah overlooked the first tee of the golf course, where we spent many pleasant hours, and learned to maneuver the steep rise of cardiac hill. The greens were sand greens; Arthur was ahead of many of his colleagues, given that as a youth he played golf on the sand greens of Australia.

We visited the market, one of the country's best. It was overflowing with handicrafts, and we always came back to Manila loaded with strawberries and vegetables that were grown in the surrounding highlands.

One of the best restaurants in town was Forest House run by two Spanish mestiza ladies. One needed to order at least a day in advance from the very limited menu. They had the best paella outside of Spain and imported their rice into a country where so many varieties were readily available. They introduced us to a variety of Spanish Riojas, many unfamiliar vineyards from this famous Spanish area. We discovered a new Riojas brand that we still sought thirty years later.

Somehow, in spite of our wonderful memories of Baguio, a sad chord resonates. Our good friend Alice Laya perished during the devastating earthquake of 1990. She was so young, beautiful, accomplished, and attentive. She was a marvelous hostess, a great mother, a wonderful companion to Jimmy, and, for us, a dear friend. We always read about disasters, typhoons, plane crashes, and earthquakes. Against the overwhelming power of nature, we remain helpless.

Meeting Mr. Marcos

We had just returned from home leave and learned that in the next couple of days there was going to be an important fund raising event in Manila. The Australian Ballet — with Margot Fonteyn, the great ballerina, as a guest star — would be performing at the Cultural Center. It was too late to get tickets. This was a great event, a gala performance, under the patronage of the President of the Republic.

What about contacting Sixto "Ting" Roxas, I asked Arthur? Ting was a leading banker, and his organization may have had tickets. Ting had not yet assembled his party. He was delighted to hear from us and immediately invited us to join him in his loge.

A dinner in his home preceded the performance. Finance Minister Cesar Virata and his lovely wife Joy were the other guests. The house was situated in the old Manila suburb of Parañaque; Ting's home was part of the large compound of the distinguished Roxas family. The antique furniture was the house centerpiece. Chinese ceramics were arranged in different settings. In one room was a splendid display of guns, pistols, and hunting rifles. Dinner was served, and I still recall the awe when the soup arrived in a large Ming bowl — a genuine museum piece! After all, if emperors in China had used these bowls in their daily life, why not a member of one of the most powerful and wealthiest families of the country? The Roxases entertained in grand style.

At the Cultural Center, we found ourselves seated in the Roxas loge, adjacent to that of President Marcos. At intermission, invited patrons aggregated in a private foyer. Elections were scheduled for the following week, and a large number of people wanted to corner the President. The Australian ambassador was keen to get his attention, particularly given that the occasion was an Australian ballet performance. The President saw me. We had met before. He came straight to me. What do you say to a President, when you are utterly unprepared? Did he enjoy the ballet? This would have been trivial. I knew President Marcos was a fervent golf player, so my gambit was to engage him in golf and let him know how much I was enjoying the game at the Baguio Country Club. He was very well acquainted with the fairway, and the sand greens. "What club do you use at the 5th tee?" Whatever I answered, we disagreed. We continued with golf stories. Time was ticking, and conversation was running out. The performance could not start without the President, who was still talking about his latest professional golf adviser.

I had to change the topic. "How is Bongbong doing?" This was his son, who was studying in England at that time. "Do you hear often from him?" He replied: "Bongbong writes every day." I had to smile and respond, "I do not believe it, Mr. President." But he explained that it was a school requirement to write every day. He was amused and remarked on the letter's content — "Today it is Tuesday" — one sentence, to meet the boarding school requirement. There were curious ears wondering what state secrets the President was divulging to this Greek woman.

After the curtain had been held for an additional ten minutes, we proceeded to our seats and the performance continued. There was a reception afterwards in the main gallery of the Cultural Center. The *corps de ballet* arrived in business attire. The lovely Margot Fonteyn appeared wearing a dazzling

Empire orange chiffon dress. She was petite, and floated in that gown just as she did onstage. She approached us, and learned that Arthur was with the Ford Foundation. She came to the point of insisting to know what the Foundation was doing for the arts: "Are you supporting the arts in the Philippines? Are there grants for ballet? Grants for training? Worldwide?" There she was, astute, with intelligent questions and insights, promoting her trade.

With gloves on

In the early '70s, the Intercontinental was the new plush hotel in Makati — Metro Manila's business district — and the only place in town where real American roast beef was available. We could even get turkey for Thanksgiving, provided that we ordered weeks in advance. The hotel's newly appointed manager was a Greek Cypriot, George Markides, and like a true Greek Cypriot, Markides enjoyed home cooking, such as a bowl of lentils or a bean soup. He found even slightly burned dishes appetizing, because they reminded him of his mother's cooking. He specialized in opening new hotels for the Intercontinental chain, and loved to recount the many challenges he faced. The hotel in Manila was his pride, as it became center of many elaborate functions.

The dinner we attended was in honor of Eugenio Lopez, the patriarch of one of the great political families of the country. His empire was vast: he was the major owner of Meralco, the electric company; his son Geny was in charge of the television stations and the *Manila Chronicle,* a leading newspaper, and his brother Fernando was the Vice President of the Philippines.

Markides saw us entering the foyer. As we were formally dressed, he realized we were guests at the dinner. He greeted us with a brisk "Hurry up!" There must have been a mix-up with time, as President Marcos was present yet no guests had arrived. We were the first ones to arrive and found the President walking aimlessly, with only waiters hovering around him. The President was wearing a tuxedo — a rarity, as he was always photographed in the traditional Filipino *barong tagalog*, a long-sleeved shirt made of translucent pineapple fabric. I was wearing white long gloves. What was the protocol? Do you shake hands with gloves on? Yes. What about holding a drink? What about sampling canapés? I abstained from any refreshments and removed the gloves only at dinnertime.

The dinner was a small affair with just 20 people in attendance, an intimate occasion by Philippine standards. A waiter stood behind each guest. The dinner was exquisite, the service unsurpassed, and there were no speeches. Eugenio Lopez had very generously donated land in Makati's prosperous business center for the Asian Institute of Management (AIM) to be erected. The Ford Foundation was providing salaries for many of the faculty. The initial team came from Harvard and the first AIM President, Steve Fuller, had been dean of the Harvard Business School. Steve was an outstanding fundraiser, able to motivate people to open their pocket books without ever asking for money. Many organizations would have loved to have him. A couple of years later, funds were procured from all over Asia, with Japanese corporations as the main donors. The Asian Institute of Management emerged as the leading business school of the region.

Dinner at the Palace

"I am going to the Malacañang dinner," I forcefully told Arthur. We had dinner guests that evening, academics from Australia, and Arthur wanted us to entertain them. "Our guests are special. They came all the way from Sydney, and I am obliged," he said. In his humble way, Arthur felt that our visitors were more important than a contemporaneous invitation to the Presidential Palace. There would be no excuse to cancel our dinner party. But I was adamant. I didn't get too many

Malacañang invitations. This was the White House of the Philippines, a rare occasion, an honor, and I was determined to go.

Arturo Tanco, the Minister of Agriculture, was my escort. It was the tenth anniversary celebration for the International Rice Research Institute, where so-called "miracle rice," a high-yielding variety that promised to reduce hunger in, was engineered. Ministers of agriculture from all over Asia were invited, with the Rockefeller Foundation president as the guest of honor.

As we entered the Malacañang gates, I became aware that we were not proceeding through the usual entrance. Arturo informed me that there was a small reception before dinner at the private apartments of the President, and that I was to join him. I never thought for a moment that I should find myself in such an intimate gathering with the President of the country and such illustrious guests. Mrs. Marcos was dressed in an exquisite *terno*, with richly embroidered butterfly sleeves. She was dripping with jewelry. Fresh from a trip to Russia, she was eager to show us her new collection of Byzantine and Russian icons.

After a while, the President asked us to join him for a walk through the garden to admire his orchids. The First Lady declined, saying it was "too windy" for her bouffant coiffure, and she opted to remain behind. We meandered through the garden; floodlights illuminated the palm trees, where a large assortment of delicate orchids was clinging.

In the dining room I found myself with the same illustrious entourage. Was I sitting at the head table? The national anthem was playing, the television cameras were rolling, and I was wondering where I would sit. There was a host of round tables with hundreds of people. Arturo Tanco came to my rescue, calling an aide who directed me to sit with Arturo's wife Pat. She was an American and a teacher at the International School. Pat was an outsider amid the other Filipino Cabinet wives. I joined her at the table with a sense of relief.

The tables had artistic displays of tropical flowers. The evening's program and menu were embossed and elegantly placed in front of one's place card. The glasses were Waterford, the dishes Limoges. The consommé imperatrice was followed by poached sole, beef braised in a Madera sauce, a Caesar salad, and a surprise for dessert. An appropriate French wine accompanied each dish. Pat, who was often guest at those functions, recognized the caterer from the menu. "It's from the Hilton, it will be good tonight."

Champagne was poured and I experienced another extraordinary encounter. I started laughing. Pat asked our waiter for a bottle of champagne and placed it under the table. What was she doing? Hoarding wine from the palace? The waiters knew her well; after all, she was the wife of a Cabinet minister. She knew the ritual, "we shall have so many toasts with empty glasses, let's get our own bottle and enjoy ourselves." This was a state dinner! Indeed we had many toasts and words of goodwill. They are all forgotten, but not the bottle of champagne that we enjoyed during the evening.

As was the norm, dinner was followed by entertainment. The famous Bayanihan Philippine dance company was performing. Rice planting was the initial dance — rice is sown, then transplanted, and after it ripens, harvested; it is then threshed, wind blown, pounded, and winnowed. All these stages were depicted in the dance. How appropriate, given that it was the Rice Institute celebration! The world-renowned *tinikling* was next. Performers danced in and out of rapidly clapped bamboo poles. The *singkil* is a dance from the Lanao province. Every daughter of royal blood in that province is expected to learn this dance, which takes its name from the bell-bracelet worn around the ankle. The *aasik* was my favorite. It was reminiscent of Persian markets, a slave dance of the classic type. In the Muslim southern Philippines, this dance is usually performed by the lady-in-waiting to the daughter of the Sultan.

A glamorous young lady was sitting next to the President;

she had not been at the reception. Her long blonde hair reached nearly to her waist. Who was she to be seated, next to the President? The rumors and gossip were buzzing. Arturo had to find out; after all he was at the head table. At the end of the evening he approached her. She was a guest at the palace for the weekend, a granddaughter of Franco. He asked her what she thought of the President. "Boring" was her less than diplomatic answer.

I recounted this evening many times. I regretted that Arthur had not been with me, but then if he had accompanied me I would probably never have had this remarkable experience.

Closing a chapter

Our stay in the Philippines was coming to a close, and it was time to take care of our staff to find them jobs and possibly direct them to new careers. Siri decided to join her daughter in Alaska! I am sure she missed the balmy weather of the Philippines. Our driver Ponciano had been going to school at night, taking accounting courses. The Press Foundation came to his rescue and offered him a job. He was still holding it twenty years later.

Our gardener Ernesto had a very realistic aspiration. He wanted to become a tailor. We intervened a year before our departure. We sent him as an apprentice three times a week to a tailor shop, paid his daily wages, bought him his sewing machine and a few essential tools for his new trade, and helped him open his first shop. He needed customers, but didn't have to look too far and too long to find them. The Ford Foundation drivers had their blue shirts meticulously sewn by Ernesto. A new career was launched.

It was time to close a chapter of our lives. The Foundation policy was to limit assignments to a tour of few years, since longer-term people tend to their objectivity; the Foundation did not provide a long-term career along a bureaucratic path. Young people with fresh ideas were brought aboard. Arthur decided to continue his development work and joined the United Nations Development Program (UNDP). Our next assignment was a regional position in the South Pacific, head-quartered in Western Samoa.

Arthur was surprised and honored when President Salva-dor Lopez and the Regents of the University of the Philippines cited him before his departure as having "served with schol-arly discernment and a deep understanding" of the needs of the Filipino people. It remains the highest honor he received.

With Educators
in Indonesia

I first met Fr. Orlando Quevedo more than 30 years ago. He was part of a small group of young Filipino scholars, Ford Foundation grantees on a study tour to observe how Indonesian universities "relate to their regions as resources in development." Besides Fr. Quevedo — then president of Notre Dame University in Cotabato — our group included Prof. Gerardo Calabia from the Institute of Planning of the University of the Philippines, Prof. Raymondo Fonorella of the Agri-Business Center of Central Mindanao University, and a Prof. Torres of Mindanao State University. Prof. Goodman, a Ford Foundation project specialist, accompanied us.

We landed in Jakarta after a short flight from Singapore. It was for all of us our first visit to Indonesia. Jakarta, the capital, was a sprawling Third World metropolis. The glittering skyscrapers that adorn the city today had yet to be built, and bicycles and motor scooters dominated the traffic.

The Asoka Hotel was our home for couple of days. Our budget did not permit accommodation at the plush Hotel Indonesia, the most comfortable hotel in Jakarta at that time. We were taken aback by a sign posted in each of our rooms:

"Massage available from midnight to 3 A.M." As we returned from dinner one evening, Lou Goodman was accosted by some "ladies of the night," who turned out to be transvestites. It was an interesting encounter.

The Ford Foundation office was modest in comparison to the plush office in Manila — reflective, perhaps, of the level of economic development level of Indonesia then. On arrival, Jack Bresnen, the Foundation's representative, briefed us on Indonesia's political and economic status and on the Foundation's activities and programs. The delegation's aim was to spend less time in the academic centers of Jakarta than in the rural areas, so we could understand the intricacies of land tenure and of the cooperation between provincial governments and local universities. Could observations gained by the team prove useful and transferable to successful approaches in the Philippines?

After Jakarta our first destination was Sulawesi — also known as the Celebes — a disheveled starfish of an island between Borneo and the Molluccas. For centuries Sulawesi, especially the southern part of the island, commanded the lucrative spice trade routes, making its major port Makassar an important, much fought over place. Pepper, cloves, nutmeg, vanilla, and the many derivatives of coconuts made fortunes here. The Makassar we saw was a dusty city and we did not venture to any of the famous tourist spots vividly described in the colorful brochures.

We visited Hasanuddin University and met with the South Sulawesi Planning Board, headed by the Governor General Idris, a brigadier general. It was a very formal session, during which questions arose about the ability of local government to respond to the needs of the population, community groups, and citizen's organizations. Provincial government officials, together with policymakers and scholars from the local university, generated approaches to contribute to the well-being of the rural people.

The province was rich, laden with whole mountains of pure asphalt, and oil exploration was well underway. In addition to its natural resources, the province was receiving generous aid from a number of countries. The French had donated the water purification system, the Yugoslavs contributed the electric generator, the Czechs had built the sugar mill, the Swiss brought in hotels and textile manufacturing. The key was the close cooperation between the local government and the university. One percent of the province budget was earmarked for research; clearly the military was the paymaster. University students carried out projects in rural areas, disseminated information to farmers, and supported innovative projects. It was obvious that the involvement of universities in regional development was due more to the Indonesian military's pressure than to any academic inclination.

Hasanuddin University, a provincial academic center, seemed prosperous. The faculty was given free housing and the deans were furnished with a car. Salaries, however, were dismal by any standards. Dr A. Hafid, the rector, invited us to his house. It was spacious home — bright, airy, furnished with oversized bamboo sofas and chairs puffed with quilted batiks. The furnishings were complemented by antique Chinese pieces. Both the rector and his wife spoke excellent English; we were offered a sumptuous tea and sweet meats. There was the traditional exchange of gifts. I was presented with a beautiful piece of yellow silk sarong, woven in the province; my lovely Filipino embroidery was graciously received. I was not included in most of the meetings, but this gave me the opportunity to roam in town and visit the local markets. I learned later that Arthur and the Filipino team were interviewed by Radio Indonesia, and provided their assessment of the role of Filipino provincial universities in rural planning.

A necklace of lights

Makassar at first sight was an ugly city, dirty, with an unkempt waterfront. But later at night, the unkempt promenade along the beach came to life as dozens of wheeled food stalls arrived and set up shop end to end, creating a necklace of lights. Fish sizzled, *satay* grilled, beer flowed, and Makassar took on a different air.

From Sulawesi we flew to Surabaya, in the northeast part of Java. We stayed in a charming old hotel, a reminder of past colonial administrations. There was a large verandah and high ceiling with swirling fans, but what we most vividly recall were the bathrooms all decorated with Delft tiles. Arthur ordered dinner that evening; he miscalculated and missed one order. Ray was left without his fried chicken, and we all waited for the missing order to appear.

Next day we crammed ourselves into a minivan and drove from Surabaya to Yogyakarta, our next major destination. It was a long eight-hour drive across one of the most varied and spectacular parts of Indonesia. There are more than 20 volcanoes along Java's spine. Many eruptions through the years have created one of the most fertile spots on earth. The countryside was lush and green but also so crowded. We would have loved to eat al fresco, which would have been more enjoyable than dining in a large restaurant. But was it safe? There were food stalls set up along the road offering fried *goreng*, or noodles with many wonderful tidbits, and satay, meat grilled on skewers and served with a peanut sauce. Many concoctions of beans and peanuts in colored rice were also available. The aromatic smell of the satay was most appealing, but we were not ready to risk it. Water was unsafe and ice in any drinks was to be avoided; we saw blocks of ice dragged over the dirty streets. We indulged in buying bunches of mangosteens and feasting on them, this wonderful fruit was difficult to find in Manila at that time and was so abundant in Java. We had pomelo, juicy and sweet, a distant cousin of grapefruit. As we were driving, we would encounter the smell of durian, which could have come from a vendor selling it along the road; more likely the fruit was transported in an open lorry moving ahead of us with the omnipresent smell trailing behind.

A merchant sold spinning tops, a child's toy. We could not resist; we had to stop and have a whirl. He had to be recompensed for all the photographs we took; after all we were using his capital as a backdrop of our pictures.

Although it was not the rainy season, scattered showers were not uncommon in the tropics. We saw a little girl, three or four years old, stark naked, holding a pink umbrella over her head, gingerly walking along the road. Her feet were covered with mud. We wondered what the future would be for that child, one among millions in this beautiful but overcrowded land.

Yogyakarta was a significant stop; the Klaten, a "model rural development project" under the auspices of the German government and now sponsored by the German NGO Heifer International, was a key to our visit. When we arrived, 18 village chiefs from surrounding villages were waiting to receive us, all wearing their finest and most stunning costumes. They brought along their wives, not one but two or three sometimes four wives. Some of the wives were obviously pregnant. They asked me how many children we had. A stunned silence met me when I responded that we did not have any.

A trusting partnership

The Klaten was supporting farmers in the region with their livestock. Farmer groups had won national-level awards, and a local dairy cooperative served as a model for other dairy cooperatives in the region. Farmers were trained in practical business and organizational matters, such as micro-credit; thus they became part of a self-reliant and more prosperous community. Expatriates, mostly Germans, represented various disciplines. They included a livestock consultant, an agronomist, a veterinarian, a soil and agronomy consultant, a livestock nutritionist, an agriculture socio-economist, and an anthropologist. The rural community was transformed into becoming more self-reliant and sustainable. This was done by building a trusting partnership between the villagers and the German experts, by building the local organization, and by sharing knowledge, especially on livestock. The roads around the area were better kept, and the farmers' housing looked more prosperous and substantial than in other parts of Java.

In a moving ceremony, with military honors, the village chiefs presented Arthur with the Klaten insignia. It was a green and yellow silk banner on which rice and kapok were embroidered with gold thread. We treasured it for many years.

At Gaddjah Mada University in Yogyakarta, a discussion on land tenure was on the agenda. With Fr. Quevedo, we visited an Islamic college. Dr. Muktar Ali, the rector was a distinguished Islamic scholar who later became Indonesia's Religious Minister. He received us in his modest home, where his wife offered us a variety of home-made Indonesian delicacies for tea. She was a busy lady with six children to take care and did all the baking for us. She mentioned that it was too expensive to buy those delicacies in the market. They were poorly recompensed. This was the home of the rector; we wondered how difficult it must be for a junior faculty member. Fr. Quevedo invited the rector to visit the Notre Dame University in Cotabato. A young Catholic priest initiated an interfaith collaboration.

The Buddhist cosmos at Borobudur

Our stay in Yogyakarta included a visit to the great monument of Borobudur. Built around 800 A.D., it is the largest Buddhist structure in the southern hemisphere and one of the biggest in all of Southeast Asia. It was in desperate need of repair. Designed as a massive tantric mandala, it depicts the Buddhist cosmos starting with the daily world on the bottom and spiraling up to the realm of nirvana. We walked clockwise, as is proper for all Buddhist monuments.

Images of elephants, kings, warriors, and dancing girls lined the terraces, a stunning similarity with temples in Cambodia. The upper three circular levels were a dizzying spiral of Buddhas sitting in meditation in their lotus-shaped stupas. Most of the Buddha heads were missing, either by vandalism or because they had been destroyed by earthquakes and volcanic eruptions. The Buddhas had been there for centuries. Serenely they greeted the sun every day, silently, asking for nothing. It was said that Mount Merapi spewed forth her ash and buried the site for almost 900 years. I could imagine the Buddhas sitting peacefully for centuries and meditating. We walked around, reaching the upper level. At the top there was a huge empty stupa. The unaware might think the statue was taken, as many were by the Dutch in the late 19th century, but the emptiness represented nirvana. With no face, each one of us can form his or her own image, as a matter of faith.

In the 1980s, Borobudur was finally restored with funds provided by UNESCO. Seven hundred men worked six days a week for ten years cleaning, repairing, and reassembling more than one and half million stone blocks. I revisited Borobadur in the late '90s. There are four staircases providing easy access to the top, but using them you get only the view, you do not experience the journey. Reconstructed, Borobudur had not lost its mysticism; it rises majestically in the plains of central Java. It is a sight not to be missed, second only to Angkor Wat in grandeur. It remains a magnificent symbol of peace and harmony, a heritage of the civilized world.

Yogyakarta was and remains the artistic center of Indonesia. Dances, gamelan, batik weaving, shadow puppets are still honorably practiced. We met students from around the world learning the intricacies of the batik making process. We encountered old women bend over wax, designing batik fabrics; we met young men who would surround us, eagerly asking us to visit their shop.

One of the great Indonesian painters, Affendi, had his house opened to the public. We decided to visit, but he was away in Europe for the opening one of his exhibits, and so we never met this great Indonesian master. His home — partly a gallery today — is run by his daughter and is a national museum.

Central Java's spiritual seeds have grown into a bountiful harvest. All around Yogyakarta are rich fields of rice, coffee, tea, sugarcane, and cocoa. With tropical temperatures and steady rain throughout the year, farmers manage three harvests without depleting the soil. These fields are so fertile they have been in continuous cultivation for the past 2000 years.

Home in Yogyakarta was the Ambarukno Palace, where I stayed again 30 years later. Luxurious hotels have been erected since then: the Hyatt, the Amanresort. The Ambarukno, however, remains the choice of the seasoned traveler, a traditional Indonesian hotel, spacious, air-conditioned, with a friendly atmosphere and attentive personnel. But most importantly it is a hotel that is not cut off from its surroundings. During our first visit, it offered a limited menu of Western and Asian dishes, which were all superb. Arthur indulged himself in lamb chops Provencal. In the evening, at the main dining room, there were performances of Javanese dancing based on the Ramayana story. Gamelan orchestras imbued dances and *wayang* or puppet shows with their hypnotic music, which seemed to have no beginning, middle, or end, just repeating beats and refrains. But nothing was more memorable or mesmerizing than the *jailing* or trance dance in the courtyard of a near by hamlet. There was a full moon, and the only other light that shone during the dance came from the flames from burning coconut husks placed in the middle of a circle.

It was during this trip across Java, crammed in our minivan, that our little band forged an *esprit de corps*, a camaraderie, with jokes being shared, life events compared, and friendships developed that endured through the years. We would follow the career of Fr. Orlando Quevedo, who was a simple priest at that time, an educator. Since then he ascended the hierarchy of the church, first as a Bishop, then as Archbishop, and now president of the Bishop's Association of the Philippines.

From Yogyakarta we flew to the capital city of Jakarta. A visit to the University of Indonesia was in our schedule, and a meeting with renowned journalist Rosihan Anwar attuned us on the role of Islam in development.

From Jakarta we drove to Bandung. There is considerable scenic beauty in this forested area, with every turn and every valley providing another wonderful vista. Bandung got world attention as the site of the first Afro-Asian Conference of Non-Aligned Nations in 1955. We visited the Institute of Technology and its satellite communication center. We had dinner with a UNESCO expert who introduced us to his favorite local restaurant, and we understood why — the food was so good, the service superb, there were linen tablecloths, and the cost was no more than a dollar a head.

We had more projects to observe, and universities to call on. We went to the island of Sumatra, a large volcanic island about the size of California. Compared to Java, Sumatra was sparsely populated and mountainous, with dense tropical growth. As our plane approached through long mountain valleys, Padang, the capital of West Sumatra, unfolded as a low-rise city of white walls and red-tiled roofs punctuated by the breathtaking Minangkabau spires.

A matrilineal society

West Sumatra is peopled by one of Indonesia's most sophisticated cultures, the Minangkabaus. They once enjoyed 500 years of independence as a kingdom that survived into the early 19th century. They have created an unusual culture in these mountains. They are devout Muslims, but they are also a matrilineal society, with an egalitarian social system and economy in which women own all the property. Banking is completely in the hands of women. Inheritance is passed from mother to daughter. If there is no female in direct line, inheritance will be transferred to a sister. Brothers play a more prominent role in the family's wealth distribution than husbands.

Daily life is governed by intensely complicated and arcane rules of etiquette. I am sure we breached many of the rules.

The ladies, all Minangkabaus, invited us for dinner. It was an elaborate buffet. I was warned not to sample some innocuous meatballs, but no one warned Arthur who sampled them. They were pure dynamite. He had to gulp down barrels of water, potable or not, beer, and ice cream just to cool his palate. Hours later he was still burning inside. Arthur talked to the young men. Part of growing up among the Minangkabaus was a stint abroad in the *rantau* — a word that means, roughly, "anywhere but here." One young man admitted, "These women own me." No wonder anthropologists are drawn to those hills.

Our Grand Hotel in Padang had cement water containers in the bathrooms. We encountered the same structures in our hotel in Makassar. At first we thought the containers were small bathtubs!

After Sulawesi and Java, we were surprised to learn how poor the province of West Sumatra was, contributing only 2 percent of Indonesia's national budget. We visited Andalas University in Padang and met Governor Herun Zain and his planning staff. The governor was articulate, energetic, a visionary. So many governors ruled like warlords but Governor Zain was an outstanding administrator. He wanted to bring the potential of his province to the attention of investors. Sumatra was so rich in mineral wealth. He had Western Sumatra participate in international trade shows, and he enlisted the collaboration of the university in his plans; it was obvious that under President Suharto, the military held sway in regional development.

When Governor Zain later visited us in Manila, we hosted a dinner in his honor, and among the guests was the Dutch ambassador. The two of them talked animatedly, and I asked if they conversed in Bahasa Indonesia. No, they communicated in Dutch. In spite of any nationalistic fervor, the language used by educated Indonesians was still Dutch in the mid-1970s.

Our team returned to the Philippines with many promising ideas, in education, in training, in experimentation. For Fr. Quevedo, a University president, his aim was to hone his skills in human relations. All the participants became aware of the importance of developing working relations with key people in formal and informal settings, of improving attitudes toward development, of the necessity of social research, of involving students in social research programs, of the desirability not only of upgrading the quality of teachers, but also of focusing on pragmatic technical and vocational education. The participants planned to advocate elsewhere the development efforts they observed in Indonesia. They all found that besides the unprecedented demand for education and training, people had a growing interest in understanding the various facets of their identity in this world.

In the South Pacific

I could tell you about Samoa in 1972. It was a new era in the history of the world. The astronauts had already landed on the moon, but this was the year when an American President, Richard Nixon, crossed the Bamboo Curtain and visited the Forbidden City in Beijing, China. This was the year that Kurt Waldheim was elected Secretary-General of the UN. This was the year that Bangladesh was born. I cannot say if we could call it a peaceful year, as the explosions and shootings in Belfast continued, as did the conflict and fighting in the Middle East. It was the year of a daring criminal massacre in Munich during the Olympics, and hijackings were becoming rife. There was another French nuclear test in the Pacific. But for Western Samoa, what was important was that it was the tenth anniversary of this young nation of 150,000 people scattered between the two main islands of Upulu and Savai, two little specks in the vast ocean.

We landed in Western Samoa, the heart of Polynesia, on a grass airport. Flights there were infrequent, and the arrival of a plane was an event for the locals. Arthur had been assigned here as Deputy Regional Representative of the United Nations Development Program (UNDP). The region was immense, encompassing Western Samoa, Fiji, Tonga, the New Hebrides, the Solomons, Niue, Nauru, and the Cook Islands.

The island lies in the South Pacific halfway between Australia and Hawaii. It was and still is isolated from mass tourism. The road to the capital, Apia, provides one of the most scenic drives in the world, following the coast with blue lagoons stretching for miles, palm trees swinging in the wind, glorious tropical flowers, and churches at every bend. Here was Robert Louis Stevenson's last home.

Picturesque villages sat along the road. Samoan houses called *fales* stood in a semicircular way that suited the climate ideally and kept them open to the breeze.

Samoan fale

The center house belonged to the *matai* or chief who held the family title and was responsible for organizing and managing the family's resources. Matais represented the dignity and honor of the families in the village council and other forums of political and social affairs.

Our house, a large wooden frame with a huge verandah, was the former German Officers' Club.

Our house in Apia

Western Samoa had been a German colony before World War I. However, the British had sent in a New Zealander expeditionary force to occupy the island at the outbreak of the "war to end all wars." Western Samoa became a New Zealand mandate under the League of Nations, and New Zealand's protectorate under the UN after World War II (what about the war to end all wars?). The island gained independence in 1963. Independence was, however, somewhat of an illusion, as the country was and remains nonviable as an economic entity.

A break in the isolation

The official accredited community was tiny, composed of the New Zealand High Commissioner, the UNDP Representative, and the Peace Corps Director.

Communications were primitive, adding to the isolation. This was, after all, the time before the Internet, computers, faxes, or even the telex. A half duplex phone was our contact with the world. We got accustomed to the long pauses required between callers. At home we had a party telephone line. The Hill household's number was 36, three rings. It was not unusual to have people listening in.

One of the things that helped me in this desolate spot was the Apia Public Library. They had quite a good small collection. In addition, they had a budget for new acquisitions, and were most willing to purchase the titles I wanted to read. Among others, I believe I read the whole oeuvre of Solzhenitsyn.

Another break in the isolation was provided by the UN families, who came from every corner of the earth. We had wonderful dinner parties as, when we were invited, they cooked the best dishes of their country with supplies that they had carried back so preciously from home leave or from Fiji. The Chinese (Taiwan) were wonderful, as were the Indians and the Ceylonese, but the very best were the Czechs. I still remember the great dessert that Nadia, the veterinarian's wife, produced in those primitive conditions.

There were no medical facilities worth the name (except for a doctor from New Zealand who could fix poisonous coral cuts), no hairdresser apart from a filthy barber, and no basic food supplies. For a medical emergency one had to fly to New Zealand. This was not simple, however. The UN experts assigned to the Western Pacific came from different countries. Our Czech veterinarian, a citizen of a Communist country, was not permitted to enter New Zealand; he had to bully his way through New Zealand immigration when he brought his daughter to be treated for an emergency. A Taiwanese family was not allowed to land in Australia, as only mainland China was recognized. Citizens of Taiwan could not even obtain a transit visa.

Our lifeline for food supplies was the *Tofua*, a boat from New Zealand. It arrived every three months. You could then find flour in the store and have bread delivered at home. It was not unusual among the UN families to call and ask if you had any spare sugar, and in many dinner invitations the hostess would ask whether the guest had any onions left at home. We had duty-free privileges and lived on canned food shipped in from Denmark. As for liquor, a Seventh Day Adventist ran the government liquor store. You can imagine the size of the selection.

There was a market on Saturday. You could see the Prime Minister's wife wearing thongs, her truck parked outside the market, or the New Zealand High Commissioner's wife looking for an eggplant, perhaps a green pepper or an octopus. Sometimes we would find a turtle. The lovely lagoons,

Arthur and an outhouse in the back ground

however, were decimated by dynamite and pollution from toilets built on jetties, which left the Samoans to eat low-grade canned mackerel imported from New Zealand and Japan, in addition to their basic diet of taro and boiled green bananas. We were fortunate to have a lovely garden filled with a wide variety of tropical fruit trees and plants. These had been put in place at the time when our house had been occupied by the

Secretary of Agriculture. More than once the PM's wife came
to our garden to pick mangoes and avocado.

Reef worms and a narcotic drink

We did not experience many festivals in Samoa. The most
memorable was the night of the *palolo*. This is a special kind of
fishing that occurs before dawn on the sixth to eight day after
the full moon in October or November when the palolo worms
rise from the reef. Samoans consider palolo a great delicacy; it
tastes like caviar, and many come for the rising to those villages known to have them in abundance. Draped with flowers
to welcome these annual visitors, the people quickly scoop
them up before they melt in the morning sun.

Festivals are usually accompanied by drinking *kava* —
the narcotic Polynesian drink made from the roots of the kava
plant — giving speeches, distributing fine mats, and eating,
singing, and dancing. Kava ceremonies are a must at meetings
of matais when entertaining important guests and on occasions of particular rejoicing or great sorrow. Ceremonies unite
distant branches of families and provide opportunities to fa-
miliarize and solidify relations. History and legends are often
reenacted, and it is on such occasion, that chiefs embroider
their speech with proverbial sayings.

Flowers were plentiful — hibiscus, frangipani, orchids, bird
of paradise, and ginger torches. A woman's marital status in
Western Samoa is revealed by the way she wears her hibiscus.
A single woman wears the flower in her left ear, a married
woman in her right ear, and a married and available woman in
both ears.

There was a jail in the country and the best vegetables
were cultivated in the prison's garden. Prisoners were off on
weekends, which were treated like holidays, during which the
country was closed. Not surprisingly, thefts occurred on the
weekends and we all had our share. Indeed, Samoans do not
have a word for theft. You share everything. The Peace Corps

volunteers brought clothes and books for their assignments, but within days all their belongings were shared in the village. The attrition rate was enormous. We could not persuade Sita, our house girl, to use the towels we gave her, but soon found our towels in her room. She was not stealing them; she was simply sharing. The wife of the Peace Corps director commented that I was lucky that Sita was so fat. Her servant was wearing her underwear!

No use for PhDs

The water bill was based on the number of faucets. Hence we had only two faucets inside the house and one outside for the garden. There were no meters or filters. The water came straight from the river, and to our amusement, small shrimps emerged from the faucets. Through cracks in the shower, green foliage regularly emerged almost every night. A tiny bit of mold on the ceiling in the evening would expand to cover one-fifth of the ceiling by next morning. We had to wipe book jackets and record jackets with vinegar to prevent mold growing, and lights were on all the time in our closets to protect shoes and leather belts. A lovely batik art piece bought in Malaysia was ruined by the mold in that humid environment. I was so proud of Arthur — in fact, I considered it his biggest achievement — when he actually put glass in our bedroom windows for the first time and installed an air conditioning unit imported from Denmark! PhDs were of no use there, where installing an air-conditioner required special talents.

A lovely landmark along the coast was Plum Pudding, a striking set of rock formations springing from the ocean. The drive there passed through lush tropical jungle and plantations of coconut, cocoa, and bananas. Vegetation grew lush, the result of heavy rainfall, tropical temperatures, and fertile soils. The beach surrounding Plum Pudding was white sand, and the 80-degree water made it a beachcomber's paradise. The sand was like white sugar, and the sparkling beach was embedded with coral and shells of all sizes, shapes, and colors. As we sat on the rocks, the clear water revealed startling flashes of brightly colored fish darting here and there, and to swim among them was an experience of pure fantasy. No aquarium or oceanic institute could match the excitement of seeing those colorful tropical fish, right at your feet.

The local golf course had only nine holes and was in need of a manicure. The insects, flying bugs, and cobwebs did not make for a pleasant encounter. But now and then the game paused to allow the players to take in the absolutely spectacular view of the emerald green waters of the Pacific.

A visit from the "leftenant"

Everyone came to Samoa — the Pope, Prince Charles (whom we met twice), the Prime Ministers of Australia, New Zealand, Fiji, Tonga and Niue, even the President of Nauru. The yachts of the super-rich docked in Apia harbor, which could be seen from Arthur's office window. Within a few weeks of our arrival we had a VIP visitor, Undersecretary Rafael Salas, the head of population planning of the United Nations. We had to entertain Salas, but our airfreight had just arrived with some bare essentials and only few plastic dishes. The electricity also just happened to be out that day. We had to do with these plastic dishes and with cold sandwiches. Luckily, Sita came through; she cleaned our huge garbage can and filled it with the splendid orchids growing in our garden. That centerpiece proved priceless in New York. Years later, Rafael Salas still remembered our centerpiece.

Our brush with royalty came when Her Majesty's Ship *Jupiter* arrived in town for an official visit, with the then-lieutenant (that's "leftenant") Charles aboard. It was a time when President Nixon was close to impeachment. Without any media present, Prince Charles' reply to the question, "What do you think of President Nixon?" was priceless. Almost without a pause he replied, "If he were one of my ancestors, his head would have been chopped off."

The Prince spent at least ten minutes with Arthur asking about the UNDP, the function of the agencies, and their interrelationships. He admitted knowing little of the UN development programs compared to his knowledge of the deliberations of the Security Council. His informality culminated when he said "I was last week with my parents in NZ. They were a lot of people at the airport. I asked them where they were from Ireland, Wales, Scotland, Midlands. Where were the New Zealanders hiding?" Arthur laughingly assured him they were all in Samoa.

In a reception aboard the *Jupiter*, Lt.Charles, a junior officer, was relegated to the job of a waiter. Tray in hand, he was very attentive in refilling the guests' drinks. A young Samoan had a crush on him. In a nonchalant way, Charles placed his tray with drinks on a table, gave her a big kiss, and told her that she had been "kissed by a prince." He then took his tray and continued his duties. She was awestruck.

Aggie Grey, a legend in the South Pacific, was among the guests that evening. She was part-Samoan and part-English, a vibrant personality and the driving force of Aggie Grey, the best hotel in town. The hotel served as a meeting place of American soldiers on R&R during World War II, of movie stars in the fifties. James Michener was said to have been inspired by Aggie and based on her the character of Bloody Mary in his book *Tales of the South Pacific*. By now Aggie was an old woman. She was coaxed to perform a Samoan dance. In spite of her age, she obliged. She was very graceful, with a lei around her neck, a rhythm in her movements, and a twinkle in her eyes. The Prince was asked to join, and as a good sport he did, making a fool of himself, pulling his tongue, and delighting the audience. He shook hands with Aggie at the end.

The Prince asked if he could do anything for us while in Apia. We asked if one of the *Jupiter*'s helicopters could fly over the primary school. The children had never seen a helicopter before. Next day before departing a helicopter was circling the local school. What a joy for the kids.

Tourists from the cruise ships competed with the natives in their attire. Sometimes one thought that the only clothes they owned came from the Folies Bergeres. The yachts stocked up on orchids, ginger flowers, bird of paradise, and anthuriums, and within 24 hours they were gone. Occasionally we had a Greek merchant ship in the harbor. On these occasions I became a professional beggar, inviting the captain for lunch and then asking if he could spare some Greek cheese.

A short-lived diet

Sita entertained the tourists.

Sita, a Polynesian beauty

With coconut trees and travelers' palms shading our expansive garden, the tourist buses stopped for a photograph. Sita was there waving and flashing her broad smile. They must have ended up with more pictures of Sita than of our garden. Luckily video recorders were not in fashion in 1972.

Sita must have weighed 250 pounds, not untypical for a Samoan. She weighed herself daily and in no time ruined our small bathroom scale. One day she decided she wanted to slim down. We encouraged her, suggesting she eat fish every day and refrain from the starchy taro, the staple of the Samoan diet. Her diet lasted three days. By the third day the garbage can was full. I could not resist my curiosity. I counted 42 peels of green bananas. That was the end of the diet.

Sita loved to play cricket, and was head of her village team. Fans crowded the field when she was playing. Sita's weekly village job was to shave the lawn surrounding the matai's fale with a bush knife. She was clever avoiding it, offering the excuse that we needed her for extra work. In the evenings she frequented a local bar, where sadly, once, she lost an eye to a broken bottle in a brawl.

It was not uncommon for idle young men to throw rocks at passing cars, and one of our UN colleagues was hit near the eye by a rock thrown through the windscreen as he was driving through the village at night.

Rita Tamasese was the Prime Minister's wife. She was a plump but attractive woman with expressive eyes, and yellow shells strung on a length of coconut fiber as her only jewelry. She always wore thongs, and proudly drove her utility vehicle. Once Rita picked up a lost tourist. Escorted back to the hotel, the tourist commented on Rita's good English and inquired where she worked. Rita told her she was the wife of the Prime Minister. She recounts how the tourist started to move closer to the door and got a look to say "She must be nuts"!

The Prime Minister the Honorable Tupua Tamasese Lealofi IV and Rita were invited to an official visit to Taiwan. Upon her return, Rita recounted the official dinner with Chiang Kai-shek. There had been only chopsticks on the table. Tame, as she called the Prime Minister, politely asked for a knife and fork but Rita was willing to try. "Half of the food was in my mouth and half on my dress," she recalled.

The Peace Corps Director was a political appointee of the Governor of Michigan. He had never traveled outside the United States; this was his first overseas assignment. It tells something of the US foreign appointments at that time. One day he called Arthur to ask what a naval attaché was. The US naval attaché was coming from New Zealand to Apia. The reason was that "The Russians are coming."

The aptly named Frog Evans, a UN expert, was the harbor master. He arranged for us to visit aboard a Russian submarine and the mother ship. We were fortunate to have our Czech veterinarian along, as he spoke fluent Russian. It was not a nuclear submarine but still not very many Americans, including the naval attaché, had the opportunity to visit a Russian submarine. Of course we did not know where to look or what questions to ask. We just went for a ride.

The nightmare was the UNDP representative, an ex-US navy officer, protocol-mad, and most probably CIA. When he was not traveling, which he did 50 percent of the time, he was on the tennis court with his wife, a Thai princess who was surrounded by a staff of Thai servants. All the rest of us, UN families, had to survive with the local help. The Princess required all wives of UN personnel to participate in volunteer work in her house every Tuesday. Even when she was traveling, the meeting was scheduled at her house. I was delegated to report on who was absent. One activity was to make cut-and-paste and coloring charts to be donated to the local primary school. Every Tuesday, when the Princess was there, she had a new dress (one of her staff was a seamstress), and offered us a new recipe for cookies or dessert. In two years we never had the same refreshments. My Somali friend decided to get pregnant, just to avoid the Tuesday "*Casa de Moda*" gathering.

Reflections on the UNDP

We stayed two years in Western Samoa, a tough assignment. Samoans were of great anthropological interest to Margaret Mead, but not to live with on a day-by-day basis — and certainly the government was not able to provide office support to a United Nations regional office.

While working in the Pacific, Arthur became thoroughly convinced that new approaches were necessary to provide sensible assistance to the tiny island countries. It was unrealistic to think that countries with populations of under 200,000 and sometimes considerably less could provide all the technical personnel to run a complex modern economy. In the '70s, not a single Pacific islander was director of telecommunications in his own country, and it was doubtful if some of the smaller countries would ever be able to identify, train and retain one of their own nationals in this, or similarly complex, posts.

Some of the island countries had need for a veterinarian but certainly not for more than one. If they did succeed in getting a national veterinarian, it would not be justified to begin training another immediately, but if something happened to the single veterinarian (emigration, illness, death) it would be at least several years before another national could be trained to replace him. Clearly, more suitable approaches had to be found to meet the unique circumstances of countries and territories with very small populations.

I joined Arthur in New Caledonia on the occasion of a meeting of the South Pacific Forum he was attending. It cost us a fortune in airline fares (it was so expensive to go anywhere within the South Pacific) but I needed to get out for my sanity. There were no frequent flyer miles at that time. New Caledonia was the *dolce vita* of the French, a tropical paradise of blue waters, white sands, lazy warm days, and balmy evenings. Called the island of "eternal spring" it was a French colony since 1853, and in 1946 it became a French overseas territory — a small if distant piece of Southern France, much like Provence.

The French government paid an extra allowance to its administrative officials according to the distance from Paris. Noumea was further away than Tahiti and hence officials there received higher pay. The private yachts in Noumea made for some of the greatest agglomerations of yachts we had ever seen. Frenchmen ran the country from shops to schools and hospitals, and even operated the trams. The poor Melanesian laborers had to return to their dwellings in the outskirts of town. It may have been a pleasant place for the visitor, but it was also colonialism at its worst.

The French UTA Airline brought in wheels of brie and other French cheeses, along with fresh temperate-climate fruits and other goodies a couple of times a week. After Apia, shopping in Noumea was just like doing it in Paris, with a stroll down the city avenues revealing dozens of chic boutiques, rare French imports, and the latest in lingerie, hats, and jewelry. Noumea had the facilities of any major Pacific port and the yacht-crowded harbor provided the perfect venue for a host of water sports.

The aquarium in Noumea held probably the most interesting collection of tropical marine life in the world, where strangely beautiful plant life shared the water with teeming tropical fish. The all-embracing darkness kept alive and thriving the most delicate creatures of the sea: fluorescent corals, live anemones, cowfish, and the nautilus.

As we were leaving New Caledonia, we loaded ourselves with a dozen bottles of good wine and filled our suitcase with a variety of French cheeses and patés. We had to stop in Fiji, as there were no direct flights to Apia. We arrived there at midnight and Arthur, usually so reserved and calm, had to make a lot of fuss to obtain a room with a refrigerator in order to keep the cheese cool. Once back in Apia, it was time for a party. Selected friends were invited, those who had long missed and would really enjoy the delicacies that were oh-so-rare in Samoa.

It was not uncommon for the electricity to conk out and, of course, it happened that evening. Candles were lit, the breeze was cool, the wine was good, and the cheese remained fresh. Later in the evening the power returned; the fans started swirling, we began dancing, and cameras immortalized the gathering. Years later in Normandy, with our friends Pam and Max who had retired there, we gaily recalled what had come to be known as the Hills' Zorba party.

A Fijian feast

Fiji was paradise in comparison with Samoa, and was the place to stock up on necessities. We flew often to Suva, the commercial center of the islands. The UN families always gave me a shopping list: paper napkins, doilies, anchovies, electric light bulbs (screw-type and push-type), and medicine, even condoms. We made good friends with Minister of Culture Ratu David and his lovely wife Andi Davila Toginavalu, a Fijian princess. A whole village was put to work to give us a genuine Fijian feast. A long table was covered with banana leaves and decked artistically with red hibiscus to complement a variety of specialties from octopus to turtle soup, and a local dish called *palisami* that can be described as resembling a spinach soufflé.

Andi Davila inspecting a Fijian feast

Ratu David invited us to the sacred island of Mbau where Fijian chiefs were buried. It was a rare honor for a foreigner to step on Mbau. Arthur had an uncle who used to be a missionary in Fiji and was still remembered. Our standing with Fijian chiefs was enhanced as they recalled Uncle "Wally," the Australian missionary.

When we visited New Hebrides, the British-French condominium, I was surprised by the very confusing way they had chosen to run a country. While Arthur met with the British officials, I met the French officials as I speak fluent French. The two groups had such a divergent philosophy about running the place. The British hospitals were wood-and-brick structures resembling those in England, while the French hospital looked more like a giant Samoan fale — built on stilts, its roof made of coconut husks, and exposed to the air. We stayed in a lovely modern resort called the Pandanas, run by a French couple. Years later, at a restaurant in Antwerp also named the Pandanas, Arthur discovered that the owners were indeed the same couple who had hosted us in New Hebrides.

Entering New Hebrides, the British had to go through British immigration while the French went through French immigration. As a citizen of neither of the two countries, one had a choice, but the choice would also determine the laws governing the individual during the stay. We went through French immigration, as the line was shorter. When we departed, the French were closed as it was a Sunday, so the Brits stamped us out.

I joined Arthur when he represented the United Nations Secretary General at a conference of the Law of the Sea in Nuku'alofa, the capital of Tonga. Tourist literature describes Tonga as the crown jewel of the Pacific, a fairy-tale Polynesian kingdom steeped in history and ancient tradition. Indeed the islands had never been colonized or occupied, but a fairy tale?

Nuku'alofa was the sleepiest, the dustiest, the slowest, and the poorest of the Pacific ports. The road from the airport was riddled with potholes. All the roads were appalling, and the buildings were grim as well. Offices were empty or locked when they should have been open. White frame homes and a few businesses lined the beachfront, where a sign caught my eye: "Bus Service, General Merchant, Taxi, Clothing Center, General Theater."

General store in Tonga

The Royal Palace resembled a rural Christian church, wooden and white with a bulky steeple. Christianity came into full power in Tonga with the approval of the monarchy.

Holiday for prisoners

Tongans went to church three times a day on Sunday and condemned anyone who failed to go. The law said the Sabbath was to be kept holy. No person was to practice his or her trade or profession. No planes landed or took off on a Sunday. No one was allowed to play games or to swim. Tongans were fined or given three months in jail for violating the laws. But the jails were emptied on the weekend; the police, the jail, and the fire department closed during the Christmas holidays. Prisoners could go home!

Tonga had no investors, no immigrants, hardly any expatriates, and hardly any tourists. It had no desire to see strangers and outsiders were actively discouraged from prolonged visits. Tongans had little understanding of and no interest in the outer world. Men and women, old and young, walked slowly. There was something extraordinary and unmovable about Tongan torpor — it was regal, sensual, and languorous.

HMS *Jupiter* had visited Tonga as well. Arlington Davis, the British High Commissioner in Tonga, recounted that Prince Charles had asked for a bicycle for himself and his security man. Seeing the two cyclists the following day, Tonga's Prime Minister commented to the Prince that he had recognized him by his bicycle. There was a cruise ship in the harbor, but none of the tourists recognized or guessed that one of the young men on a dilapidated bicycle was the heir to the British throne.

Tonga is situated on the International Date Line, and thus is the first country in the world to greet each new day. As we arrived a number of delegates were jet-lagged and amazed that with a 24-hour difference, we were so fresh. Needless to say Samoa was only a one-hour flight away on the other side of the date line.

Nothing locally was made for sale in Nuku'alofa except postage stamps. What money it had came from the remittances of Tongans in New Zealand and in the US, mainly Hawaii, employed as gardeners, car washers, and tree trimmers. Another source of revenue was the issuance of Tongan passports. For $10,000 someone who was stateless could become a Tongan Protectorate Person and carry a Tongan passport, with the freedom to travel in any country in the world — except Tonga. Mrs. Imelda Marcos, the Philippine First Lady, obtained a Tongan passport, for whatever purpose it may have served her.

Majestic and drenched

There are not very many kings left around, and while in Tonga Arthur decided to take the opportunity to pay a courtesy call on His Majesty King Taufa'ahau Tupou IV. The meeting at the Royal Palace Court was arranged by the Prime Minister. It was an open room where he met the King, who had no entourage. They were photographs of old Tongan kings, of the British Royal family, and of Queen Salote — the beloved queen who had more or less upstaged Queen Elizabeth at her own coronation in 1953. It had rained hard that day. Tongan customs insist that in order to show respect you cannot imitate the actions of the persons you honor. At the first sign of rain Queen Elizabeth's footmen put up the hood in her carriage as it rolled towards Westminster Abbey. Hoods were raised on the rest of the carriages in the procession, all but one, that of the Queen of Tonga. She sat, vast and majestic and drenched. From that moment she earned the love and affection of so many people in England. There were framed letters, one of them from "Your Good Friend Elizabeth R."

The King, a graduate of Sydney University, weighed somewhere around 425 pounds. One could hear his heavy footsteps and even heavier breathing as he descended the stairs. He was very excited by a Boeing 707 that the Japanese government was offering him. He wanted to do nothing else but talk about his new toy. It never occurred to him to think about landing rights or the length of runways in other Pacific islands. The Prime Minister was worried, if indeed the offer was accepted, that the cost of running such a plane would bankrupt the country.

Arthur tried to steer the conversation to nuclear policy in the Pacific, Polynesian migration, tourism. No avail. Agriculture? This opened an opportunity for the King to speak freely — about, of course, his plane. He was planning to ship the temperate-climate fruits that Tonga produced to the other tropical islands. On Arthur's departure, the King asked an aide to give him a couple of cantaloupes from his garden. And so Arthur emerged from a royal audience with a crumpled brown paper bag stuffed with two royal cantaloupes. They were delicious.

At the Crossroads of the Ages

After Western Samoa, Arthur was assigned by the UNDP halfway around the world to landlocked Afghanistan, where — long before the turmoil following September 11 — we spent two very happy years.

We came to Kabul in the aftermath of the 1973 overthrow of the king by his brother-in-law and cousin, General Mohammed Daud, who became President of the Republic of Afghanistan. Daud governed until the Communist takeover in 1979. We had visited Kabul years before, so it was not our first encounter with the country, but now we were making it our home.

Our belongings from Western Samoa took nine months to arrive. As there were no professional packers in Apia, Arthur did all the packing, using every scrap of newspaper he could find in the country. His carpentry skills were very limited, however, so the wooden crate he built looked more like a chicken coop. From Apia our belongings were shipped to New Zealand, then transshipped for the long voyage across the Pacific, through the Panama Canal, and then over the Atlantic before landing in Rotterdam. Permits for the delivery took quite some time to be processed, as our shipment had to go through what was then the USSR. After a few months in storage, our belongings were loaded on a train destined for Moscow. Another rail journey brought them through Uzbekistan near the Afghan border. It was late fall and the Oxus river separating the two countries had not yet frozen. Our shipment, now loaded in barges, finally reached Afghanistan, and a lorry brought it to Kabul. Nothing was broken, nothing was missing. I was so proud of his diligent packing, and thanked our good fortune. We still recall the happy reunion with our treasures, accumulated through many peripatetic years. We had clothes again, as well as dishes, but most importantly, we had our books and tapes. The new music equipment, purchased in Hong Kong and carried to Kabul by plane, was already in place, and our home once again reverberated with music.

We were excited to be assigned in Afghanistan, a harsh but beautiful country. Its rough, rugged terrain has produced some of the best fighters in the world, and its stunning scenery of great mountains and lush green valleys has been an inspiration to poets. For thousands of years it has been fought over and disputed by many conquerors. It was through Afghanistan that pilgrims and traders working the Silk Route carried Buddhism to China and Japan. Alexander the Great conquered Afghanistan and Central Asia and went on to invade India, leaving behind a new vibrant Buddhist–Greek kingdom. Other invaders included Darius, Genghis Khan, Tamerlane, and Babur, the founder of the Mogul Empire. Czarist Russia and Britain vied for control of Afghanistan in the19th century, because of its strategic location as a gateway to India. Both suffered defeat. No European country would ever colonize it.

However, the series of invasions resulted in a complex ethnic and religious mix that was to make nation building very difficult. When we lived there, both Russia and America were attempting to woo Afghanistan with economic aid.

After Apia, Kabul, a city of half a million people, appeared cosmopolitan. The modern section of town with its thorough-fares was built with an eye to the future. It was the enclave of about two dozen embassies accredited to Afghanistan. The road from the airport, lined with sycamore trees, ended in Pakhtunistan Square, which sported a huge fountain lit by colored lights and an outdoor café. Strollers crowded the square and the surrounding streets. Men wore well-tailored suits and Italian-style shoes. Most likely they were government employees. The only feature distinguishing them from their Western counterparts was their karakul, or lambskin cap. To my surprise, there were quite a few women wearing well-cut suits and high-heeled shoes.

Scorpions to scoop

Still, Kabul was an untidy, sprawling city, struggling for form among the hills. Outside the modern enclave, the box-like houses made of mud or mud brick climbed steeply beneath the precipitous walled skyline and kept their rectangular shapes, with doors and windows well set to bar the winter winds.

We were assigned to one of the loveliest houses in the country, in the suburb of Wazir Akbar Khan. The area was a diplomatic enclave. Occasionally, it still mentioned on CNN. A German architect built the house, which looked like a Swiss chalet. Its steep roof was ready to receive the heavy snowfalls of the Kabul winters, and the wood-burning fireplace was a joy. The heating was primitive, but adequate. Like all the other foreigners, we used *bukharis*, the Afghan heating units, with their pipes running across the ceiling. They were fueled with diesel, and the smell was inescapable. Electric heaters in the bedrooms supplemented the bukharis, although the supply of electricity could be quite unstable.

The summers were cool and pleasant as Kabul lies on a plateau at 5,500 feet. Our living room opened to an inviting terrace, where grapevines spiraled over the pergola posts. We even had a swimming pool. Every day there were a few scorpions to scoop, an endless task for our gardener.

We studied Dari — the Afghan version of Farsi and one of the two national languages — with a professor at Kabul University. Our tutoring was carried out in the United Nations office. Our tutor would not accept an invitation to our home as we, UN and other foreign representatives, were required to provide a list to the Department of Foreign Affairs of the names of the Afghans we entertained at our homes. After two years of practice, I became fluent in Dari, but Arthur lacked a facility for languages.

Our landlord General Aref was a very distinguished man. He studied in France and spoke excellent French. He would often send us sweet melons grown on his farm, or a basket with a variety of grapes. But much like our language teacher, he never accepted our invitations. They did not want to be on any Foreign Affairs list.

Arthur was fortunate to work closely with the Minister of National Planning and his staff, and also with many senior officials of government in a number of ministries. These were men (no women occupied posts at that level) who almost uniformly had studied abroad, most often in Germany or France. Many had European wives whom we met. We never met the wife of the Minister of Planning, who frequently came to our home but who maintained a traditional, conservative Afghan household.

Caryatids in the bazaar

It was the real people of the country who chiefly crowded the bazaars, pushing past us with turbans askew, their round skullcaps gold-embroidered in Kandahar; it was the only bright spot in their costume, with everything else the color of dust. Their *sharwal* or baggy cotton trousers, a style unchanged for centuries, flopped loosely under a *kameesh* or shirt that came to the knees, and a shorter Western jacket worn above it took away any hint of splendor; the style was in keeping with the rather dingy aspect of the long uneven streets. They were not the bureaucrats of the modern section of town, but the real people of Kabul, who in the past had shaped the history of their country, and who now preserved its distinctive culture.

Women flitted about under the fragile silk grill hiding their faces. The *chadri*, a voluminous, shroud-like veil that Muslim women wear in this part of the world, made their heads charmingly small and flared round their ankles in a sprightly bell of plissé, giving them a look of gaiety when they moved. But when they stood shrouded on the sidewalk, seeing but unrecognizable, they might as well have been caryatids to the passerby. However, it was not uncommon to see in the bazaar few Afghan women modestly dressed in slacks, although jeans had not yet arrived.

We loved to venture away from the modern section of town. Meandering in the endless back alleys towards the bazaars, we first encountered that omnipresent smell suggesting mutton broiled in oil, mingling with the odor of fried rice with raisins and nuts. We followed our noses and ended up reaching one of the typical Central Asian teahouses. The furnishings were simple. People were sitting or squatting on long wooden benches. As I spoke Dari, we were immediately welcomed, and offered a cup of strong black tea with lots of sugar. "Where are you from — Russia?" "No, we are with *mullalah moutahed* (United Nations)." "What is that?" Met by silence, I claimed my true heritage. "I am from Alexander the Great Country." "Oh, Iskander! You are doubly welcomed." As the time for prayers arrived, there was an exodus from the teahouse. Men congregated facing westward towards Mecca, kneeling and offering their prayers to Allah.

The bazaars were always full of vegetables and fruits of temperate climates: mulberries, pomegranates, apples, apricots, peaches, fresh pistachios, grapes, and melons.

Julie at a fruit stall in Kabul

Indeed wonderful melons! Marco Polo described the melons of Afghanistan as the finest in the world. The most expensive fruits were the lemons imported from Pakistan, and the lemon vendor was considered a rich man.

Julie and lemon vendor in Kabul

Oranges, however, were abundant, and in the wintertime, we muddied our boots on the icy pavements just to purchase glorious juicy blood oranges by the case. They were grown in Jelalabad, a town with a milder climate at a lower altitude.

The butchers carried lamb and we feasted often on grilled kebabs marinated in the local yogurt. In the winter we had wild duck. Yousouf, our cook, was able to prepare duck in great many innovative ways. One day, Yousouf announced that a beef filet was available; we thought a shipment had arrived from Pakistan. Beef was a rarity, and I was so proud to offer it to our distinguished guest, the German ambassador. When the filet arrived none of us could cut it, much less chew it. You could bend your fork on it. It was worse than rubber, and no wonder — it was camel filet! We all had a good laugh. After all, we were living in the primitive conditions of landlocked Afghanistan.

With diplomatic privileges, we were able to obtain wine, cheese, butter, chocolates, and many Western goodies from Denmark. There were numerous exchanges of food supplies with the American diplomats. We never lacked anything, unless we really wanted Vermont maple syrup. Who had the best cheese? Who carried the best feta cheese — the Bulgarian or the Yugoslav embassy? The water supply was either nonexistent or intermittent, but Nazir, Arthur's driver, brought water from a purification center at the American Embassy, for which we were so very grateful.

The carpets of Afghanistan

The carpet market, like so many in Central Asia, was a labyrinth of small shops where rug vendors offered their wares. An Afghan could tell you — just by looking at the colors, the designs, and the density of the knots — the part of the country where the rugs were made. Carpets were expensive even in Kabul because they took up to a year to be woven. The techniques of creating the complicated geometrical patterns were difficult to acquire. All dyes were natural, and the process involved, for example, boiling the skins of red onions, white onions, pomegranate, beetroots, and flowers to produce a red dye. Only black dye had to be purchased, and it came from Germany. The process was not very scientific; close examination of a large Afghan carpet yielded subtle variations in tone. No two batches of dye were exactly the same, but this was part of the rug's charm.

The real carpet expert was an Englishman, Dick Pearson, the only resident foreign businessman in town.

Dick Pearson perplexed by the origin of carpet

Dick could even recognize the year a carpet was woven, given it fell somewhere in the preceding decade. No questions went unanswered. How much lanoline was in the wool? Had it rained that year? Were there enough green pastures during a particular summer? Dick represented Harrods of London and major German department stores. He bought forty percent of the Afghan production. He was well known in the bazaars and spoke the language fluently.

Dick was perplexed by a couple of rugs we owned. The design originated from one tribe and the knots from another. The designs and knots never mixed. He asked if he could take them to the bazaar to show them as "the traders surely know," But even merchants were confused. Here was Turkoman design with a *yak tara* single weft knot. Impossible! Where were those rugs woven? More shopkeepers got involved examining, wondering, discussing. I wrote to ask my father, who was at the time living in Athens, if he knew anything about those rugs, and he solved the mystery. The rugs had been woven by Greeks who migrated from the Caucasus in 1917 after the Russian Revolution. They had brought their craft to their new home, and were not restricted by tribal traditions.

I found a splendid rug on our living room floor one day. It was sheer poetry. Dick had sent it for our consideration, and we could keep it for a few days. It did not take long or us to decide, and we bought it. Another time, a richly patterned *parda* arrived. This type of rug is used as a divider in Afghan village homes. Its design has been standardized, so that there was a long fringe only on the bottom, as the rug was intended to be hung and not to cover the floor. The colors were rich and vibrant, but we decided to return it for some reason. A week later we regretted our decision. We went back to Dick. Could we get it back? "It's already packed in a truck ready to be shipped to Beirut. It will cost you an extra hundred dollars to unpack the truck and locate it." We obliged. The colors have mellowed through the years, and I wish I could see it in a hundred years. What a masterpiece! We purchased these rugs at cost; Dick would accept a bottle of scotch as a commission. He did not have diplomatic privileges and alcohol was not available in the market.

Curios and coins

The curio shops catering to tourists were in the modern part of town. They displayed old-fashioned handguns, a kind of lute, and hookahs or smoking pipes made of bright blue pottery. The visitor feasted on an eye-catching showcase of traditional Afghan crafts, swords, lamps, bowls and jewelry worn by the women of nomad tribes.

Julie with of curio shop in the background

One of our greatest joys was our visit to the coin bazaar. It was icy cold in wintertime. You crawled in through a small entrance. The sooty ceiling was low and the room dimly lit, with only a brazier keeping the tiny space warm. A carpet hung at the door to the bazaar alley. You sat on cushions; a blanket was given you to cover your legs. A cup of hot tea was offered. Then the merchant would pour from a burlap sack his coins, thousands of coins, and the search ensued. We spent hours in the coin shops on Thursdays, the beginning of the Moslem weekend. The coins were silver, bronze, old, new, real, and fake. Coins from all over the world had somehow found their way to those remote alleys of Kabul. In the summer time, the brazier was gone and the blankets were rolled away. A refreshing piece of watermelon was offered.

Hakim Hamidi was the leading numismatist in town. He introduced us to the most trustworthy coin merchants. His catalog of modern coins of Afghanistan was a valuable resource to us novice collectors. Gold coins were always kept in a safe, and it took several visits before the shopkeepers would open a safe for us. After a few months, we became more cognizant of Afghan minted coins and were searching for some of the rare examples to complete our collection. There was a particular coin from the reign of Amir Abdul Rahman that had eluded even our numismatist friend. It was reported in his catalog and he knew about it, but had never seen it. Could we find it? The word was out in the bazaar. If we found it, would it be a fake? One weekend, one of our favorite shopkeepers went to the countryside. His assistant remained in Kabul, but was vague about his boss's travels. Another week passed, then a third. A month later, the shopkeeper was back. This time he opened another safe underneath a pile of carpets, a new secret place we had not seen before. Here was the gold tilla of King Abdul Rahman, the six-gram variety! We bought it without bargaining. Years later it was authenticated at the numismatic museum in New York City, to which it will be donated.

While revisiting a coin shop in Ghazni, 100 kilometers south of Kabul, we found a bronze Olympic medal. It was from Pakistan's polo team in the 1956 Olympics held in Melbourne. Arthur did not know what he would have done with it, but even today it is one of the few things he regrets not having purchased.

Our cook Yousouf

Yousouf was one of the most dignified human beings we ever encountered.

Yousouf our cook in Kabul

He was over six feet tall, handsome, well built, powerful and strong. He had served as the personal attendant of King Mohamed Zahir Shah, who returned to Afghanistan in 2002.

In the 1970s, the King was in exile, and his cousin Daoud was the president. New banknotes were printed, but Yousouf insisted he be paid with the old notes with the King's picture on them. He showed us a letter from the Queen asking him to join the King's entourage in Italy. Yousouf had refused. He told us he would never leave Afghanistan. As the palace was only few blocks from our house, Yousouf would visit his old friends who were working for the new President. He will tell us about the visitors the President received. Was the Russian ambassador a frequent guest?

Every morning, Yousouf would buy a huge piece of the flat wonderful bread, *nan*, a staple throughout the entire Central Asia. It is delicious when fresh. When stale it gets indigestible. Yousouf would take his bicycle, and for the grand price of two cents, purchase a nan, place it inside a pillowcase, and peddle back home. The nan would be still warm and we would spread it with honey. It was, and remains, one of the best breakfasts we ever had. Another of Yousouf's jobs was ironing. He loved to iron and Arthur never had his shirts so perfectly pressed.

Years later, talking with an Afghan waiter in a local restaurant in San Diego, we mentioned Yousouf. We learned that he had left the country when the Taliban had made survival so difficult and moved to San Diego! However, by the time we learned this, he had passed away. Arthur was saddened that we were unable to see Yousouf again, or help him in some way, especially when he had been so close by.

We always believed that the staff in our house should have a medical checkup. We arranged for them to have an examination at the American Embassy clinic. When the results came, the doctor discovered Yousouf had a variety of intestinal parasites. Pills were prescribed. A few days later we saw him digging carrots from a field next to our home, and eating them straight from the ground. What good would those pills be?

Entertainments and receptions

With so many embassies in Kabul, there was always a diplomatic event or other to attend. Besides their national day, some countries celebrated their military days. More than once we attended Iraq's military day! It was during our stint in Afghanistan that Chairman Mao passed away. Arthur vividly recalled the number of mai tais he had to drink. He inscribed "Long life" upon signing the official registry at China's Embassy. As a UN representative, he was most welcome. Most likely, the Chinese were unaware that he was an American citizen. The US had not yet recognized China, and bilateral relations were tense.

A number of countries sponsored goodwill tours for their prominent artists. We never lacked for invitations, despite the fact that, as UN Representative, Arthur was at the bottom of the diplomatic list, making which was the key to the invitations. We enjoyed the performances of leading ballet dancers, musicians, and opera singers from around the world. We would hear one particular Bulgarian soprano years later at the Metropolitan, and she was thrilled that we had heard her in Kabul. Performances at the German and Polish embassies were always a treat. For most UN families, it was difficult, however. There were no movies, no television, social life was limited to intimate dinner parties.

Kebabs were the most common fare at the embassy receptions. However, the Czechoslovakian Embassy was the exception. The Ambassador requested the cooperation of his community in preparing specialties from their country. The Czech teachers at the Russian school had no choice but to be recruited, and we very much enjoyed their treats.

The American Ambassador entertained by showing movies, followed by a dessert. It could not have been a greater *faux pas* when, one evening, with the German Ambassador present, he showed *Casablanca*. There was a long silence after that. Another guest that evening was the Afghan Foreign Minister. He recounted that as a teenager he lived in Berlin where his father was the ambassador to Germany. When the war came, his father stayed behind while the family moved to Switzerland. Casablanca held a special meaning to him, as well.

The United Nations had declared 1975 the International Year of the Woman. I was asked to be the UN official delegate to the celebrations. As I spoke Dari, one of my main functions was to give speeches written by Arthur's staff at high schools.

For the occasion, the American Embassy mounted a major photographic exhibition of prominent American women. Pictures of Eleanor Roosevelt, Barbara Walters, Billy Jean King, and others were proudly displayed. Who had ever heard of these women in Afghanistan?

The Russians used their budget to promote a nutrition program over the radio. It seemed a much more meaningful contribution. There was no television in the country, and most women were illiterate. The radio program was able to reach a wider audience.

Diplomatic dames

As a Greek with a United Nations passport, I was sought by both Eastern and Western camps alike. I was always amused to see all the Western diplomatic women sitting together, the Poles, Bulgarian, Czech, and the Yugoslavian dames of the Eastern bloc sitting together, and the ladies of the Arab and Muslim world congregating together. I just walked and sat wherever I wished, and was often used as a conduit for communicating. The president of the diplomatic wives was Madame Abu Zeid from Egypt. She conducted the meetings with superb efficiency and tact. We usually met at the Intercontinental.

During one of the events, the wife of the Russian ambassador, Madame Puzanova, a physician in her own right, was wearing a pair of small sapphire earrings. She was keen to let us know that she had purchased them with her own earnings, and hence, was not like the Queen of England with her inherited jewels. You could see the long face of the wife of the British ambassador. The Russian lectured us on the merits of USSR's system and the importance of the Woman's Day in the Soviet Union, describing how it was celebrated and how mothers were venerated. Before long, Madame Emmoniere of the French Embassy simply could not resist the temptation. A chic Parisian, she swirled around in her glorious mink coat and responded, "In our country, Madame, it is woman's day every day . . . ."

Madame Karazanova, the wife of the Bulgarian ambassador, wanted to buy clothing material. Mrs. Newman of the US Embassy volunteered to take her to the remnant bazaar. This nearly resulted in an incident. "Do the Americans think that we are so poor that we cannot afford material from a department store?" Only later did she realize that the Kennedy remnant bazaar was the best shopping place for these items.

I was elected as a member of a negotiating team. The issue was to decide the date of the diplomatic wives bazaar. The Russians wanted to hold the bazaar in November during the International Year of the Woman. They had problems with storage if the bazaar was delayed and with winter it would have been difficult for them to transport the goods across the frozen river at the border. The Americans wanted to postpone it, arguing they needed extra time to gather donations from the United States for this fund-raising event. Cosmetics, deodorants, shampoo, and hairspray were the best-selling items in the American booth. The arguments were not trivial. It was a matter of transport, of storage, and also of coordination with the President's daughter, the patron of the event.

I had been to the Russian Embassy before, but this was an intimate gathering. The wives of the British and Polish ambassadors were part of the team. Madame Puzanova, our hostess, greeted us very amicably. She was wearing a cute wig, a fur trimmed dress, and of course her sapphire earrings.

The Russian Embassy was grand, airy, and bright with spacious rooms. On the green walls there were large paintings of Russian artists of the Impressionist school. They were very pleasing pieces. The embassy had central heating, a rarity in Afghanistan. I wondered how many cameras and microphones were hiding in those heating vents recording our movements and discussions.

Tea was served from giant samovars that were in desperate need of polishing. The china was cheap porcelain, white and orange with a ghastly gold trim. The tablecloth could have used Yousouf's ironing skills. It was a feast of sweets: cookies, cakes, piroskies, cream puffs, pies, spicy nut breads, chocolates, and tiny tarts decorated with pink and green sugar. Coca-Cola from capitalistic America was also offered. The whole spread was so provincial. What a waste for just five people. Madame Puzanova had to have her translator along.

The team voted unanimously for the Russian schedule. We wanted to raise the money that particular year and not postpone it. It was also easier for me to achieve the UN pledge, as we would sell UNICEF Christmas cards better in November than in April. After our meeting we were ushered in a giant ballroom, just the five of us, to see a film. It was a superb artistic production of Tchaikovsky's *Swan Lake*. It was a brilliant performance of the star, Valery Panov, one of the great Russian dancers. He had defected to the West only few months before, and ironically, though understandably, his defection went unmentioned.

Balloons for a bazaar

I was the chairperson of the United Nations' yearly bazaar. I unearthed the talents and creativity of so many international wives. We crafted beautiful Christmas decorations that could have been displayed in any major department store in the West. Our stuffed animals were most popular and homemade baking was in high demand. A substantial amount of money was raised for a good cause, the local hospital.

The diplomats' wives were also engaged in various charitable causes. With the money from the wives bazaar, we supported the local orphanage, which housed approximately a hundred children. Built by the government of Czechoslovakia, it was a white elephant, an immense, empty, and cold building of marble. Who needed marble in Afghanistan?

At the end of Ramadan comes the feast Eid'l Fitr, a three-day holiday. A big celebration, it can be likened to our own Christmas festivities. The bazaar was loaded with stacks of sweets. At one of our diplomatic wives meetings, we decided that a basket of goodies should be distributed to each child. The ladies requested every embassy to provide a small item for the occasion. One was to supply the baskets, another pencils, another oranges, another candy, etc. Balloons were to be my contribution.

Having learned the word for a balloon, *pokona*, Arthur and I were off to the bazaar to procure my contribution. We searched along the alleys the appropriate shop, which we entered and asked for "pokona". Silence. We repeated "*besyar pokonas*" (lots of balloons). The proprietor looked at Arthur, then at me. Flashing a big smile, he produced a box of condoms! A package from the U.S. Agency of International Development, Pakistan, a gift from the American people. Eventually, we got the message through. We got the balloons. For three days, the Hills' pokona story was buzzing around Kabul's cocktail circuit.

In the style of Lord Curzon

New Year's Eve brought an invitation from "Her Britannic Majesty's Ambassador . . . . For a dinner dance and see the New Year . . . ." It was to be a black-tie affair, but after the informality of Samoa, Arthur did not have a tuxedo. A dark suit? Perhaps Arthur could wear his ten-year-old white dinner jacket. In December? Well, this was Kabul, not London.

The compound of the British Embassy was enormous, a conception of Lord Curzon. The gardens were marvelous. The complex was guarded by centenarian Gurkhas. The residence itself was so grand as to be comic. It boasted the largest pediment and pillars between Delhi and the neoclassic opera house of Ulan Bator. There was a disco band, and the ballroom was full of people dancing. Most of the guests were Afghans, a few of them coming with their European wives. To honor Afghan Islamic traditions, no alcohol was served. Just before midnight we were given 12 raisins, which we were supposed to eat one at a time as Big Ben struck. There was so much confusion, so much noise, no one heard Big Ben. Some guests received thirteen raisins, others ten. We ate ours all at once. As we were leaving an American lady commented this was a "Lord Curzon-style" evening of neo-colonialism.

We attended a number of memorable events. One of them was *buz-khashi*, a kind of polo with whip-wielding horsemen trying to grab the carcass of a headless goat. It was played only on national days or at special events.

Buz-khashi was the most popular sport among Afghans, like baseball is to Americans or cricket to the Brits. Secretary of State Henry Kissinger was in town, and a game was arranged in his honor. We did not know the rules (if there were any). The ball, so to speak, was a beheaded goat. The animal had been disemboweled, filled with sand, and placed in a hole in the middle of the field. Two opposing teams surrounded it. Each team consisting of a dozen players on horses sought to get the carcass out of the hole and carry it around the "goal posts" hundreds of yards away. We could not see much except a cloud of dust around a central mêlée.

And a mêlée it was. The riders with arms dangling down were trying to grip the carcass. When a goal was scored, the rider lifted his whip high in the air and the sponsor of the event — and all the spectators — quickly and vocally decided whether or not the rider had scored and rated a prize thereby. Kissinger was the sponsor, and all eyes were on him. He donated a turban cloth for the winner. There were really no teams and no rules for the sport as such, and it invited comparison to Afghan politics. We were all dusty and thirsty at the end of the match. As a souvenir, we bought a buz-khashi whip, another of those treasures that we would carry with us back to America.

Sorties to Peshawar

We took a number of trips to Peshawar in Pakistan. The scenery was breathtaking as we descended from Kabul's 1,800-meter altitude through the Maipar Gorge to Jelalabad at 600 meters. Near the top, the road dived in and out of tunnels cut through the rock and although stark and forbidding, the views could only be described as magnificent. Lower down, as the steep slopes leveled out, all became tranquil. The river slowed and widened with views of agricultural land.

It was February, Kabul was blanketed in snow, and the temperatures were hovering around zero. The road was slippery with ice. There were several places where an incautious driver could slide off into the gray-green Kabul River. We felt a sense of relief upon reaching the very pleasant 20-degree warmth of Jelalabad.

And then we were off towards Peshawar, through the mighty Khyber Pass.

Julie at Khyber Pass

Arthur became very resourceful with his UN passport and UN number plates. He could cross two immigration posts in less than half an hour. This ordeal took a day for most regular travelers. Afghans drive on the right side of the road, Pakistanis on the left. A portion of the road at the border was no man's land. It was frightening experience coming down the gorge and seeing a Pakistani driver heading straight toward you. Fortunately there was not very much traffic, and in spite of the terrifying bends we made it safely every time. I could not resist taking a picture of a sign depicting the camel trail.

There were few signs along this historic road. Small square forts bristled on every hill. Names of regiments — British, Pathan, and Indian — were carved on jutting rocks.

Regiment plaques at Khyber Pass

Afghanistan had been a pawn of the superpowers of the 19th century — and apparently remains so today. In 1841, the British were retreating from Afghanistan. They invaded the country in 1839, to secure trade and to prevent tsarist Russia from moving in. Both British and Russians were driving for territory, natural resources, and international power. A force of 16,500 perished — fighting men, Europeans, and Indian sepoys, infantry, cavalry, families, camp followers — at the hands of Afghans in the Khyber Pass. Only one survived, a medical doctor who recounted the horrible massacre, one of the greatest of British debacles. Much blood has been spilled under the rocks of the Khyber Pass, blood dried out by the sun.

Travels in Afghanistan

We were privileged to travel extensively in Afghanistan — much more than most foreigners. After a second application and some "facilitation" of the process by Arthur's contacts in the Ministry of Foreign Affairs, we were granted permission by the Ministry of the Interior to travel all around the country, including the highly sensitive areas along the borders of Iran and the Soviet Union.

Afghanistan had only four main asphalt roads to tempt the tourist and not too many sites to crowd a traveler during his summer stay. The road down from Kabul to the west leading to Kandahar and then to Herat was the American-built highway, but our journey was to take us through unpaved roads, tracks, and areas with no roads at all.

Our travels — a modern caravan with two four-wheel drive vehicles and a good supply of canned food, water, and petrol — took us south from Kabul to Kandahar. Charles Rutledge, a UN expert, traveled with us in the other jeep. We passed through Ghazni; the town was wrapped in the deep dream of provincial peace, and the castle ruins, seen through an archway, drifted like a mirage. We drove on over lovely hills. In this comparatively inhabited region, mud-brick houses plastered with more mud and straw stood behind high compound walls — a traditional defensive feature of Pashtun homes. Narrow, dusty alleys that turned into mud baths in the rain connected village homes.

We proceeded to Kandahar, Afghanistan's second largest city. It was an oasis town in the desert. Surrounding the city were lush green fields and shady orchards producing grapes, melons, mulberries, figs, peaches, and pomegranates. It was dusk by the time we reached the comfortable guesthouse of the USAID.

Kandaharis have always been traders, as the city stood at the intersection of ancient trade routes. Its numerous bazaars had been famous for centuries. The best skullcaps, waistcoats, and fine white shirts were still stitched and sold in the Kandahari bazaars. We spent a short hour among them the next morning before we set out on our long day across the desert to Herat.

Herat, the cradle of Afghanistan's history and civilization, is also an oasis town, encircled by fertile, irrigated farmland, and rimmed by mountains. The rampart of the old city was still visible, with a grand bazaar around it. In medieval times, the city had been a center of Christianity, then a major center of Sufism — the spiritual and mystical side of Islam. Indeed, located amid the competing Turkic and Persian empires, Herat had been an early convert to Islam. Built in the seventh century, the main mosque had been rebuilt many times, and it was decorated with exquisite blue Persian tiles. The mosque held inscriptions from the Koran and famous Persian and Afghan poems. This strong Persian influence indicated Herat's strategic role as a gateway to Iran. The *madrasah*, or religious school, was attached to the mosque; 50 students were attending that year. The day of our visit, the marble of the inner courtyard was too hot to walk on in bare feet. As soon as a lesson ended, the students rushed out to buy ice cream from a vendor stationed right in front of the school. Outside the mosque, an old blind mullah listened attentively while a child painstakingly read the Koran, line by line.

A blind Mullah listens while a child reads the Koran

From Herat we traveled north on the edge of Badakhsan via Qali Nao, Bula Murghab, Maimana, Daolatabad, Sribagan, Mazar, and Kunduz to Ai Khanum. The exotic names came from and evoked a very distant past.

Tea on the roadside

Morning was still young when we left the paved road. A thin cloud of dust began to rise around us and soon covered everything. The green wheat fields were dotted here and there with red opium poppies. The road appeared to cut haphazardly through the hills. Teahouses were spaced out along both sides of the road. The mud wall huts of the teahouses held no more than a single, dark room. Outside was a covered terrace where travelers gathered. An old man sat on a threadbare carpet laid out on the ground. He enjoyed the sights, the arrival of lorries, the dismounting of passengers, and the unexpected meeting of friends traveling in opposite directions. People were dressed according to the province and tribe to which they belonged, in wide shirts or close fitting tunics or spreading cloaks.

An Afghan traveler

They wore turbans that were either loose and flowing, or wrapped firm and tight: astrakhan kulahs, brilliant silk caps, or tall hairy sheepskin hats. They delighted the attentive ear with their astonishing and inexhaustible supply of tales, stories, and lies. A man in a brown wool caftan, here called a *chapan*, was of Uzbek or Turkoman origin, a horseman of the northern steppes.

The tea was bubbling hot. Charles informed us that it cost one afghani, or five US cents, with sugar. A hookah with hashish changed hands among travelers and moved from one pair of lips to the next. Lungs were filled with water-cooled smoke. One afghani for three puffs — what a way to start the day, to dream, to wonder, to extract the most from sensual delight.

Chaishambe — Wednesday — was a charming village perched along the road. Legend had it that an emir stopped here on a Wednesday, hence its name. This was not uncommon in Central Asia; Dushambe is Monday, a town in Soviet Turkestan.

Coming down the Subzak pass the view was breathtaking, a vast panorama reminding us of our own Grand Canyon. The car was loaded with extra petrol, spare tires, water, maps, a supply of food and sleeping bags. We were now traveling on unpaved roads. The mud was unbelievably sticky, the passes had shimmering sheets of ice, and the streams became torrents as we proceeded. The road had a disturbing habit of disappearing altogether. We negotiated unexpected sharp curves, washed out patches, detours, and streambeds, and crossed 33 streams with the water level often dangerously close to our feet.

Crossing streams

Poppies and lilac bushes dominated the vast panorama of hidden valleys, purple shadows, and lofty peaks crowned with slate gray slopes. The magenta cliffs were sprinkled with gnarled dark green pistachio and juniper, which the high winds had whipped into exotic shapes. We descended a series of hairpin bends — on one side the saw-edged cliff, on the other a bottomless void. Huge ruts, slopes, and bends followed one after the other. The violent corners grew steeper, harder, and more dangerous.

It was here that we picked up our favorite Afghan expression "*baghal, baghal*" — "up, up" — used when the four-wheel vehicle was creeping up a 45-degree incline. We traveled four days from the time we left the blacktop road to when we reached it again near the environs of Mazar-i-Sharif. Our maps were meaningless, as they did not agree with each other.

Riding country

The accommodations along the road were primitive. Our first evening, we set our sleeping bags on grass nibbled short by summer herds. The river ran close by with unobtrusive noises. Another night we stopped in a hamlet of just five mud houses. What was described as a hotel offered a covered balcony for our sleeping bags. The place sank into darkness after sunset, with one light shining until, at eleven at night, another vehicle came down from nowhere, and the balcony that had been offered to us was filled with sleeping figures rolled in their quilts with their heads covered like cocoons. Another evening, we reached a provincial town. It had a hotel, a long barrack-like structure, bare and cheerless, with a broken-down sofa in the foyer. The tariff was 120 afghanis, six dollars, an additional 10 afghanis for some water to be heated. The rooms were furnished with simple charpoys, the local beds, four wooden posts holding hammock netting made of strips of bamboo. It was so dilapidated that the hammock touched the ground. We placed our sleeping bags on top of the rugs. We were more fleabitten than we ever been before or since.

Food had to be purchased from the outside. Nazir, our driver, bought his *shurwa* for dinner.

Nazir our driver

It was a greasy meat broth, served with dry bread. Nazir tore the bread piecemeal, steeped it in the broth, then ate with his fingers. He told us the fat tasted good. We survived on nan and canned food, as we were unwilling to take any risks. As long as there was a bazaar in a village we could find the wonderful flat bread.

Nan in Central Asia

This was riding country. Nothing on wheels except for a jeep or a land rover would defeat the terrain. A rider sitting on embroidered saddlebags met us on the narrow way that ran between hillside and river. He was a trader and his mule, loaded with pottery. A man could make a living here just by simply trafficking goods from one small town to the next — a marginal sort of life that required knowledge of local prices. He could buy a woven wool blanket for a hundred afghanis in the village. In Mazar he could sell that for threefold profit, then buy cooking oil, hurricane lamps, batteries, and sacks of tea, and return to the village. And how were the roads? "Terrible, a man could get killed."

The inhabitants of theses provinces boasted the finest astrakhan sheep, the most precious carpets, and the breeding of the swiftest horses to conquer those steppes. Their ancestors had come from Central Asia on the same horses. Their children learned to ride when they learned to walk.

In villages, the arrival of a four-wheel vehicle was an event. Curious faces immediately surrounded us. We, the travelers, had a valuable commodity to exchange with the locals: news of other towns the state of the roads and the passes. "Where are you coming from? Are you government officials?" Nazir passed a photographic document from hand to hand: "This is called an identity card; the government is giving them to every one in Kabul. See, that is my picture." Imagine the government giving people photos of themselves to carry. And it was free? "God is great!" I wished I had a Polaroid camera, but I didn't. I took out my camera to immortalize the scene. Without exception, everyone wanted to be photographed.

Stories and samovars

To get the pulse of the area, we stopped at a teahouse. These were very special places for Afghans; there, people came to meet each other, to play a popular game of marbles called *karoum*, and to exchange pieces of information and misinformation. This teahouse had a transistor radio, and the locals were keen to show us that they could pick up the Voice of America, even though we received the strong signal of Radio Peking. The innkeeper was very proud of his samovar. "It is a Nikolaev, you know, the best kind." Samovars, a 19th-century innovation from Russia, give special character to those towns in the North. Samovars have lent their names to the teahouse — to the point where only the most deracinated Afghan would refer the teahouse as a *chai hana* (literally teahouse).

Smoke from the samovar had blackened the roof with soot. Photographs hung in cheap wooden frames, pictures of the innkeeper and of the deposed King Zahir Shah, the decorative value of whose image the revolution had not diminished.

A squatting man mesmerized the villagers with his tales. He had a flat face, a great solid chest, and powerful arms. How old was he? What was his origin, his tribe? The only sure thing he was not a Mongolian. He may have come from the Persian frontier, or India or Baluchistan, that savage land. His face was so worn that the signs of race and the marks of ancestry could not longer be read on it. He spoke the language of the province. He was not a dervish or a guru or a shaman. He had traveled the highways, paths, tracks of the whole Afghan road. The shores of the Amur Daria were familiar to him. He had trotted the everlasting snows of the Pamir and the burning deserts had scorched his soles. How long has he been traveling? What was the power, the dream that drove his unquenchable thrust of knowledge? He had never been seen to read. Yet, he seemed to remember all the happenings and all the men who had left their mark upon the mountains, the passes and the steppes of Afghanistan for hundreds of years. He spoke of Zoroaster, as though he was a disciple, of Iskander as though he had followed him from conquest to conquest, of Balkh the mother of cities as he had been born there, and the massacres of Genghis Khan as though he has been soaked in the blood of slaughtered nations and buried under the ashes and ruins of strongholds. The teahouse, the samovar, was more than a pot for boiling tea or the room above it. For the people it meant the whole world.

As we entered, the conversation stopped. Men were surprised, looked at me with curiosity, and asked Nazir how many camels I was worth — a foreigner speaking their language. "You are welcome. Please have tea." A young boy appeared, slapped cups on to a tin tray, and offered them to us. We accepted.

Along the road, we stopped at the provincial capital of Maimana. Nazir had a sister, third wife of a wealthy landowner, and we were invited for dinner. I am sure they were pre-warned, as a feast had been prepared for us. Our host, Khalil, was a fair-skinned man in his late thirties who owned an extensive piece of fertile land along the river. Carpets were spread on the ground. We had the afternoon to relax. We were offered tea and introduced to neighbors and relatives. We waited for the *arbab*, a headman of the area, to join us for dinner. It was uncomfortable sitting cross-legged, so we stretched our legs, moving together, first one side then on the other, but later you became numb and forgot your discomfort. It was a sumptuous meal of kebabs infused with cloves, cumin, and cinnamon, chicken, pilaf full of nuts and raisins, potatoes, spinach, and plenty of yogurts. The nan was fresh. Sweet melons completed the meal. It was all washed down with refreshing cardamom tea. I could not follow the conversation well, and Nazir translated periodically. It was evident that the topic was drought. "How can I irrigate? No rain this year." "The pumps come from China, Russia and Pakistan. Do you know which are the best?" "The water level in the river is so low." Flowing water is almost a religion in this part of the country; it helps to purify what it touches.

A wife weeps

After dinner, I asked if I could visit the women. They

seemed to anticipate my curiosity and I was ushered with alacrity to the women's quarters. Behind the impenetrable mud wall, I found myself in the shelter of a large family: brothers, sisters, wives, and children. Carpets were lying on the floor, piled one on top of the other. Carpets were also hanging on the walls, serving as dividers from room to room. This was a display of wealth.

I met Khalil's four wives. They were beautifully dressed, wearing at least three layers of necklaces, Turkoman bracelets, and heavy make-up around their eyes. They were attractive, but not beauties. The eldest was powerfully built; she could easily have passed for a Greek. Nazir's sister was very fair with expressive blue eyes, and wore the simplest attire. Again I was a subject of curiosity. They had never met a foreigner before, and here was a foreigner who could speak their language. They touched me, examined my watch, combed my hair, felt the fabric of my slacks.

It was the language that broke the ice and the questions started flowing: "How many children do you have?" When I answered we did not have any children, they gasped, "Is your husband planning to have another wife?' The second wife was in tears as she did not have any children and she was concerned that she may be divorced. I asked her if she had seen a *hakim*, a doctor. "I cannot visit a male hakim." I explained that there were women doctors in Kabul, perhaps even in Herat. However, these towns were not part of these women's horizons; they might as well have been on the other side of the earth.

The questions continued. "What gifts did you receive at your wedding? Did you receive any cattle? Any jewelry?" I was hard-pressed to explain about the cattle, but for jewelry it was easier. Yes, "Brides receive jewelry from their families." That was the opening they needed. Immediately, they went to the communal chest and brought out their jewels. Incredible silver pieces, necklaces, bracelets, pins, tiaras. I recall a heavy necklace with ornate silver balls, interspaced with beads of coral, lapis lazuli, turquoise, and black onyx. It was so artistically designed, just strung on a simple piece of string. It could have been on display in a showcase in New York or Paris and stopping crowds. "Is there anything you need that you would like us to give?" They presented me with a gift, a beautiful Kuchi piece, embroidery of large multicolored flowers on black velvet. I was dumbfounded. It was from their wedding trousseau. I accepted gratefully this treasure to carry back from Afghanistan. My gift of tea, sugar, and a tin of fruitcake looked so meager in comparison.

I was interested to know whether the women always wore their chadri when walking outside their compound or going down to the river. The answer was simple. "You do not walk naked inside your house, and we feel naked if we are not covered up." I delved into a question that worried me most. I struggled to find the right words in Dari. "What is it like for four women to run the household — is wife number one the most powerful one, or perhaps the youngest one?" I could not use the word favorite. They greeted my question calmly, but the answer had more emotions than anything else said that evening. "We are all sisters, we always had four mothers." It appeared that the interminable captivity had forged between the four wives a bond of intimacy that would never be completely broken.

To lighten the mood I asked about celebrations. "Our man always fires a gun when a child is born, fires into the sky." This is how they celebrate the birth of a *pesar* son, a brand-new warrior. The first thing the male baby hears is the sound of a bullet; the second thing he hears is the name of Allah.

These women, virtually uneducated, would hardly ever leave their village in a lifetime. They would never clamber the chalky slopes above it except for gathering some wild rhubarb now and then. Their flat-roofed house built of earth was their life, but also their grave.

Mud houses in Central Asia

The woman's life was the least happy aspect of Afghanistan.

I spent two hours before I joined the men. For a moment, Arthur thought I had been kidnapped. Those two hours behind the mud walls in Maimana remain the highlight of my international experiences.

Market day

It was market day when we reached Shereen Tagao (Sweet River), another small dusty town along the road. Carpets were on display and I could not help exploiting my bargaining skills. It was a game for me. 70,000 afghanis? 50,000? 40,000? Half an hour later, I was still at my game. By then I was committed and a purchase had to be made. It was less than a hundred dollars. Arthur paid in crisp new notes — another source of great excitement. The village people had never seen clean, brand-new notes. When we stopped in another village to buy nan that evening, the local teahouse was buzzing with the news of the foreigners paying all that money for a carpet! Looking at our pictures years later, we recalled the bargaining and the fun we had.

Carpet merchants in Shereen Tagao

The bazaar of Daolatabad was one of the oldest in the province; it retained the order, smell, shape, and customs of the marketplaces in Central Asia. It was a maze of narrow, winding lanes and blind alleys, stalls, shops, and warehouses. The sun filtered through the straw mats and the foliage, set up to shade the alleys, produced zones of strongly contrasting light and shadows in which clothes, faces, materials, cooking utensils, and provisions assumed a mysterious richness. A ragged old chapan took the appearance of costly velvet. The great copper samovar turned to fiery gold. This was where trade was carried, following long traditions, the same exchanges, same rites, same persuasions, same crafty and passionate bargaining, same cups of green or black tea passed around. The entire length of the maze was a tangled, milling swarm of men and beasts. Rank and wealth counted little in this closed pocket of confusion.

On the last leg of the unpaved road, the local governor provided us with a guide to ensure that we would not get lost in the maze of rutted tracks that had been worn by earlier travelers across the roadless desert. Osman was a rogue, but he knew the road well and guided us skillfully. Yellow dust seeped through our jeep. We were moving at a slow pace, perhaps at ten miles an hour. With all the jumping and bumping of the car, the lid of the jerrycan of petrol opened, soaking Arthur and Osman, but it could have been worse. Finally, the green valley of Shirbagan appeared. We passed a few markers for oil exploration on the way. Russians were exploring the area with huge drilling equipment.

After four days, we finally reached the paved road. We stopped at Acha for a glimpse at carpets. This was the last outpost to seek nomads' jewelry. We purchased a beautiful Turkoman necklace. We had it framed and hung it proudly on a wall of our home in California.

The days on the dusty road had made us eager to reach Mazar-i-Sharif, to find a hotel with hot water, and to recharge our energies. The food had become monotonous, so we ordered chicken, an appreciated change. Most of the hotels in Afghanistan are in a grove of pines, oak, or almond. The one we stayed in while in Mazar was no exception. The garden was well kept. As spring had arrived, tuberoses and geraniums were blooming. The charpoy chairs were comfortable, and it was time to relax among the pine trees. The hotel swimming pool, however, was pretty filthy, lacking filtration. How could we forget the energetic efforts of those young men trying to clean it?

At sunset, the garden woke up for the enchanted night; small electric bulbs began to shine and the rose scent that wafted in the air was rich and voluptuous. The gardener left his tools — a hose, a spade at the root of the rose bushes. He squatted in a corner with the youngest of his many children and smoked the cigarette of the evening.

Only 70 miles from the border of Central Asia, Mazar was

home to the blue-tiled Shrine of Hazrat Ali, Prophet Mohammed's son-in-law and the fourth Caliph of Islam.

The Shrine of Hazrat Ali, Mazar-i-Sharif

It was a must stop. We were running out of film. In every town the attraction was the bazaar, and this was also the case in Mazar. Children played on a merry-go-round, and merchants sold roasted peanuts and sesame-based candies. Upon seeing us foreigners, the seller of corn, entranced among his doves, threw a handful of his capital for nothing. Peddlers unpacked their wares, spreading them on threadbare carpets: old watches, padlocks, enormous keys, pottery. Blind musicians tuned their instruments. A scribe sat in front of a long black box decorated with pink flowers wielded a pen, an inkpot, and a little board with a blank paper attached to it. A letter done with his help cost ten afghanis.

It was in Mazar that we met an Iranian rug merchant who invited us to his home, wanting his teenage daughters to meet foreigners. He arrived in his red Mercedes to take us to his home. He was obviously a rich man, with a Western kind of house and carpets everywhere. We met the family, his brother, his six sisters, and the four girls. Two of the daughters were engaged; the eldest was getting married in a week. We had a fashion show of all the dresses that had been sewn for the wedding. The colors were bright and rhinestone embroidery was in abundance. The girl was happy, having seen her fiancée once and now planning to live in Kabul. The younger one was not thrilled with her fate, however. Hers was a marriage arranged by the family, and the fiancé was wearing a turban. Both worried that if they would not produce an heir, another wife would be added to the household.

These young women had received some education. They were neither confined behind the mud walls, nor wore a chadri when they walked in the street. Just a veil was required. They were interested in my dress, a Hawaiian muumuu, and wanted to copy the design. There was a real dichotomy in this household, the father being a successful businessman dealing with foreigners, bank accounts, exchange rates, and insurance, but still maintaining a traditional household and arranging the marriages of his children. We were served cold drinks, cakes, and coffee. No tea this time: the Iranian merchant had heard that Americans liked coffee.

Balkh's blossoming silence

Near Mazar lay the ruins of Balkh, which invading Arabs in the seventh century called the "Mother of All Cities." It was here that Zoroaster preached 3,000 years ago. It was here that Alexander the Great had set up camp and met his beautiful Roxana. It was here that the Persian poet Rumi was born. Balkh had flourished for centuries as a center of continuous civilization and Zoroastrianism, Buddhism, and Islam. Since Genghis Khan, however, the focus of culture and trade shifted to Mazar. Balkh, once the greatest city of Central Asia, was scarcely a town now, a blossoming silence. We were immersed in history here at the crossroads of the ages.

We were perplexed to see so many new rugs spread along the main asphalt road. Cows, horses, donkeys tramped over them, urinating; the trucks drove over the rugs. After a few days of this regimen and a few days in the hot sun, the rugs were "antiqued" and ready for sale to the unsuspicious German tourists. We were no less amused than bewildered.

After Mazar we traveled east to Faizabad, which was our launching pad northwards along rutted dusty tracks across the desert to the border of what was then the Soviet Socialist Republic of Tajikistan. Reaching the Amu Darya River after a hard day of driving, we could see, across the river, a number of Soviet military vehicles in motion on blacktop roads. Only hours before, in stark contrast, we had passed nomad caravans that were moving their herds and camps to high pastures for the summer.

Here we visited a French archaeological team excavating a Greek city, Alexandria-on-the-Oxus or Ai Chanoum. It was here in this strategic northern corner that Alexander the Great had brought his army. The Greek settlers he had left behind remained in possession of Balkh for two centuries. We were hot and dusty and our necks hurt from so much bouncing. We were offered French anise, a welcome change. But first we needed water, which we gulped down in huge amounts. We were thirsty and beyond caring whether the water was potable or not.

In Ai Chanoum we were taken to see the archaeological sights. Here was Alexandria on the Oxus, a Greek city. We saw the mosaics covering the palace floor, the temple, an arch leading to a palestra, Ionic columns, vases, and coins from the Greek period. The archeologists had been working for eleven years and were convinced that the hill in the west hid a Greek theater — and also that the site was not Bactrian but pure Greek. Their work was cut short, however, when the Russians invaded Afghanistan a year later.

The long trip back

Our return trip was via Kunduz. We started early in a misty morning, and encountered nomads again with their flock of black sheep, whose karakul coats were one of the chief exports of Afghanistan. Their shearing, which was done very roughly, left them tousled with a touch of modern bravado. The Afghans still walked their herd to grazing grounds — perhaps a ten-day march or so, three times during the course of the year. The shepherds and the dogs remained unseen, lost in the sea of sheep, whose pace they controlled.

We met these nomad detachments at intervals, always on the way into some side valley. A melody traveled through the silence of the steppes.

A man was leading two camels; his four wives were carefully balanced on huge baskets, each on a side of a camel. The women were wearing flowing silks; one was dressed in a harsh blue, another in strong crimson, and another in fiery yellow, while a somber gray adorned the last one. They wore many broad thick necklaces, heavy bracelets in their arms and ankles. They appeared to be wearing armor.

Nomads in the Northern frontier

As we drove along, a man stepped out toward us and stopped us. We saw through his weather beaten clothes and scorched face that he was a young man. He told us that the hamlet where his parents lived had not received any food for three days, and he asked us if we could deliver nan a few kilometers down the road. We obliged.

It was another long ride in the desert. I could not recall the number of soft drinks, water bottles, and cups of tea consumed on that journey. We were permanently dehydrated. Once, we ran out of petrol. It took hard bargaining and lots of cash to procure some fuel until we could reach a larger town.

It is notable that the roads built by Soviet aid, which ran from the USSR border through the 10,000-feet high Salang Tunnel (also built by Russians) down to Kabul, were engineered to carry tanks — as was demonstrated during the Soviet invasion. The roads built by the USAID from Kabul south to Kandahar and west to Herat were quickly destroyed under the tanks, however.

From the Salang we headed for the valley of Bamiyan (where the 7th-century Buddhas were later destroyed by the Taliban) and Band-i-Amir in central Afghanistan. Bamiyan was the center of Buddhism and an important serai, or resting place, for the camel caravans on the ancient Silk Route, which linked the Roman Empire with Central Asia, China, and India. Bamiyan remained the protector of Buddhism for the whole Central Asia and India after the Islamic conquests. We reached the valley around dusk and were confronted by two magnificent, 2nd-century A.D. Buddha colossi carved into a sandstone cliff face. The two statues, one 170 feet and the other 115 feet tall, were weathered and cracked. Their hands were gone and the oval of the head was smooth but faceless. However, the impact was stunning. The figures were draped in Greek robes, representing the unique fusion of classical Indian and Central Asian art. The Buddhas' heads were once entirely covered with Buddhist devotional art. They had been one of the wonders of the ancient world, and visited by pilgrims from China and India through the centuries.

Giant Buddha in Bamiyan

Numerous caves dug into the cliff surrounded the main figure. These gigantic holes gave the appearance of an enormous beehive. Thousands of Buddhist monks once lived in the caves and grottos in the cliffs alongside the statues.

Beehive caves in Bamiyan

It was time to proceed toward Kunar Valley, a showpiece of the UNDP program. The valley lies in eastern Afghanistan, and is the setting of Kipling's wonderful story "The Man Who Would Be King." A team of UN engineers was doing wonders by digging canals and diverting water to accommodate the farmers' needs. Poplars, a valuable building material in a land that lacks timber, grew on both sides of the canal. I inquired about the price of a sapling. To my surprise, the answer was 200 afghani, or ten dollars at the official rate — a very high price for such thin wood.

Before entering the village, we paused to admire the outlet for the wells from which water gushed to an open canal. What an invigorating sight! Fish, black shadows in the bright sunlight, darted away as we approached. The water was collected in a pond, from which it was conducted into the village, lying securely behind its thick mud walls.

We proceeded to the Panjsher Valley, home of the leader of the Northern Alliance Ahmed Shah Masood until his assassination in September 2001, just before the attack on the World

Trade Center. With the mountains in the background, the valley was home of apricot, peach, and pistachio orchards a valley as green as anywhere in the world, so beautiful, so peaceful and safe. It is no longer tranquil, no longer an exquisite escape; bloody and threatening encounters are the norm today.

Our access to the people was unusually good because of the fact that we were not seen as representing any country or power bloc. Afghans were generally cautious in expressing political views, but we managed to breach their reserve on a number of occasions, and gained some remarkable insights into the country and its culture. Islam was at the very center of their lives. Whether it is saying one's prayers five times a day, fasting in Ramadan or giving *zakat*, an Islamic contribution to the poor, few people in the world observe the rituals and piety of Islam with such regularity and emotion as the Afghans. In this conservative society, Islam has been the bedrock for the unity of Afghanistan's diverse and multiethnic peoples, while jihad frequently provided the principle mobilizing factor of Afghan nationalism, during the resistance against the British and the Russians. Rich or poor, communist, king or mujaheddin, it makes little difference. Today religion has proved a useful tool for warlords, many of whom gained power through waging jihad.

We are saddened by the way the society has been devastated by invasions, uprisings, and civil war over more than twenty years, and are frankly pessimistic that this failed state can easily, if ever, be reconstituted in the form that we knew it in any remotely decent way. The Taliban and their generation were born and or raised in refugee camps, which were populated exclusively by Pathans, educated in madrasahs. They learned nothing about the history of Afghanistan, they had no memories of their tribes, their elders, their neighbors, nor the complex ethnic mix of peoples that often made up there villages and their home lands or the fact that the people lived in harmony in multiethnic villages before the Soviet invasion.

At the time we were there, education was being encouraged, women were being liberated slowly, and the country was moving in the direction of a modern, secular state. Unfortunately, the Soviets captured this modernizing segment of the population, while the US and its allies, interested only in doing harm to the Soviets, backed their enemies, the 14th-century fundamentalists, who completely destroyed the modernizers or drove them into exile. The result we see today in the form of the Taliban and the terrorists they harbor and supply.

Four Years with the UNDP

A rthur spent four years with the United Nations Development Program (UNDP), the "banker" agency of the United Nations. He served in two least-developed countries (LCDs) — Western Samoa and Afghanistan.

UNDP's work was undertaken exclusively through government channels, i.e., through various ministries. The program was vastly broader than the Ford Foundation and had the potential to make a substantive difference in people's lives. Besides education and agriculture, it encompassed projects in infrastructure development, health, and basic social services.

These projects were run by experts from relevant UN agencies such as UNESCO for education, ITU for telecommunication, FAO for agriculture, WHO for health, etc. The experts were drawn from various countries — Scandinavians with their "neutral" nationalities were well received; US experts were a minority within the United Nations system, which the British dominated.

As an international organization, UNDP had to adhere to the political realities of the system it represented. Individuals with limited education and experience could attain high positions derived uniquely from the political backing of their government. Thankfully the organization could also count on many well-qualified civil servants, dedicated individuals with broad international experience in their fields of expertise.

The effectiveness of a country's development program was determined not only by the magnitude of investment in relation to Gross National Product (GNP) but also by the method it was financed. No matter how large, a development program predominantly financed by foreign aid was bound to fail without a strong government commitment and domestic resource mobilization.

Adopting the country program approach posed a prime policy dilemma for UNDP. Under the system, the government had the authority to determine how the funds would be used, within the terms of reference of UNDP. These terms of reference were the few props left to the local office to enable it to deny proposals which the representative and his team, as development professionals, felt were improper uses of UN development assistance.

There were occasions when Arthur would have liked to respond positively and could not, but more often it was convenient to have a basis on which to rest a refusal. UNDP headquarters in New York wanted to loosen many of the existing constraints. Arthur believed that a redefinition of the terms of reference could be most valuable, provided he could still reasonably say no to unreasonable proposals. The Malaria Control Project in Afghanistan was a case in point of the way UNDP used its terms of reference to deny a strongly pressed government request. UNDP headquarters' answer would have been very different.

Always a gray area

There was always a gray area of assistance. Arthur thought important the largely neglected area between "bankable" projects and UNDP's technical assistance, where high-risk in vestment projects were to be found. He wanted to encourage governments to take a less conservative approach to high-risk investment projects which also had the possibility of great rewards.

The whole area of education and training was very important and he pushed strongly to have it re-examined. Arthur believed that local students should be able to avail themselves of the regional educational institutions that UNDP supported in their countries. He also thought that these institutions needed to adapt themselves to local conditions, or become irrelevant and useless.

A concrete example was the University of the Philippines, and especially its College of Agriculture (UPCA). Over a 20-to 25-year period, UPCA received approximately $20 million in external assistance, mainly from USAID and the Ford and Rockefeller Foundations. There was no question that the American donors, with the full concurrence of the Filipino recipients, helped to create an American institution that simply was not viable in a Southeast Asian context. Large-scale support came to an end in 1972, and it is interesting to observe how UPCA (now the University of the Philippines in Los Baños) mutated into a Philippine institution. Had they been allowed to begin earlier, the necessary mutations would have made the transition less painful and less costly.

As a substitute for training abroad, Arthur recommended that UNDP create more ad hoc training programs, designed to take people from their present level and to give them as much additional training as could be fitted into the time available — in other words, aim for relative improvements rather than absolute standards.

Looking back on Arthur's UNDP experience, it was abundantly clear that a major obstacle to the success of his work was the government's inability to meet local costs at the agreed level and in a timely fashion. He always wished that he could have done more, but he knew — best of all people — that development was a collective and collaborative task, requiring far more than one man's best intentions.

A Return to Asia

The timing of this trip in July 1985 was dictated by our wedding anniversary rather than by any expectation of good weather. In fact, in all the places we ever headed for, it was raining most of the time. Fortunately, that did not turn out to be the case, and we were actually better off weather-wise in Tokyo than if we had stayed at home in New Jersey. Years earlier we had made an extensive trip to Japan, but this time our stay in the Tokyo area was limited.

We found Tokyo to be a bustling modern city, partly due to the fact that it was pretty well flattened right before the end of World War II, so that most of the buildings dated from the post-war period.

We headed early for what came to be my favorite place in the city. It was our first visit to Tsukiji, the largest wholesale fish market in the world. Jet-lagged as we were, it was easy to be up before 4 a.m. and take the subway to the market. A map in English outside the station gave clear directions to the place, which was only a couple of blocks away. When we arrived, the auction was already advanced. They had started with hundreds of 500-to-1,000 pound flash-frozen tuna lined up like torpedoes in the rising mist.

Blowfish and barrows

We were told that 3,000 tons of fish were sold here in a day, including forms of life I had never seen in my wildest nightmares: large, rose-colored octopi, their tentacles tucked under them like huge baseball mitts; tanks of live eels; ready-to-pop blowfish; oysters like dinner plates; and at least a dozen varieties of shrimps from the gigantic tiger to the miniscule river shrimp. It was a frantic but friendly place, and we were welcome to stroll around. Dozens of giant refrigerated trucks were parked outside the market, ready to carry and distribute the auctioned fish to smaller markets and restaurants. Motorized barrows raced by at 20 miles an hour and we got quickly drenched. We were prepared, wearing our oldest clothes and shoes, but rubber boots would have been more appropriate foot attire.

After some time observing the auction, we wandered around the outer market. There were many stalls selling everything for cooking, as well as the best-priced handmade ceramics in the city. Other stalls carried dried fish and were well patronized. We stopped at a beautiful little shrine where people prayed for the soul of the fish. It was time for breakfast; why not enter one of those sushi-noodle stalls nearby? We pulled up a stool next to some market workers having their breakfast meal. Arthur pointed to what looked good. A huge bowl of ginger was placed in front of us, and, as he loves ginger, he helped himself generously. By the time we returned to our hotel it was still early in the morning. Our clothes stank. Another shower, and we were ready for a full day of exploration in Tokyo.

We spent the rest of the day visiting the Meiji temple, a welcome contrast of serene solemnity to the consumerism exuded by the shop-filled streets of the city. We revisited the fantastic Japanese department stores and Akihabara, the high-tech area, with its endless multi-storey buildings. We took a trip out to Nikko, an hour and a half from Tokyo by train. Nikko is famous for the Toshogu shrine, but also it is a national park of great beauty. In Japanese trains, the stops and

connections are announced over a loudspeaker system throughout the train. Although we were literally the only foreigners
on the train, they made all the announcements both in Japanese and English — only for our benefit!

We had clipped from the travel section of *The New York
Times* some reviews of restaurants in Tokyo, and we tried some
within walking distance of our hotel. They were splendid.
Arthur had long been a lover of all sorts of Japanese food, and
I bore with him somewhat reluctantly. However, on this trip I
got more engaged, and came away about as enthusiastic as
him about the delights of Japanese cuisine.

From Tokyo we went to Fuji-Hakone National Park, nomi-
nally in the area of Mt. Fuji, although we remained without a
view of it because of the clouds. One day, our first one at the
Fujiya Hotel in Miyanoshita, it rained pretty steadily all day,
so we took the opportunity to just stay in our lovely corner
room, relax and watch the clouds coming up the valleys and
obscuring the mountain opposite. It was very beautiful and
made us understand better why Chinese and Japanese artists
painted mountains and clouds like they did — this was, indeed, how they looked.

To reach Miyanoshita from Tokyo, we traveled by another
private railway to a point where we changed to a narrow-gauge
train, which literally zigzagged up the mountainside to where
we were staying. Two stops further up the line was an outdoor museum, which was not there when we last visited the
area in 1967. It was quite remarkable and contained a collection of large sculptures of very high quality by international
artists such as Henry Moore and Barbara Hepworth of England and by many Italians and Germans, and some very interesting pieces by leading Japanese sculptors. Totally unexpected, the visit to this museum proved to be a highlight of our
trip, among several others.

During the three days we were in Miyanoshita we spent
one day on a circular trip by mountain railway, cable car, rope-
way across valleys in which there were boiling sulphurous

volcanic springs (quite a smell!), a steamer across a lake, and finally a bus back to where we started out. Despite our complete lack of Japanese language capability and the locals' lack of English, we were able to do this efficiently and happily, including dining in a restaurant where we reduced to pointing to what we wanted to eat. A little adventure of this kind beats going with a tour group in our estimation, and as usual worked splendidly.

From Miyanoshita we went back down the mountain to where we picked up the limited express on the New Tokkaido Line — which had the bullet trains — and went down to Kyoto. For more than a thousand years, from the seventh to the 18th centuries, this was the imperial capital of Japan. Now it was a "living treasure" city, full of splendid gardens, temples, and castles. We stayed in a traditional Japanese inn, a *ryokan* by the name of Hiiragiya. A ryokan stay is almost spiritual in nature; it was another of our highlights. Upon arrival you take off your shoes and put on a pair of slipper-type scuffs provided by the inn. You are then ushered to your room and immediately tea is brought in. This process is repeated every time you return to your room during the entire period of your stay. Our room had a small Japanese garden outside the window, and a deep square pinewood bath in which you could sit and soak after the exertions of the day. A scroll and a flower arrangement were displayed in the alcove, both to evoke the season and to accent the restrained appointment of the room. Basically there was no furniture of significance. You sat on cushions on tatami mats on the floor. Breakfast and dinner were served in the room on a very low table. The service was exquisitely polite and the food was absolutely superb.

Good health, good food

Every day brought new treats. The first day, we experienced the elegant meal *kaiseki ryori*, so famous in Kyoto.

Arthur enjoying a kaiseki ryori dinner in Kyoto

All the senses were unforgettably involved in this culinary delight. We took in the scent and flavor of the freshest ingredients at the peak of the season; the visual delight of a continuous procession of porcelain dishes and lacquered bowls — each a different size and shape — gracefully adorned with an appropriately shaped morsel of fish or vegetables to match. Another day we had *tempura*, battered seafood and vegetables lightly fried, another time *yakitori*, a kind of barbecue meat on a skewer, and the last day *shabu shabu*, a kind of lightly cooked stew, which was prepared on the table in front of us. I had never seen as a plethora of mushrooms in a meal. The fruits were outstanding in taste after the supermarket fruit we got in the US, most of which had been picked before it was ripe and artificially ripened to the great detriment of the eater. One morning I surprised Arthur by ordering a full Japanese breakfast, something in which I did not join. I must admit that at 7:30 in the morning, he was not quite ready for raw and smoked fish, pickles, rice, and seaweed. Most days we had a Western breakfast, which they kindly provided.

I really cannot do justice to all the treasures of Kyoto. We spent every ounce of energy we had visiting temples, castles, imperial villas and gardens. Even after three visits, we would have been happy to return to that city and to that particular ryokan.

Among the lush green bamboo forests of Western Kyoto stands Kokedera, the moss temple. A permit was required, and it had to be obtained weeks in advance. The temple and its garden were open only a couple of days a week and the suggested donation was steep, limiting the number of visitors. As a requirement, before entering the garden, we had to participate in a Zen ceremony. We sat uncomfortably on tatami mats, while priests gloriously dressed in purple and yellow silk robes proceeded with the ceremony. Gongs and cymbals broke their chanting.

We were asked to record our wishes in calligraphy. Brushes, a pad of black ink, rice paper, and a piece of bamboo were provided. It was a challenge for us to master the use of those fine brushes, but we were able to record in English "Good Health." The head priest then blessed our fine writing. All that was a precursor for entering the celebrated moss garden.

It was created seven centuries ago by a monk skilled in landscape gardening. It had brooks, streams, a pond, and islets large and small connected by earthen, wooden, and stone bridges. As we strolled, the pond disappeared entirely from view and then suddenly reappeared expansively. The whole surface of the garden was covered with moss of more than a hundred kinds. It had no lanterns, but an image, carved ages ago, was enshrined in a cove. Gardeners shaped branches and removed leaves to allow a limited filtering of sunlight so that another variety of moss could flourish. We marveled at the scenic beauty reflected here. It was misty even in July. I wish we could return in the fall when the Japanese maples turn their brilliant colors. It was so simple, quiet, and tranquil. It remains for us the most beautiful garden on earth.

We also traveled to Nara, an even earlier imperial capital. Although it was somewhat cloudy and overcast, and on a couple of occasions we had a light drizzle, Arthur succeeded in getting a nicely sunburnt nose before we departed for Osaka, and then on to Hong Kong. Although Japan was not cheap, we did not find things all that expensive because of the strength of the US dollar vis-à-vis the yen, and indeed the Hong Kong dollar. While in Kyoto, we bought an interesting bamboo wall hanging piece, including a fan and a bamboo vase for flowers, which we later installed on our dining-room wall. It is really beautiful. However, because of its size and shape, it was a bit of a drag to carry from Kyoto on, although well worth it once we had it at home.

An anniversary in Hong Kong

In Hong Kong, we were met at the airport by a Rolls Royce and taken to our hotel, the legendary Peninsula. We had a lovely view of the harbor, and as usual found the service at the Peninsula quite extraordinary. As planned, we had our wedding anniversary dinner at Gaddis, still the best European restaurant in Asia. It was a lovely and memorable celebration. We had champagne to mark the plotting of another 25 years of the perfect marriage.

Unfortunately, two of our good friends were away from Hong Kong at the time of our visit. Nevertheless, we were able to spend an evening with a business colleague from Hong Kong Telecom at his club, and to dine at a few interesting eating places of Hong Kong including both Cantonese and Szechuanese food. Would you believe that our favorite restaurant for the latter was named the Cleveland? There was quite a bit of uncertainty in Hong Kong about what the future would hold for the people, and many of those who could were moving themselves or their businesses out of the colony before it got too close to the Chinese takeover.

Hong Kong was a dynamic city full of vitality. We also took a day trip to Macao — which was, in stark contrast to Hong Kong, was a poor and sleepy Portuguese colony just a little over an hour away by jet foil across the mouth of the

Pearl River from Hong Kong. One of our friends was the chancellor of the University of Macao, Dr. Hsueh–Shen Hsue. We tried to contact him during our short visit he was away from his office at a meeting so we did not reach him. The contrast between the two colonies was quite amazing.

Back to the Philippines

From Hong Kong we flew back to Manila. I remarked as we were landing there that I had landed in Manila more often than any other airport in the world, even though it had been more than eleven years since I was there last. We had somewhat mixed feelings about our return, but it proved to be a complete triumph of a homecoming. We were met at the airport by Solita del Castillo, Arthur's former administrative officer from the Ford Foundation, and one of the Foundation drivers. Even before unpacking we visited a couple of art galleries and some of our remembered haunts.

We had lunch with half-a-dozen of the former employees of the Foundation. It was a wonderful get-together. The occasion enabled us to get news of many people we had lost track of. In the evening we had a family dinner with Jimmy and Alice Laya and their four children, including our 11–year-old godson Jamesy. Jimmy was now Minister of Education and chairman of the Philippine National Bank, after having been the fall guy earlier in the year when he lost his job as governor of the Central Bank because he did what he was told to do by President Marcos, which the IMF didn't like.

The Layas were a lovely family. Their home was a traditional Filipino home filled with antique furniture and art items Jimmy had collected over the years. We used to do a lot of the looking together and we had a sprinkling of the same kinds of treasures in our home here in California.

Back at the hotel, we found a beautiful vase of roses addressed to Mrs. Hill with a card from Prime Minister and Mrs. Joy Virata. I was thrilled. When Cesar Virata was dean of business administration at the University of the Philippines and then Minister of Finance, I used to be with Joy in an exercise class to keep fit and trim. Joy was not in Manila, so I did not see her. We had dinner with the Greek consul-general Alex Adamson and his son Milton. His wife, my good friend Lillian, was in the US and so we did not see her, either. So many traveling friends!

Jimmy gave a dinner in our honor at a restaurant in Intramuros, the old Walled City of Manila, which he was responsible for having completely restored to its Spanish colonial grandeur. He sent a car to pick us up in time to visit a museum for which he is the driving force, and personally came to show us around the exhibits. While we were waiting, the director of the museum — who was most impressed that the Minister was coming to show us around personally — chatted us up. They even kept the museum open beyond its usual closing hour for our benefit.

Eleven friends gathered at the restaurant. The group included three cabinet ministers (one of them the Prime Minister), two university presidents, and the Greek consul-general. Subsequently Alex Adamson told me on the phone that having Cesar Virata come to a dinner in our honor was a real coup, as he did not go anywhere socially and that it was easier to get an audience with President Marcos than it was to get Cesar. It was a lovely, relaxed dinner with much discussion of the past and of the things we had done together when we lived there and of people and what happened to them.

After the dinner broke, Jimmy suggested we go upstairs and see a sort of sing-along place they had established. There was a small group celebrating a birthday, so you could imagine we made something of an impression when our party walked in. The group had a big birthday card and one of them came over to get the autographs of these important party-crashers on the card. They wanted to know where Arthur and I came from, and I am sure they must have speculated endlessly without having an inkling of the truth. The organ they had upstairs wasn't very great, so Jimmy sent down to the restaurant where we had been and asked their orchestra to come up for a while, whereupon he and another of the guests began singing along with the orchestra. It was very enjoyable, and most memorable for all. Arthur told Jimmy that it was the first time he had ever been anywhere when someone sent out for an orchestra.

I could go on and on about Manila, but will not. The hotel where we stayed had not yet been built when we lived there, but it was only a couple of hundred yards from our old place. We walked by our house and found it empty. We could have moved right back in. This is symptomatic of the economic mess the country was in. It was going to be some time before their financial problems could be solved, and there was a serious question as to whether this could be done under the prevailing political leadership. The peso had been devalued again before we arrived there so everything was very cheap for us but it was very hard for the people who only had pesos. We saw our former family driver, Ponciano Tabinas. He told us how hard it was for him to educate his children. Was there a likelihood of an overthrow of the government? Would there be continued protests, but no substantial change? Rather than see a light at the end of the tunnel, one economist I talked with told me the Filipinos would have to get dark-adapted.

Our last visit in 2000

The last time we were back in the Philippines was 28 years since our assignment there, in the spring of 2000. It was my last business trip before retiring, and Arthur decided to join me. There is always trepidation in going back, as you want to keep the happy memories at a standstill, intact.

Since our last visit, the nation's leadership had changed. The so-called People Power Revolution was instrumental to the fall of President Marcos. A series of coups d'etat had threatened the new democratic government. Elections had been held; new administrations had come to power, new challenges had emerged. Typhoons had once again devastated the country, the currency had been devalued, new scandals had erupted, insurrections had increased, and kidnappings were not uncommon. The population had exploded, and Manila had become even more crowded, teeming with people. The pollution was worse, old buildings had been demolished to make room for new glitzy high rises, and gigantic malls and multiple screen movie theaters were surfacing in the suburbs. Traffic in the country was as chaotic as ever, although a metro train system was getting built with Japanese funds. The roads were in disrepair, and even in Makati, the business center of the country, driving was a bone-shaking, dust-eating, tire-puncturing encounter.

Starbucks was the mecca of the wealthy younger generation. Cellular phones had become immensely popular. While the old telephone company still struggled to meet its landline commitments, text messaging had become the rage. Priests on Sunday celebrated mass in air-conditioned malls, attracting more worshipers than in their churches. Malls were fully stocked with goods that were cheaper than anywhere else. Plush international hotels had been built but tourism remained low. Many areas of the southern island of Mindanao were simply dangerous, and the magic islands of the Sulu Archipelago had become the center of much guerrilla activity.

Reading the newspapers was depressing. Any one of them told stories of kidnappings, rape, bribery, scandals — sensational stories that sold newspapers. Why not highlight, I wondered, a factory opening, or the entry of a substantial bit of foreign investment? There were pictures of crowds protesting here and there, but this was not Tiananmen Square.

We returned to see old friends and once again we were overwhelmed by their hospitality. Our hotel turned into a florist shop, as tropical flower arrangements were delivered. Friends remembered our fondness for mangoes and baskets appeared overflowing with the delicious fruit. A new technique of pollination had been developed for mangoes to grow year-round, rather than in the hot summer months alone.

Brother Andrew Gonzalez – a La Salle Brother and an old friend – was now Secretary of Education (ministers reverted to secretaries after Marcos left). He recalled my famous mango dessert when we visited him. How many people can recall a dessert eaten thirty years earlier?

The Adamsons were still in the paper and chandler businesses, passed now to the younger generation. They still represented the Greek government in an honorary capacity. They had built an Orthodox church in this Catholic country, and the Patriarch from Istanbul had come to inaugurate it and to participate in the festivities. Milton Adamson was awarded the sacred title of "Archon" for his well-deserved contribution. The Philippines has been good to this expatriate Greek family.

Archbishop Orlando Quevedo, another friend from thirty years ago when he was a young priest, arrived from Cotabato to join us for a Chinese dinner at the hotel. Cotabato was where Arthur was stranded on his first visit to the provinces. It was now connected to the world. The Archbishop read *The New York Times* on the Web and completed the crossword puzzle daily. He had been elected president of the bishops' association, and was a discerning critic of government policies. His name appeared often in the press. The Catholic Church in the Philippines remains a major force, the conscience of the country.

Jimmy, after years in service for the nation at various ministerial capacities, was now in the private sector as the chairman of an auditing and consulting firm. His love for antiques and collecting santos had not diminished. His days of browsing antique shops over, traders were now seeking Jimmy out to market their newfound treasures. Jimmy's books, essays, and letters formed a marvelous compendium and seminar on Philippine cultural life. He remained an advocate of Philippine culture, a champion of artists. Part of Jimmy's antique collection was donated to the Ateneo, a leading Jesuit university, and thus became a gift to the people. It was good to see Jimmy, to learn about the children's careers, and to celebrate their achievements. There were photos of grandchildren to share, a new generation of the Laya family!

With Jimmy we had lunch at the Polo Club. Time had stood still in this urban oasis. The club had not changed; there had been no renovation in thirty years. The same old swirling fans were there, as was the same mediocre food. Even the waiters seemed the same, only older. The club evoked old money. Pictures of past presidents hung on the walls of a wood-paneled room. The initiation fee was now a staggering sum, considering the Philippine economy.

Cesar Virata, the former Prime Minister, was also in the private sector, as chairman of the Rizal Commercial Banking Corporation. He continued to be sought by new administrations to head a committee, to join a task force, and to greet heads of another influential delegation. His integrity was legendary, and he held the unparalleled respect of the international community. With Joy, he gathered old friends on our last day for a farewell dinner. This was the last time Arthur would be in the Philippines. Cesar presented us with an exquisite lapis lazuli frame. It was a piece of art, a creation of the talented local craftsmen. It stands on my desk now, with a picture of Arthur smiling his great Aussie grin.

Our love for the Filipino people remained unchanged to the end, and I can only hope that life comes right for them.

The Expatriate Life

So many people travel to the ends of the earth and never leave home. Most Americans in Thailand or the Philippines, when we were there, lived within the confines of their own communities, and knew the local people as servants or traders. Expatriates had working contacts in their area of work, but their wives largely remained in their golden ghettos, with their clubs, comfortable homes, and social relations mostly limited to Americans. Many expatriate advisers were in those countries only temporarily, seeing little sense in getting more deeply involved with the local culture.

In Bangkok and Manila, the American group had succeeded in transplanting suburbia; they were enmeshed in a net of cocktail parties and ladies' luncheons. In the morning the women went swimming or bowling at the Royal Sports Club in Bangkok, or the Army and Navy Club or Polo Club in the Manila. They conversed with other American women.

The majority attended parties which all seemed oddly alike, going from one home to another. Proper American housewives abandoned their home uniforms, their blue jeans, sneaker shoes, and squashy galoshes, and adopted attire that they had previously worn in the farthest reaches of their fantasies. They had shoes made to match every outfit, in green, gold, pink, and lavender. Their cocktail dresses and evening gowns, all beaded, were made inexpensively by local seamstresses. They did not patronize the couturiers of Manila's elite. They wore masses of junk jewelry, especially long dangling earrings, not the gems the wealthy Thais or Filipinos displayed. Foreign women spent hours at salons having their nails and toenails painted, getting elaborate bouffant coiffures.

There were monthly luncheons in Bangkok. It seemed an unwritten requirement to be there. American women met in huge groups, sitting at tables of six or eight with other women they hardly knew. In order to avoid accusations of gossip, they clustered limply around such stultified topics as servants and the inconveniences of life.

At my first and only luncheon, my conversation proved unacceptable. I was a Greek, with an Australian passport at that that time. I avoided the next luncheon. I got myself a job.

In the Philippines most of us had a retinue of servants. The cook did the daily shopping at the market and proceeded with the family cooking; the *lavendera* or washerwoman cleaned, ironed, and did the dishes. The division of labor was strictly maintained. The driver skillfully chauffeured us to markets, clubs, exercise centers, airports. He delivered and picked up the dry cleaning, polished the car, and filled the car with gasoline. The gardener was the artist who maintained a manicured lawn, mowing, clipping, trimming, fertilizing, planting, potting, and sweeping the paths. If one had a swimming pool it was added to his chores. Foreigners with larger compounds had additional helpers. Americans were generous with their staff wages; a sack of rice and a large container of cooking oil were also supplied. The cook and *lavendera* generally lived in; they had their own accommodations within the compound, their own kitchen, and their own cooking utensils. The gardener and driver reported early in the morning. They had a day off during the week, not particularly on Sunday, although it was the preferred day. They were all Catholics in the Philippines and attending Mass was part of their life.

The habit of servants

Expatriate wives acquired the habit of servants in exactly two minutes. The servants seemed to foment delusions of grandeur. So many women had excessive leisure time and alcohol was the route of least resistance. It was not unusual to see, around the pool of our apartment in Bangkok, women in shorts and beaded shirts, holding a martini in their hand from 10 o'clock in the morning. Alcohol was available through diplomatic channels for most foreigners and from the PX for the official American community.

Many women fired whole set of servants every two or three months. They sat with pursed lips and chronicled the outrageous actions of their help. I had the sneaking suspicion that they had never had a servant in their life. They complained that vegetables had not been soaked in the right strength of permanganate solution; the water had not been boiled for exactly 12 minutes. They all followed some archaic hygiene rules described in obsolete State Department pamphlets. Water in Manila during the time we were living there was perfectly safe. If an item was missing or went astray, it was always the fault of the servant, whose masters never realized that they may have misplaced it themselves.

When I was asked about our staff I could only respond that I was delighted. I was ecstatic. I refused to talk about them. I never had so much help in my life. We had such a hardworking crew, especially in the Philippines, so cheerful, so honest, so appreciative, so willing, irrespective of whether we had five or 30 people for dinner. They were part of our family. Thirty years later I still seek out my driver Ponciano when I visit the Philippines. Thirty years later he still gets his Christmas bonus.

It is true that the mechanics of life were different. The inanimate mechanical world wheezed to a sickening halt sometimes. We operated so many appliances on so little amperage that every two or three hours in Bangkok all the fuses would blow. We became experts in recovery fuse boxes. But what wonderful experiences to attend the Loy Krathong or a ploughing festival, or to wander through the glittering magical exotic temples of Bangkok, or to view the rice terraces of Banaue, explore the great Cathedrals of Ilocos, or meet another artist in his well-hidden atelier.

At first sight the cluster of fruit was unfamiliar, but it did not take long to acquire the taste of the marvelous tropical fruits. Meat cuts at the market were peculiar, a minor inconvenience in comparison to the rich experiences available to us. We feasted on buffalo bourguignon and prune stuffed duck in Thailand. In Manila the plethora of goodies at the Makati supermarket was staggering.

The weather was hot and humid. But air conditioning was available to all of us in the bedrooms providing a comfortable sleep. Why complain? Americans never discussed snowstorms and ice storms blanketing so many part of the U.S.

The children were spoiled rotten. A chauffeur took them to school and picked them up later in the day. It became absurd, as drivers would actually handcarry children's briefcases to the entrance of the international school. Parents would ask the servants to be stern with them, but the little ones were expert in manipulating the staff. Every piece of clothing was dropped where they took them off no matter how much parents ranted. The servants picked them up. Children never made up their room, never put their toys away. Upon returning to the United States, of course, they were misfits. They could not adjust, they missed their old friends, and their new classmates would find their recounted experiences incomprehensible.

Young children missed their carefree American neighborhoods, the block party, the laughter, the chaos, and of course the telephone. The telephone meant a party line in Bangkok, and was not always reliable in Manila.

If it was a difficult adjustment for American children, it was doubly difficult for those of foreign diplomats. What was the choice of the Korean ambassador? Send his kids to the international school? There were no boarding schools in Korea. Leave the children with relatives back home? What about the next assignment? Another international school? Send them to a boarding school in the UK or the United States? Where did those children belong? Which country? Where would they undertake their higher education? In which language?

Muddying my feet

Returning back home was an adjustment for all of us. I did not join the ladies' luncheons and found myself working in Bangkok. I made an effort to learn Thai, to attend lectures at the Siam Society, to travel all over the Philippines, to understand the culture, to join colorful festivals, to visit barrios, and to sit under coconut trees. Living in Asia, one of my ambitions was to plant rice. I achieved it. My feet and hands got all muddy. I did not have to bend much; my planting was very limited, carried out in an experimental plot at the International Rice Research Institute in Los Baños. However we lived in the comforts of the golden ghetto of Makati, a gated community with a wonderful staff taking care of the mechanics of living. I never once put gasoline in my car while living overseas.

If life in the capital cities was unreal with its privileges, life was very different for those families assigned in the provinces.

The Foundation had families in a couple of remote towns of Mindanao, with its predominant Moslem population. It was not dangerous to live there in those days, but still these were tough assignments. As the only foreigners with the exception of a missionary priest, they had to cope not only with the demanding climate, but also with unreliable electricity, staff unaccustomed to Western hygiene, non-existent medical facilities, and a limited choice of Western food supplies. A most welcome gift to bring to those families was a couple of slabs of cheese and a fresh head of lettuce. For them it was a true treat.

Life was easier for advisers involved in their jobs. There were wives who withdrew inside their homes to take care of their plants and who complained constantly. Others, however, found their niche and loved it. They immersed themselves in their communities, learned about the culture of the region, volunteered to teach at the local Catholic college, mentored underprivileged children, and even "adopted" Filipino students. Becoming part of the local community, they were invited to weddings, birthdays, and celebrations. They developed camaraderie and friendships that lasted for years. They thrived at enduring typhoons, earthquakes, and hardships, emerging as winners.

We were all middle-class professionals with advanced degrees, but otherwise authentic nonentities before we arrived overseas. Arthur's job provided us an entrée to a privileged elite. We were well aware that we did not belong in this distinguished group. None of us came from prominent families, but we mingled in Thailand with high-ranking civil servants and members of the royal family. In the Philippines, we were entertained by top government, academic, and business leaders. In our own country we did not have that level of access. We did not meet the politicians. We met the technocrats who were running the country, cultured, idealistic, with long family roots and traditions. We were humbled to be so well received and honored.

Cairo and the Middle East

From 1981 to 1982, Arthur commuted to Cairo, as the head of a major project in the Middle East for ITT. He would one day be in Kuwait, another in one of the Gulf States, or Saudi Arabia. His work also brought him to the Sudan, although I am stretching things a bit by putting Sudan in the Middle East. Cairo served as his base and I would join him occasionally if his stay became too long an absence from home.

On one occasion, what was supposed to be a short two-week stay stretched to seven months. Unlike in Asia, in Cairo we did not get established in a household, but spent our entire time at the Sheraton hotel. The hotel was managed by ITT and we were offered the best possible accommodations.

What can I say about Cairo? I was born in Egypt, spoke perfect Arabic, and had a least some understanding of the Arab mentality. As a city, Cairo with its 12 million people was very old and at the same time very new. Its older sections, its bazaars, and its mosques evoked pleasing echoes in one's memory of what one expected the East to be; its newer parts were alive with the energy of people who had played a leading part in the progress of civilization. Now they were striving vigorously to overcome the difficulties of any developing country.

While Arthur traveled around the region, I stayed alone in

Cairo at the hotel. I joined the Ghezira Sporting Club, where I improved my tennis game, meandered in the bazaars as I loved to do, ventured in the mosques of medieval Cairo when it was appropriate, took classes learning the making of papyrus paper, and revisited the stunning, mindboggling archaeological museum. On long weekends we drove to Alexandria, my city of birth; we visited Port Said and crossed by ferry the Suez Canal to the Sinai. The statue of Ferdinand de Lesseps, the canal's French engineer, once stood at its entrance but had been long removed during Nasser's time. Again we enjoyed the light and sound performance among the great temples at Luxor in Upper Egypt.

A divided allegiance

As an Alexandrian born of Greek parents, I had a divided allegiance. Being Greeks, my parents had been obliged to leave Egypt under Nasser, joining an exodus of more than half a million foreign-born; my father's business was nationalized and our home was confiscated. But it was also in Egypt that I received my early education, and it was in Alexandria that I learned and used fluently a number of languages. Whoever is born drinking the water of the Nile cannot easily forget.

I was back now with Arthur, sponsored by a major American corporation. The local press reported on Arab investments, on another factory passing to Saudi or Kuwaiti interests. The alcohol refinery was built and run by Kotsikas, a Greek industrialist from an entrepreneurial family. It had been nationalized a few years earlier, but now the Sadat government was selling it to the Kuwaitis. I could not resist and asked: "You throw out one lot of foreigners, you nationalize their properties, their agricultural lands, their factories, their businesses, and now you are selling it to another lot of foreigners." Kuwaitis were not particularly liked in Egypt, as they flashed their wealth in Cairo's casinos.

The answer was philosophical. "Their purchases are only on paper. With another signature, we can take everything back, it is our land." It wasn't very comforting if you were in international business; the rules had apparently not changed since Nasser's time.

The Sheraton hotel was our home, and almost all of our meals were taken there. We tried every item on the menu, but with prior notice to the chef, it was possible to order specialties such as pigeon *au ferik* — pigeon filled with fresh green cracked wheat, a complicated dish — or *Om Ali*, a pudding filled with pistachios, raisins, and nuts delicately scented with cinnamon. They were a testimony to the fact that great cooking could be found in any cuisine of the world.

Imported wines were very expensive, so we limited ourselves to the locally produced Gianaklis wine. I remembered the Gianaklis family, Greeks who had owned vineyards in the Alexandria region for 50 years. The vineyards had been confiscated and had passed into Egyptian hands, but the brand name remained. The land was fertile and the climate was perfect, but with no further investments, new developments in winemaking had not been adopted. It was not unusual to find, among a dozen bottles, at least one that had turned completely to vinegar. Unceremoniously returning a bottle of Gianaklis wine was perfectly acceptable; the sommelier was accustomed to it, no questions asked.

As days became weeks and weeks became months, hotel food grew monotonous. We were longstanding residents now; we did not need to look at a menu, and the chef was most willing to prepare a simple dish of fresh noodles or poach an egg for our dinner. There were, however, many restaurants, humble affairs serving charcoal-grilled chicken or kebabs and *kefta*, minced lamb shaped into small cakes and served with pepper sauce. Egyptians being great sugar addicts, tea and fruit juices were served sweetened. In the afternoon it was common to adjourn to a patisserie for coffee and gatcaux, with pastry shops to be found on any corner. Fresh dates were available only for a couple of months of the year, and they were addictive. We were hungry for home cooking, but a home invitation was rare; how tasty was the apple pie prepared at an American friend's home!

Service at the hotel was erratic. The waiters were eager to please and very courteous, but giving the customer their attention and providing efficient service was not part of their training. When a senior executive from ITT headquarters joined us for dinner and had to get a waiter's attention, he took the large silver candelabra gracing our table and held it above his head. Three candles were flickering; he looked like the Statue of Liberty with a three-prong torch. Even this gesture did not catch the waiters' attention immediately.

Working hours in Arthur's office stretched from morning to noon, the Egyptian staff went home for lunch, followed by a long siesta. The office reopened at five, and work continued past nine in the evening. By that time, I would walk along the Ghezirah Bridge, to Arthur's office, unperturbed, blending completely with the locals. It was perfectly safe.

The world's noisiest city

Driving in Cairo was not an easy task, requiring nerves of steel. Traffic was chaotic. Arthur had a car and driver during the day, needed for appointments at different ministries in different sections of the city. Cairo was in perpetual gridlock with drivers unwilling to give way, especially at major intersections. The worst was at Tahrir Square, the giant Independence Place in the center of Cairo. I pitied the policemen who tried desperately to maintain order. As in so many large overpopulated cities in the developing world, public transportation was crumbling. Buses were overflowing, with people overhanging from every door, even every window, and sometimes they sat on the roof. This was not in a rural area; this was in the center of the major capital of the Arab world. It was the noisiest city on earth, worse even than Teheran. Every driver had his hand on the horn, blasting his way, a national pastime. Mark Fishetti, one of the consultants and part of Arthur's team, could not stand the noise registered from our car; he would tip a pound — equivalent to couple of dollars — to the driver, with the stipulation that he not use the horn. The incentive worked, most of the time.

Telephone communication was virtually non-existent. Calls got through within the same area, but if the call had to reach the other side of the Nile, it was another story. Tom Olson — another consultant and a Middle East expert long resident in the region — tried one day to place a call to Ghezirah, an island on the Nile, just a couple of kilometers from the hotel. He was unable to get through; the telephone cables under the river must have rotted since they were laid there a half a century earlier. Tom took a taxi, but then got stuck in traffic. It would have been faster to wear a ghelabia and walk.

Arthur once wasted 24 hours in our hotel suite waiting for the international operator to place a call through to the United States. It was so frustrating; it would have been easier for him to take the 90-minute flight to Athens, make his telephone calls from the Greek airport, and return the same day!

General Adel Meguid El Abd, the Deputy Minister of Manpower, was Arthur's counterpart. We called him the "Doctor," and he loved the title. He was trained in Sandhurst, the United Kingdom's prestigious Royal Military Academy, and moved up the ranks in the Egyptian army. During Nasser's time it was advantageous to learn Russian, which he did, earning a PhD at Moscow University. Now, under Sadat, the Americans were back in favor, so the "doctor" covered his bases and sent his children for studies in the United States. His wife was the daughter of the past governor of Cairo, a distinguished family of Turkish origin which had been very powerful during the era of King Farouk and the British Protectorate.

The "Doctor" was tall, trim, and very fit. Every morning at

dawn, he took his canoe and rowed along the Nile for an hour. His military training was part of his upbringing, and he was one the few Egyptians for whom punctuality was a prerequisite. He was very sensitive and Arthur's diplomatic skills were tested during many negotiations.

He traveled often with Arthur to Jeddah, Saudi Arabia. There, he would take an afternoon off, trade his smart Western suits for a long white garment, and went to Mecca for prayers. A devout Muslim, he never touched alcohol. Islam indeed was a sacred part of his life.

Once, when Arthur was in Saudi Arabia, the Red Sea Palace — the hotel where he usually stayed in Jeddah — was fully booked. A solution was to share a room with his colleague Phil Parker, the marketing VP. The next day, as Phil was paying the bill, he looked at the invoice made out to "Phil Parker and Friend." You can imagine the faces and innuendos when ITT's accountants looked at this receipt!

Home to a snowstorm

After a few months in Cairo, and with Arthur on business in the Sudan, I decided to return home. A major snowstorm hit the East Coast the day I arrived, dumping two feet of snow. I regretted leaving the balmy weather of Egypt for the tundra of North America. While in Khartoum, Arthur heard on the radio about the major snowstorm that blanketed the Northeast. African news does not usually report on US weather, but this was a major event.

Arthur was worried and called me. After his experience in Cairo, he doubted that he could reach me, but after only a few minutes we were connected. I was thrilled to hear his voice, eager to relate my adventure of reaching home in the midst of a snowstorm.

The next day, Arthur met with the Telecommunication Minister of the Sudan and congratulated him on Sudanese telephone efficiency. The minister laughed. "It does not happen this way.

Everyone must be shoveling snow in New York, and they are not in their offices. This is why our circuits were open."

Arthur stayed at the Khartoum Hilton. One evening, while he was having dinner at the coffee shop, he noticed a group of Americans carrying a voluble conversation at the next table. Being alone, he started eavesdropping, and began to hear the names of common friends being mentioned, names from our Philippine times. The group was having a meeting with the Agricultural Development Council of Sudan. He could not resist and decided to introduce himself and join them. One of the gentlemen immediately recognized him and said, "My wife and I had dinner in your home in Manila!" He recalled the occasion, even the fact that another of our guests, Arturo Tanco, the Minister of Agriculture, was late in joining us for dinner. What a small world! Arthur then remembered the occasion.

The desert kingdom

Saudi Arabia was financing the project Arthur was heading in Cairo. With the quadrupling of oil prices in 1972, money was pouring into Saudi coffers at unspendable rate and the sleepy desert backwater was rushing headlong into the 20th century. The Saudis had launched colossal modernization programs to spend their vast oil revenues, around $90 billion in 1979. They rebuilt whole cities block by block. They erected new factories, ports, and military bases. They provided free education and medical care to all citizens and sent their gifted young men to study in Europe and America. Conservative, devout Saudi Arabia became a country on the make — with all the inevitable strains between the old and the new, between rising expectations and mounting concerns for traditional values.

Foreign workers — Yemenis, Palestinians, Filipinos, South Koreans — provided the manual labor at Saudi Arabia's oil fields and construction sites. In 1979, they needed trained manpower and asked the Egyptian government to provide it.

It was for the Saudis a way to help their brothers in the Arab world. Manpower was available in Egypt and ITT was contracted to provide the technical training. A major feasibility study was underway. The Doctor, as Deputy Minister of Manpower, had vast contacts in the Middle East. This was how Arthur was brought into contact with Prince Mohamed El Faizal, grandson of King Abdel Aziz Ibn Said and brother of Saudi Arabia's Foreign Minister. Arthur met the Prince many times at different locations: his palace in Jeddah, his Dakota apartment in New York, his castle in Ireland, and his stunning apartment at the Ile de la Cité overlooking Notre Dame Cathedral in Paris. The same decorator had furnished all locations, which were all very modern, with an exquisite collection of Oriental rugs thrown in.

Prince Mohamed was tall and broad-shouldered, with the characteristic hooknose of his Arab heritage. He had studied at the Sorbonne and at Harvard. In Saudi Arabia he wore traditional robes, but changed to smart business suits in the Western world.

While in Cairo he offered us his suite at the Sheraton. It overlooked the Pyramids; fresh flowers arrived daily, and the telephone kept ringing for the Prince. When I greeted him as "Your Royal Highness" in the hotel lobby, many heads turned to look.

It was Ramadan time and many negotiations were undertaken late at night. Once, the Prince invited the ITT team for dinner at his palace in Jeddah. A servant was assigned behind each chair. Not knowing what was coming, Arthur took a second helping of rice when it was offered again, not realizing that a dozen more courses — succulent French and Arab delicacies — were to follow. The coffee was extremely strong, served in thimble-size cups. As there was no place to put them down, they were constantly refilled. Arthur learned that shaking your cup indicated no refill. Ultimately one of the American guests got the shakes, and the staff got the message.

Icebergs to Arabia

The prince recounted one of his favorite projects: floating an iceberg from Antarctica to the Red Sea. Those icebergs, as large as Rhode Island, were to be wrapped in plastic to reduce the melt. They were to be powered by sails, or perhaps by a generator. But how were they to be steered? How long would it take for them to stop? How would they cross sea-lanes? His French advisors had a solution. In order to get to the Red Sea, the iceberg had to be carved into a million slices. The impact on climate to the region would have been enormous, with effects on agriculture, fisheries, marine life, and obviously the weather. The Prince was enthusiastic and finished with a grin: "Next, we shall have the Winter Olympics in Saudi Arabia!"

The company limousine brought Arthur and the "Doctor" to the Prince's Dakota apartment in New York. The Prince was financing a feasibility study. After clearing security with the concierge, they arrived at the apartment. A maid opened the door and the Prince offered them a hand in greeting, while the other hand held a telephone to his ear. In two separate living rooms were businessmen waiting to see him. "You are here to fix the money?" was his greeting. "How much is it?" He took an open checkbook from his pocket and wrote a check for $330,000 on the joint account he held with his wife Princess Mona at Irving Trust, One Wall Street. He did not record the amount and put the checkbook back in his pocket.

Back at ITT headquarters, the first question of the Marketing VP and Controller was "Did you get a letter of credit?" They said no. "I told you so," came the ironic answer.

"What about a check, in cash, the full amount paid in advance?" It took little time for the controller to call ITT's treasurer, who in turn called Irving Trust. Upon reaching the right individual and mentioning that they had a check from Prince Mohamed El Faizal, a voice came back: "The check is clear." "But I have not told you the amount of the check — " protested the treasurer. "It does not matter, the check is clear."

Prince Mohamed El Faizal was in charge of administering the family finances at that time. With oil revenues at $6 million a day, I could easily imagine Princess Mona on her way to Tiffany's to buy another bauble.

The Deal Maker

You set up a hot Silicon Valley company with a technology that could fit into an AT&T service. Who do you call to make a deal? Corporate and New Business Development. Arthur was part of this team at AT&T World Headquarters.

The 20-person team was only a year old, and already it had negotiated 60 partnerships with high-tech companies such as Netscape Communications and Net Object. The team was committed to serve AT&T's operating units by focusing on key companies, businesses, and strategies that could help the company to grow. They had to deal credibly with small firms and avoid flaunting AT&T's size and resources. The team also helped AT&T sell off assets that were no longer strategic. It worked closely with Legal and Finance to ensure that all three shared the same practices and philosophy. The strategy worked. These people were not bureaucrats; they were world-class matchmakers.

Arthur was involved in a number of those deals, both in the US and abroad. He would be dealing with Samsung in Korea for data services one day, and with the Chinese government in Shanghai the next, negotiating a fiber optic network in Pudung, the business and economic center of that city. But what engaged him most was his assignment in Luxembourg.

He would take the late evening plane for Europe, have

breakfast in Germany, fly to Luxembourg for the board meetings, have dinner in France where he would be billeted, and fly
back the next day to the US on the fastest possible connection. Frequent-flier miles were not available in the mid-'90s,
so I never was able to take advantage of the thousands of air
miles he clocked.

Europe Online was a multilingual online service launched
in 1995 to provide Europe's homegrown version of America
Online or Prodigy. The company was based in Luxembourg
and the board meetings brought Arthur to that country for
couple of days every month. AT&T had a 15% stake in the
company. The largest shareholder was Burda, a big German
publisher. Others were Britain's Pearson (part owner of *The
Economist*) and Matra Hachette, the French conglomerate that
provided a strong link to the French market.

Melting moguls

But Europe Online was launched too late, as others were
already in the market; it was based on a proprietary system,
while the world was moving to an Internet-based structure. It
should have been centralized, but it was running separate services from different countries, an arrangement that soon proved
too expensive; it should have been financed by subscription
and not by advertising. It could have been profitable, but it
was not.

The optimists on the board claimed the services were getting 300,000 hits a day, and that users could find what they
wanted on Europe Online faster than on rival services — something that Europe's high telephone charges made vital.

One of these optimists was Candace Johnson, the
"Satellady" who brought competition to European television
and German telephones. Candance Johnson was an American
and a booster for Europe Online. She had been successful in
launching the first privately-owned European TV station and
Europe's largest private satellite communications, allowing

corporate networks across Europe's well-guarded borders. In her inevitable run-ins with monopolists and regulatory authorities she deployed two fearsome weapons: her connections and her charm. She had the best contacts in the European communications business. She rounded them for elegant soirées in Cologne or at her husband's embassy — he was Luxembourg's ambassador to Germany — where he played the piano, she sang Schubert, and middle–aged chairmen and regulators melted.

But melting moguls could not see her through her latest venture: Europe Online. The major shareholders were losing money and were pulling out. Arthur's job was to extricate AT&T from this mess — quietly, away from the newspapers. The giant telephone company had various investments in Europe and did not want to hint at any change in strategy.

Board meetings were to be conducted in English. The chairman was Dr. Christian Schwarz-Schilling, the former Minister of Telecommunications in Germany, and with Burda's representative being another German, the language at the board meetings often reverted to German. Arthur had to vote for one resolution or another, possibly without knowing what was being discussed and what he was voting for. Fortunately his Luxembourg lawyer, a multilingual fellow, was there to fill him in and to advise him on the right course.

The shareholders were unwilling to back the company further; they wanted out, and sought a return of whatever assets the company owned if it was acquired or went bankrupt. Arthur had persuaded his management to write off AT&T's investment. It was a significant amount but AT&T did not require any residual assets. The board was relieved at having one less shareholder to pay. Arthur became a hero.

Europe Online did not survive. The company was dissolved. Candance Johnson reproached her backers for failing her dream. AT&T's name never hit the newspapers. Arthur got a promotion.

The Scripps

*I*n May 1986, the hematologist to whom Arthur had been referred for further testing pronounced a death sentence. "You have leukemia," he was told, "a rare form called hairy-cell leukemia."

A sample, aspirated from his bone marrow, was stained and placed on a slide. The doctor invited us to look at it through the microscope. The smear revealed hairy cells, little tentacles protruding out of many cells. These were not the spherical cells portrayed in biology textbooks; they were different; they were diseased. We could not believe it. Leukemia? Arthur was feeling fine. We were both perplexed. What was next? How serious was it? The doctor proposed three steps for attacking the disease. He stopped after the third step, and although he never exactly said it, the message was clear: "Call the undertaker."

Arthur did some research on this condition. The disease struck only about 600 patients each year in the United States. It could kill within months, or gnaw at the body for years, condemning the victim to constant fatigue as it consumed oxygen-carrying red blood cells and destroyed infection-fighting white cells. The average life expectancy after diagnosis was about four years.

Four years later, in April 1990, Arthur had come down in

weight from 160 to 135 pounds. This was after a not-so-suc-cessful period of treatment with alpha-interferon, which bore unpleasant side effects. He was told by his oncologist that he would have to try another and even less pleasant form of inter-vention. We had reached step three.

Arthur was hospitalized with a bout of pneumonia. His immune system was way down, and he had lost so much weight as to be skeletal. But he never lost hope and thought of him-self in humorous terms. He entertained the idea of becoming a movie star by offering himself to Steven Spielberg as an extra in a movie about the World War II "Death March." He always looked at the bright side.

Hope in San Diego

We spent Easter in Greece to digest this news and to de-cide how to proceed. On the day after our return to New Jersey, where we lived through this whole experience, Arthur read in *The New York Times* about a report in the *New England Journal of Medicine* of an experimental drug, 2-CdA, developed at the Scripps Research Institute in San Diego to treat hairy-cell leukemia. It had been tested successfully at the Scripps Clinic. His New Jersey oncologist was skeptical, however: "All trials report initially exciting results that fade quickly."

Arthur made it his business to find a way to become part of this trial. His oncologist agreed to support his request to be admitted into the Scripps clinical study.

We came to San Diego that summer — our first time to visit after nearly 25 years. The city, the balmy weather, the breathtaking natural beauty of the cliffs, the wide sandy beaches, and the landscaped parks enchanted us. We stayed at the Sheraton — reverted to the Hilton of La Jolla now — and walked every day the few yards to the Scripps Clinic.

Arthur became the 66th patient to receive the drug. 2-CdA was administered just once — dripped into his arm over a week through a tube connected to a small portable pump, attached to his belt, like some high-tech family pack. There were six other patients participating in the clinical trial that week, coming from all over the country. None of them had learned about the treatment from their oncologist. Without exception they all found out about it from the press or from television programs. Some patients were gripped with fever and admitted to the hospital; Arthur was among the few with no fever recorded. He was checked daily and his blood counts meticulously monitored. He never thought of himself as a guinea pig.

After one week of treatment as an outpatient, he was pronounced completely clean and clear of any trace of leukemia. I still remember when Alan Saven — his doctor at the Scripps, then a clinical fellow and today the director of the Scripps Cancer Center — told him that "There is no more circulating hairy-cell leukemia." It was one of the happiest days of my life.

2-CdA is an intellectually interesting story. It was based on the work of a single junior scientist, Dr. Denis Carson, with one assistant. He had been newly recruited to the Scripps and was studying a rare immune deficiency. He came up with the idea of making 2-CdA, which he synthesized and checked for purity. There was some concern about the legality of testing the drug on humans. At that time — but no longer — the Food and Drug Administration had no jurisdiction over intrastate testing. Dr. Carson moved the process through to clinical testing.

One of the Scripps Cancer Center's unique strengths was the unlimited access it provided between scientists from different disciplines and between scientists and clinicians. Its buildings were designed to nurture informal contacts with the intention that quite separate lines of investigation will meet and merge, often in new and profitable ways.

Professional and financial support was required for Dr. Carson. These he was able to get from Dr. Beutler, his department chairman at that time. The large bureaucracy of a major university medical school was far less likely to provide support to a junior faculty member. The practical approach stands in contrast to the more generally followed practice in the academic community in which chemists with highly developed techniques search for problems to which the techniques can be applied.

There is a necessary difference between the focus of pharmaceutical companies, which must respond to the needs of the marketplace and their shareholders, and the Scripps Cancer Center. In a large pharmaceutical company, the emphasis necessarily is on common diseases striking large patient populations, and where there are no close ties between laboratory researchers and clinicians. As a non-profit organization, the Scripps Center could and did follow up on ideas that promised help to patients often overlooked by industry. Although only few patients may suffer from each specific rare cancer, cumulatively they represent a very large, even significant proportion of all cancer patients. Happily, advances in understanding and treatment of rare tumors also can often lead to insights for better treatment of common tumors.

A miracle drug

The story of 2-CdA, told through the people who identified, concocted, developed, tested, and administered it, and those whose lives were saved by it, is in a way the story of biotechnology till then — its serendipity, its challenges, its tediousness, its gaffes, its calculation, and, in the end, its payoff. Dr. Beutler describes 2-CdA development as "a scientifically beautiful story, insightful into the way medical research works." 2-CdA was one of Scripps's great success stories, and in 1992 it was approved for commercial distribution by Johnson and Johnson as Leustatin.

We stayed in San Diego for another three weeks so that Arthur's bone marrow could replenish his white cells with healthy ones. There was no trace of hairy-cell leukemia. He was cured by a miracle drug. He remained clear of leukemia until the end of his life.

As a visitor to San Diego, I wanted to visit the sights, the zoo, and the world-renowned animal park. Again I recall Dr. Saven's admonition: "There are some strange organisms floating in the zoo." With Arthur's white corpuscles still dangerously low, it made sense to minimize any possible infection. He was feeling so well. He wanted to go surfing in the inviting blue waters of the Pacific. As a youth he had loved to surf in Australia, but for someone who only days earlier had hairy-cell leukemia, it was advisable to exercise restraint. I do not believe he ever forgave me not allowing him to buy a surfboard.

For years the telephone would ring at home or in his office. "I heard you were treated for hairy-cell leukemia. What is the treatment like? Where did you receive it? What is the cost like? What are the side effects?" Arthur was always available to talk about it. There was no meeting or work deadline that was too important, and if someone needed that information he was immediately available to provide it, to counsel, to answer detailed questions.

A tranquil time

When we retired, the choice was easy to make. San Diego would be our new home. We had lived for nearly twenty years on the East Coast. We had wonderful friends, memorable holidays in East Hampton, great fishing expeditions with our friends Mel and Eileen Tublin, family reunions at Thanksgiving with cousins Ginny and Kyrie, unforgettable 4th of July celebrations, our wedding anniversaries. Yes, we would miss the change of seasons, the brilliant fall colors, the Metropolitan Opera series, the New York Theater, the excitement and offerings of a great city like New York. The pull of a more tranquil time, the medical facilities of the Scripps, brought us to Southern California. We never regretted it.

We purchased a typical California house in the lovely community of Rancho Santa Fe. We got involved in a new community, we made new friends, we took long walks on the sandy beach of Del Mar, we followed up and down the trails of the Torrey Pines Reserve, we visited times and again the animal park — something we could not do years earlier — we explored the missions, we participated in numerous events of the University of California, we received countless house guests and friends from all over the world, we became a host family to a foreign student. Every time we drove past the Scripps complex on Torrey Pines Road, Arthur would remark, "They are such a good people there, they saved my life." You could not find a truer believer.

It was time to repay the Scripps in a different way besides our annual donation. Arthur created a bequest to benefit the Scripps Research Institute in hopes that his support would lead to an even better understanding of human disease and the development of more treatments like 2-CdA. He was immensely indebted to Dr. Beutler and his team who developed the drug, to Dr. Saven who conducted the clinical trial, and to the whole concept of the medical Scripps medical programs.

He also wanted to do something tangible. He loved to write and was facile with words. He volunteered to be a writer and a spokesperson for the Scripps. He was assigned to interview scientists, doctors, clinicians, patients. He then wrote their stories for internal publications, for the media, for grant applications, for fundraising events.

Scientists at the Scripps Research Institute continued to develop new cancer fighting molecules that hopefully will follow the path blazed by 2-CdA developments. The Scripps Cancer Center is using advanced technology and sophisticated testing procedures as a means for scientists to explore ideas that they could only wonder about before. It is important to emphasize, however, that it is not the tools but ideas that are the key to unlocking the mystery of how to counter the unchecked cell growths we call cancer. For two years in a row, the Nobel Prize in Chemistry was awarded to or shared with a Scripps scientist.

Arthur spent hours as a volunteer. Scientists gave him their time generously. E-mails went back and forth; the telephone would ring for clarifications on his write-up. He learned a new lingo. Arthur had the unique ability to take a complex subject and discuss it in a manner that the common layman could easily understand. For years he could do that for his job, for things related to education, to diplomacy, to international affairs, to telecommunications. Now he was able to accomplish the same thing for a subject so different from his training, reaching as far as angiogenesis.

An award in London

Advances in research on the human genome fascinated him. *The Financial Times*, in association with Cap Gemini Ernst & Young Life Sciences, invited readers to submit an essay of no more than 1,000 words on the following subject: Will public access to genome technology divide the "haves" from the "have-nots" in the same way that education, health care, housing, and sanitation have in the past? It was an international competition to be judged by a panel selected by *The Financial Times*.

Arthur had a lot to deal with: What was genomic technology? What were the interests of the haves vs. those of the have-nots? Could he argue his points cogently enough in an essay of only 1,000 words? Banking on the knowledge he gained from his interactions with the Scripps scientists, Arthur wrote and submitted his entry.

For a while, we forgot all about the entry and the competition. For Arthur it had been just another essay to write, another argument to put on paper. Five months later, the telephone rang. It was from the editorial board of *The Financial Times*, with the exciting news that "You are the winner of the international competition." We were invited to London, where Arthur would receive the award and participate in the accompanying festivities.

The major prize was actually publication of the winning

piece in a biotechnology supplement to the FT. A lesser prize was an up-to-date personal digital assistant. "No cash, please — we're British."

We went by train through the channel from Paris — where we were vacationing — for an overnight stay in London (all courtesy of the sponsors) to participate in the Global Pharmaceutical Awards Ceremony, which was part of a banquet at the Banqueting House at Whitehall Palace. Black tie was obligatory — a fact that, fortunately, was made known to Arthur before we left California. The event began at 6:30 p.m. with champagne in the Undercroft, dinner in the Banqueting Hall, then drinks and jazz until midnight back in the Undercroft. Even the photographers were in black tie!

Some twenty awards were made. The only awardee given an opportunity to make a response was the winner of the Lifetime Achievement Award. All of it was memorable, but the highlight was the hidden royal treasure in which the ceremony was held. The great Palace of Whitehall was the sovereign's main London residence from the days of Henry VIII until its destruction by fire in 1698. The only part to survive the fire was the Banqueting House, a lone testament to the splendors of a regal past. It is one of London's several historic royal palaces and it is still owned by the Crown to this day. Nine canvases of Rubens are still in place. These exquisite paintings are still intact and provide a spectacular sight, even at the cost of a crick of the neck to view them. This brush with royalty brought us back to our meeting with Prince Charles in Samoa — suddenly so distant, in time and space.

Continuing the work

The food and the company were just as enjoyable as the setting, and I would treasure the memory of that evening for a long time. I still do — along with the multitude of other sparkling moments I was privileged to have shared with Arthur.

In August 2002, Arthur passed away from colon cancer.

Until his last days he was cheerful. He told me to take a pencil and paper and tell our friends that "I had a good life, and I have no regrets because of my wonderful wife who cared so much and still cares."

Arthur was my best friend, my only friend, the window through which I enjoyed the world. I live with the wonderful memories of 43 golden years of marriage. He touched the lives of so many people, and he lives in their memories, which is the best memorial of all.

He left me a wonderful letter where, among other things, he wrote that "Friends around the world are to be loved and treasured. I know you will grieve for me and that is right. But grieving must end and life goes on. I want you to enjoy the years you are left. Do the kinds of interesting things we always did together, and life will be good for you."

I have taken his advice — a return trip to the Philippines, and a journey to Vietnam in late 2002 is evidence that life goes on. I was asked to join the board of the Scripps Cancer Center. I am sure Arthur would have approved. In a minor way I continue his work.

THE TRAVEL DIARIES

OF

ARTHUR HILL

Mountains and Monasteries

We are home from a most memorable trip to China and Tibet.

The trip was definitely one for hardy travelers. Fortunately we had a most compatible group of traveling companions and an outstanding Chinese-speaking guide. After four days in Hong Kong we went first for a week to Yunnan province, bordering Tibet, then to Tibet itself for a week, and finally we left the group and went on our own to Shanghai for the last four days.

Ranging from 6,000 to 10,000 feet in altitude, the mountains of Yunnan province, home of the Tibetan Autonomous Prefecture, are beautiful. The tree-covered slopes and the green, green valleys are reminiscent of what you see in Bavaria and parts of Austria. Within a 50-mile span, you cross the headwaters of the Yangtze River, which flows into the China Sea at Shanghai; the Mekong, whose mouth is near Saigon; and the Salween, which flows down through Burma. All are fed by the melting snows of the high mountains of Tibet. The gravel roads were long and bumpy, the accommodations were quite basic, with hard, lumpy beds, and the monotonous Chinese food consisted largely of boiled vegetables.

The Tibetan Autonomous Prefecture is so called because

more than half of the people there are ethnic Tibetans, in this case the Khampas, who are the traditional warrior class. For whatever reason, the Chinese have no visible military presence in this area, and the culture is more Tibetan than Tibet in many ways. The monasteries, the scenery, and the people made this part of the trip thoroughly worthwhile. Yunnan is said to have the most diverse plant species in the world, and some of the mountainsides were colorful displays of wild rhododendrons, azaleas, and many other plants which we were not able to identify. It was really beautiful. Most memorable of all was the monastery we visited where we were blessed by a living Buddha. Monks attain this title by a long lifetime of compassionate devotion. This one had spent 30 years in exile in India, and in his mid-70s has returned to his home monastery to live out his remaining years. It was a truly moving experience.

In Tibet itself, you are at a much higher altitude. We were mostly from 10,000 to 14,000 feet, although we crossed one pass that was at 17,200 feet. This made us qualified members of the three-mile-high club. The beauty of Tibet is of a different quality than Yunnan. It is a stark, high desert with bare mountains (you are above the tree line), with large sand dunes (this was truly a surprise) and sometimes the soaring, snow-covered peaks that rise to 23,000 feet or more. Remember, we were not far from Everest, which tops 29,000 feet. The air is dry and so clear and unpolluted that the tops of the mountains cut a sharp line against a brilliantly blue sky, a blue that goes from a soft powder blue at the horizon to a deep azure blue straight overhead.

The Chinese military presence is very evident in Tibet. We saw military convoys of 25 or more trucks on more than one occasion, and numerous military posts. During the Cultural Revolution in the mid-1960s, many of the monasteries were damaged or destroyed and a lot of the Buddha images were similarly badly treated. Since then the Tibetan people and the Chinese government have exerted considerable effort to rebuild and repair. A number of the monasteries we visited had several hundred monks or lamas in residence, and there were many, many Tibetan and Mongolian Buddhists on pilgrimage to visit the monasteries and to make their devotions.

It is a dilemma, but as a secularizer and modernizer, I am of the opinion that the Chinese presence has made some real contributions. Tibet, which has a population of about three million in an area roughly the same size as Western Europe, was a complete theocracy prior to the Communist intervention — and I note that the Chinese have controlled the Tibetan area in various degrees for well over a thousand years. At the time the Communists came to power, the Buddhist monasteries owned some 90% of the land in Tibet and the people were really feudal serfs. Since then the Chinese have brought schools (the only education prior to this was from monks in the monasteries), health services, roads, airports, electricity and telecommunications. The people are beginning on the road from the 14th century to the 21st century. Not surprisingly, it is not exactly a smooth road, but I believe, sincerely, that the road leads in the right direction.

On the roofs of monasteries built in the 7th century, you will see a satellite dish, and in Lhasa there is a television tower situated on top of a holy mountain right inside the city limits!

The country is beautiful, the mountains are spectacular, and the people are open, warm, and friendly. Religion is obviously central to their culture and family life. They want the Dalai Lama back home. This, I am afraid, is a vain hope. He is such a political figure today that the Chinese cannot and will not allow him to return. It is only after his death that there is a possibility of some negotiated compromise that will give the people of Tibet greater religious autonomy within the framework of the Chinese nation. It is simply unrealistic to imagine that this strategically important piece of real estate will be given up by the Chinese in the foreseeable future.

On the way home we spent four days in Shanghai, a thriving, dynamic, modern city. The Shanghai Museum is architecturally splendid, and its holding of bronzes, ceramics, scrolls, and calligraphy are both spectacular and beautifully displayed. After the mediocre Chinese food in Tibet, it was a pleasure to have really great Chinese/Shanghainese delicacies at their very best.

On Top Again:
Back from Down Under

J ulie and I recently returned from five weeks in Australia — doing our best to avoid the Olympic Games, but not entirely successfully, as noted below.

During our stay I drove more than 3,000 miles in four states. The switch from driving on the right side of the road to the "correct" side of the road was made with no difficulty, as was the switch back on our return.

We last lived in Australia 37 years ago and, with the exception of a fleeting visit to Sydney and Bathurst in 1998, haven't been there in more than a quarter of a century. Our dominant impressions were:

-   Australia in the early 1960s was very much a white European, mostly British nation with a decided prejudice against other races and not too much time even for recent immigrants from Southern Europe. Today it is a truly multiethnic country. What surprised us most was the large number of young Asians who, when they open their mouths, spoke "pure" Australian, with all that implies.
-   Australia's well-documented "cultural cringe" (the con-

viction that anything created overseas must be superior to the homegrown product) has all but vanished. I can remember my parents, fourth-generation Australians both, talking about taking a trip "home" by which they meant England. That certainly wouldn't happen today.

– The emergence into the national consciousness of the aboriginals and a broad swell of support for some sort of "fair" compensation for past wrongs and a "reconciliation." This sentiment featured strongly in the opening and closing ceremonies of the Olympic Games — which you may have watched.

– More openness about Australia's convict roots and heritage. When we lived in Australia, almost no one claimed any sort of convict ancestry. Now it is a mark of pride. Even I admit to the "transportation" from County Clare, Ireland, of my forebear, Margaret Connyngham. But I don't know what was her offense!

Although we were in Western Australia, about 3,000 miles from Sydney during most of the Olympic Games, we did watch and read about them. I have been impatiently and frustratedly critical of US TV coverage of past Olympics, but I regret to say that Australia's coverage was worse! The games themselves were an outstanding success and Australia's athletes won a phenomenal 16 gold medals and 58 overall, remarkable for a nation of less than 20 million inhabitants. Each of the medal victories was breathlessly and triumphantly covered by the electronic and print media. Unconfirmed reports suggested that other nations also enjoyed some success at the Olympics, but it was difficult to be sure. In one event we watched in which an Aussie won a bronze medal, Channel 7 (the monopoly broadcaster) omitted any mention of who had won gold and silver. And never once did we hear the "Star-Spangled Banner," despite the US achievement of 39 golds.

As it turned out we couldn't entirely avoid physical contact with the Olympics. In Melbourne after the games we were returning to the city by tram from a visit to one of our old haunts when we learned that the tram could go no farther. The roads ahead were closed for a triumphal parade of Australia's Olympic heroes. So we got out to see them, medals and all. One exception was Ian Thorpe, three-gold-medal swimmer, who appeared with none of his trophies. I guess he didn't need to advertise. What was interesting and impressive was the enthusiasm of the crowds lining the parade route. There was a kind of innocence about it. We ran into some of the athletes again in Hobart, Tasmania, as they were checking in while we checked out.

Our principal reason for choosing the southern spring to visit was my long-standing promise to Julie to show her the truly wonderful wildflowers of Western Australia. We did not venture far enough into the desert (the distances are enormous) to be able to see the almost boundless fields of pink everlastings that I visited as a youth, but we were treated to a cornucopia of colors and varieties. WA's more than 13,000 species of wildflowers — the greatest diversity to be found anywhere in the world — pose prettily along roadsides and creeks, in gorges, gravel pits, and gullies, fields and forests, and on hills and coastlines. And even the smallest towns have a tourist information center staffed by friendly and knowledgeable volunteers eager to tell you exactly where to look for unusual sightings.

In the south of Western Australia we drove through magnificent Karri and Tingle forests, the largest and oldest eucalypts and among the largest and oldest trees anywhere. They are awesome. While in that region we paid a visit to Margaret River, emerging as a center for some of Australia's finest premium wineries.

We also saw — in the wild — kangaroos in four different states, koalas, thorny devils (a small fearsome looking iguana), echidnas (Australian spiny anteaters), seals and sea lions, opossums (one tried to break through the screened window of our cottage in a National Park in Tasmania), and a poteroo (a tiny pink-eyed kangaroo) on the patio of our cottage. In nature preserves we also saw wombats and Tasmanian devils. Bird life is just as different from other countries as is the animal life — black swans (Perth's river is the Swan), many, many different kinds of parrots, kookaburras, and others I cannot put a name to.

I left my hometown, Perth, in 1957 to travel to the US for graduate studies. I never lived there again. When I left it was a sleepy town of about a quarter of a million. Since then it has boomed, growing five times. To me it was almost totally unrecognizable — but somehow it still seemed like a sleepy city. Probably the remotest city anywhere, Perth is closer to Singapore and Jakarta than it is to Sydney and is physically separated from other Australian cities by a seemingly endless desert.

From Perth we flew to the nearest Australian city, Adelaide, capital of South Australia, and proud of its heritage as a free (not convict) colony. Time seems to have passed it by. When I left Australia it was much larger than Perth, but today the tables have turned as it has failed to grow. Just outside Adelaide is Barossa Valley, an important center for premium wine production, now beginning to be challenged by WA's Margaret River. We took a day trip there but were disappointed to learn that new safety regulations make it extremely difficult — in our case, impossible — to visit the cellars where wine is made and stored. We had to settle for videos and tastings. We also took a day flight out to Kangaroo Island, the site of a number of our wild fauna sightings.

Leaving Adelaide, we drove to Melbourne, a distance of about 450 miles, including a drive down the Great Ocean Road, bordering some of the most spectacular coastal scenery anywhere. Known as the shipwreck coast, many of the rocks and capes are named after sailing ships that were lost there in fogs and storms. The day we traveled this route, a piercing cold wind was blowing in across the Southern Ocean from the Antarctic. Looking at the huge waves breaking on the sandstone cliffs it did not require much imagination to see how these achieved their beautiful, sometimes grotesque shapes. This was one of the most memorable days of our vacation.

We lived in Melbourne from 1961 through 1963 while I was teaching at the university there. We paid a nostalgic visit to the campus but found it difficult to recognize as so many new buildings have filled what were then open spaces. No regrets at all about moving on, even though Melbourne is a wonderful city. Unlike Perth, it has grown incrementally and still seems familiar. We visited our favorite market (Victoria Market) and even found an Italian coffee bar, Pellegrini's, that has a table in the kitchen where you can eat a great rigatoni. The "new" owner — who bought the place in 1974 — was dining in the kitchen and was delighted to be regaled by tales of our lunches there almost 40 years ago. The rigatoni is still great.

From Melbourne we flew south to Tasmania, the island state. Its capital, Hobart, is a lovely small port city on the Derwent River. A day's excursion away is Port Arthur, one of the harshest and most feared penal settlements, where the most hardened convicts were sent. It is a sadly moving place to visit, and an awful example of man's inhumanity to man. As an aside, it is a curious example of selectivity in public education that many US students, if they learn anything about Australia's early history, learn that it was settled to dump Britain's un- wanted prisoners. What they usually do not learn is that it was founded in 1788 to replace the earlier dumping grounds lost due to a successful revolution in the American colonies!

Departing Hobart's mild, temperate location, we drove west for a day through magnificent forests and mountains to the west coast, arriving in Strahan on Macquarrie Harbor, Australia's second largest natural harbor after Port Phillip Bay (Melbourne). Here was another dreadful penal settlement, Sarah Island, ex- posed to the howling winds known as the "roaring forties," winds that come across the South Atlantic from South America, passing south of South Africa and on across the Indian and

Southern Oceans to launch their fury on this first land mass in their path. The water of Macquarrie Harbor is an inky black from the plant tannins that bleed into the Gordon River and are discharged into the harbor. Despite the color, the water is fresh and drinkable, and today it supports a substantial salmon farming industry.

Our final stop was Cradle Mountain National Park. The Lodge is magnificently located, the place swarms with native animals, and the walks and views are spectacular. We had three nights at the Lodge, and when we woke on our final morning it was to find snow falling — quite a contrast to the fine and balmy weather we had experienced for most of our trip. When we drove away around noon there was about one-and-a-half inches of snow on the car — the closest we want to get to the white stuff ever. As we descended to the plains the skies cleared and the sun came out. We flew out of Launceston under blue skies, en route for Melbourne, Los Angeles, and San Diego. We're glad we went. We enjoyed it. Five weeks is too long, though, to be living out of suitcases. We'll never do that again. Finally, we're glad to be home.

In the Footsteps of Marco Polo: Along China's Silk Road

*B*etween June 19 and July 10, 2001, Julie and I were privileged to take the road along which silk and many other goods reached the west from China, and along which "Western" ideas and goods penetrated the Middle Kingdom. Notable among these imports was Buddhism, and our trip was aptly titled "The Buddhist Trail."

A group of 21 redoubtable travelers, we journeyed together under the leadership, guidance, and tutelage of the best China guide one could find. Gerald Hatherly, a Canadian, is completely bilingual in English and Mandarin Chinese and is the guide of choice of people who demand and can afford the best. People like Bill Gates and Warren Buffet, Steve Ross (former chairman of Time Warner), Barbara Streisand, and an unnamed investor who, three weeks before us, was the first foreigner given permission by the Chinese government to land the private jet he piloted himself in cities beyond Beijing. Seven of our group, us included, traveled with Gerry last year to Yunnan and Tibet.

In the US we know well that if you want something done it is often not what you know but who you know that determines success. In China, *guangxi* (connections) count to an even more formidable extent. Gerald had connections!

For example, in Xian, home to the terracotta warriors, our guide was Professor Wang Xueli, who was a director of the dig that unearthed these treasures from its beginning in 1974 until 1989. Near Kucha, at the northern edge of the Taklamakan desert, we were only the second group in 2001 allowed to visit the Kumtura caves, home to exquisite Buddhist wall frescoes and mosaics. In the remotest part of western China, using connections that led to the person responsible for assigning space in government guesthouses (usually reserved for the most senior government officials) we were twice permitted to stay in these relatively superior accommodations. In Kucha, itself, Julie and I had the good fortune to occupy the suite used by Deng Xiao Ping on one of his visits. In Kashgar we sat in the chair used by Jiang Zemin during his visit a year earlier.

But all of this is prelude. My trip report this time comes in two parts. In this first part, I describe and comment on the highlights of our fabulous journey itself. In Part II, I will address the remarkable changes occurring in China today and reflect on their probable meaning for the Chinese, and for the US and the rest of the world.

Along China's Ancient Silk Road

Part I: The Journey — The Buddhist Trail

X **ian**: We joined our tour group in Xian, a rapidly changing and modernizing city with many new buildings and roads, including flyovers and cloverleaf intersections. In ancient times known as Chiang An, the city was the eastern terminus of the Silk Road for a total of some 1,100 years and capital of eleven different Chinese dynasties from the seventh century BC through the Tang dynasty (618-907). From here, in 221 BC the emperor Qin Shihuangdi first imposed central control on most of what is today's China, a remarkable achievement given the vast distances and primitive communications of the time. The emperor's best-known legacy today is his tomb, constructed over a period of 38 years. In it were discovered the now world famous terracotta warriors, unquestionably the most important archaeological site in China. In the first of three pits we visited, approximately 1,100 of the 6,000 life-size figures have been restored. On a previous visit we were only permitted to view the site from a high platform, and were not allowed to take photographs. This time, with Professor Wang, director of the dig from 1974 to 1989, we went down and around the figures and took pictures galore.

Professor Wang told us that he was sent to work as a farmer for ten years during the Cultural Revolution. When the first discovery of the terracotta warriors was made, then Premier Chou En Lai asked, where are the archaeologists? When told they were farming he ordered them brought back to Xian and put to work on excavation immediately.

Next we visited the Great Mosque of Xian, first constructed in 742 by Moslem Persian merchants living in the city. The present mosque dates from the early Ming dynasty and represents a unique fusion of Chinese architecture and Persian and Middle Eastern embellishments. We met with the Imam of the mosque, who told us there are some 60,000 Hui Moslems in the Xian area. The Hui are the descendents of the intermarriage between early Persian and Central Asian traders and local Han Chinese women. Later, during the 13th and 14th centuries, thousands of Central Asian soldiers were brought to China, further consolidating the Chinese Islamic community.

The Imam told a remarkable story of how, in 1966, in only his second year as Imam, he faced down the Red Guards of China's Cultural Revolution who came to destroy the mosque. When he heard they were coming, he determined to resist, but his congregation was afraid and would not support him. So, instead, he welcomed the Red Guards and diverted them with stories. Only one axe swing was taken at the center of the mosque before they went away, planning to come back later. They never returned.

Lanzhou/Xiahe: Lanzhou is a polluted city of 1.5 million people on the Yellow River at an elevation of 4,500 feet. From it we proceeded by bus, a six-hour ride, to the small rural town of Xiahe (elevation 9,700 feet) in southern Gansu province, home to the Labrang Monastery. Xiahe is on the northern edge of the Tibetan plateau, and the people here are mostly Tibetan and Mongolian. The road from Lanzhou is paved, a sharp contrast to the many miles of gravel or lesser roads we traversed in Yunnan and Tibet in 2000. Also noticeably different were the power lines evident everywhere. Altogether it is a more developed and prosperous area. Like Yunnan province, the scenery was reminiscent of Austria and Bavaria.

Along the road we passed through an ethnically diverse area with many Hui people and other minority groups. In Xiahe itself there is a significant minority Hui population. This may account for the fact that, unlike in Tibet, we saw no dogs in the monastery. Buddhists don't eat dogs. Hui do. The mosques in this area have minarets with an almost lacework construction, very different from anything we have seen before in Arab countries or in Iran or Afghanistan. At one mosque where we stopped, a young man claimed to speak, read, and write Arabic, but when Julie tried to talk with him her efforts fell flat. However, when paper and pen were produced they were able to communicate slowly, but quite effectively. He ended up writing, "I love you." Should I be jealous?

In a village along the road, a dragon boat festival captured our attention. Daoist priests were performing a ritual dance to the rhythm of drums to ward off evil spirits and the threat of disease, and a group of men, apparently under the influence of opium, were carrying a god-figure on a kind of stretcher.

The Xiahe Hotel where we stayed lacked some significant amenities — like hot water, except for rather narrow time frames in the morning and evening. There were no keys to the doors, and we were advised to leave no valuables in the room. To demonstrate that we are not the only intrepid travelers, a Japanese group carried a label on its bus that read "Hanoi-Irkutsk, 8,300 kms, 43 days." They were 21 days into their epic journey.

We spent a morning visiting the Labrang Monastery, founded in the 18th century and one of the six most important yellow-hat sect Tibetan monasteries, the only one outside Tibet proper. The setting, in a fertile valley surrounded by bare hills and mountains, displays the resplendent religious buildings beautifully. During the Cultural Revolution about a third of the buildings and many religious items were destroyed, but by now, with money from the government and devout Tibetan Buddhists, most of the monastery has been restored and rebuilt. Interiors are clean and better lit than in Tibet, as they use some electricity and substitute vegetable oil lamps for the traditional smoky yak-butter lamps. The monastery once had over 4,000 monks in residence; today the number is approximately 1,400. Large numbers of pilgrims were visiting from the surrounding area, from Mongolia and from Tibet itself. Inside the monastery halls it is somewhat dark, as befits religious buildings, and the brocades, tankas and Buddha figures were mystical and exotic.

Xiahe town has a dusty main street lined with two-story wooden shops selling a variety of goods from the practical to tourist souvenirs, although the number of tourists reaching this area is minuscule (mostly German, French, and Dutch). The racial types and their dress were exotic beyond belief. Tibetan Buddhists, Moslems and Han Chinese appear to mix amicably.

Dunhuang: Known as the "Blazing Beacon" of the Silk Road from the 1st century BC through the 10th century AD, all caravans entering or leaving Imperial China had to pass through the Dunhuang region. Locked away in the heart of the Gobi desert, then four days' camel ride from the nearest town, lies one of the least known of China's many wonders, the Mogao Caves, the "Caves of the Thousand Buddhas" at Dunhuang. It is certainly the most important cultural site on the Silk Road. The caves, carved between the 4th and 14th centuries, contain a glorious record of both the growth of Buddhism in China and are a wonderful record of Chinese cultural history. This vast art gallery in the desert deserves a proud place beside such world masterpieces as Angkor Wat, the Taj Mahal, the pyramids of Egypt, and the Parthenon.

Almost 500 caves are still in good condition, containing more than 45,000 murals and 2,000 stucco figures of Buddhas, Bodhisattvas, disciples, and donors (acknowledgement of gifts never goes out of style!). Because the surrounding desert is so dry, the wall paintings have been well preserved, in some cases for 15 centuries. One cave, the "library cave," once housed some 50,000 ancient manuscripts, banners, flags, and other materials associated with Buddhism. We visited ten caves representative of the various styles and periods and saw magnificent murals and statues, including huge Buddha figures. One soared 116 feet high (the second largest image of Buddha in China), another stood 80 feet high, and a third, a 51-feet long reclining Buddha, represented his final moments before nirvana. The impressions of this huge desert art gallery will remain with us for a very long time.

Two detours in my description of our trip are necessary here. First, there is the historical importance of Dunhuang as the site where Buddha images from the West, with obvious characteristics of Indian and Greek (yes Greek!) styling, were morphed into true Chinese figures, which then swept east into the rest of China and into Korea and Japan. Second is the damage and losses that have been inflicted on the site over the centuries. To the Chinese, the removal of manuscripts (including the Diamond Sutra, the world's earliest known printed book), murals, and Buddha images by Western adventurers and scholars in the late 19th and early 20th century was theft, pure and simple. Chinese historians today are particularly bitter because knowledge of this period of their nation's past is so meager. Today the missing items are displayed in museums in Britain, Germany, France, Sweden, India and the USA or, more often, hidden away in vaults unseen by scholars or the public. Some of the removed items were destroyed during World War II when the allies bombed Berlin's Ethnological Museum. Other German holdings, placed in safe storage, were later removed by the victorious Soviet forces and have not been seen or heard from since.

These losses, though, should be put in a longer perspective. For example, in the mid-9th century, most paintings of the Tang dynasty were destroyed during a wave of anti-clericalism which resulted in the closure or destruction of some 40,000 Buddhist temples and shrines throughout China. Later, as Moslem missionaries converted local populations to Islam, Buddha images were defaced or destroyed because of their belief that human images were sacrilegious. At Dunhuang itself, in the period following the Russian revolution, 400 White Russian soldiers who had fled to China were interned in the caves for six months. In addition to their graffiti, their campfire smoke charred the walls and roofs of the caves in which they were held, doing irreparable harm. At about the same time, local thieves scraped all of the gold leaf from the robes of the Buddha frescoes, while farmers removed images to their homes for worship, or simply took material for building or to use as fertilizer. Finally, as tourism begins, the humidity from many visitors accelerates decay. Given all of this, it is remarkable that so much has survived in place. Since the 1940s the Dunhuang Research Institute has taken the lead in research and protection of this great human heritage.

Following our tour of the Mogao caves we were caught in a *feng sha* or sandstorm, another climatic concern for the preservation of the art treasures.

Before leaving the Dunhuang area we visited a large sand dune area and had the opportunity to ride Bactrian (two-hump) camels or to take a camel cart — the driver of which spent his time talking on a cellular phone! Next we headed west through the Gobi desert to the Yumen (Jade Gate) pass, the border site through which jade traders entered China — after first obtaining the official documents to enter the imperial empire. Nearby we saw the end of the Great Wall, dating to the Han dynasty (207 BC-200 AD). In addition to the adobe structure we also saw the remains of a small garrison encampment and ruins of beacon towers used to send signals along the walls to warn of intruders.

Urumqi: We arrived in Urumqi, in Xinjiang Province, in time for the July1 celebration of the 80th anniversary of the founding of the Chinese Communist Party. There were flags, banners, balloons, dancers, drum teams, and, on TV, programs that ranged from Western classical music concerts to martial displays. Xinjiang Province, some three times the area of France, has a population of about 16 million, and is rich in oil, natural gas, and mineral wealth.

Urumqi was a real eye-opener. From what we had read, we expected to see a dusty town. Instead we found a booming, vital city of two million people. From our 23rd floor, first-class hotel room window, Julie counted 26 buildings of 20 floors or more, all of them constructed in the 1990s. This development is symptomatic of the Chinese investment in its western-most province with its significant minority Moslem population, the Uyghurs. When the US did this in Vietnam it was called "winning the hearts and minds of the people." Will it work better for China? Only time will tell. Still, it is astonishing to see what is being accomplished in terms of accelerated economic development, especially of the cities.

Xinjiang historically has been a crossroad of different worlds — the Eurasian steppe, the Mongolian heartland, and China. In the Provincial Museum we saw an exhibition of mummies that provided a wonderful visual overview of the cultural and human diversity of ancient Xinjiang. Ranging in age from 2,000 to 4,000 years, the mummies were preserved by the almost total absence of any moisture in the desert regions. Unlike the more familiar Egyptian mummies, they were not wrapped and artificially preserved. They were merely placed in their graves, dressed in their best, and with various artifacts, and proceeded to dry out without decay. Silks and fabrics were as well preserved as the bodies. They were truly remarkable.

Turfan: From Urumqi we set out by bus to skirt the great Taklamakan desert (second largest in the world after the Sahara) to the western border of China, a distance of over 1,000 miles. The first stop was Turfan, one of the great oasis cities of northwest China. To reach it we traveled south from Urumqi along a splendid new four-lane divided toll highway, completed in 1998 at a cost of $200 million. The funds came from a World Bank loan of $2 billion for road construction throughout the province. Our drive skirted the rim of the Tian Shan (Heavenly) mountains, one of the three great mountain ranges of Xinjiang. The last third of the drive crosses one of the most desolate stretches of the Gobi desert before reaching the deep greens of the Turfan oasis.

Turfan lies in the Turfan Depression which, at 505 feet *below* sea level, is the second lowest point on the earth's surface after the Dead Sea. It was hot on this July day — 114 degrees Fahrenheit to be precise — but the air was so dry that it was almost tolerable! In winter the area is said to be bitterly cold. Despite the extremes, Turfan is a major agricultural region for Xinjiang producing grapes (for raisins, fresh fruit and wine), excellent long-fiber cotton (exported to the USA) and, in smaller volumes, vegetables and fruit crops.

We visited an oasis irrigation system, known as a *karez*. Developed in ancient Persia, the system can be found in use in modern Iran, in Afghanistan (unfortunately destroyed by Soviet invaders and civil war), in Central Asia, and here in Xinjiang. The karez is a method of dropping shafts to access and direct the underground rivers of glacial melt from the nearby mountains. The channels we saw, which had been in use continuously for 250 years, run for 40 miles and provide abundant water for agriculture and household use.

We also visited the ruins of two ancient cities — one (Jiaohe) a garrison post and now a UNESCO World Heritage Site, the other (Gaochang) the seat of a powerful kingdom from the 1st through the 14th centuries — and the Astana Tombs, burial ground for the people of Gaochang. The tombs have yielded a treasure trove of funerary objects and texts that have been important in understanding the remarkable culture that flourished at Gaochang. Our final stop in this area was at Suliman's Minaret, an 18th century minaret and mosque built in the central Asian style of Samarkand and Bokhara, the only one of its kind in China.

Turfan to Korla: Along this 275-mile route we left the Gobi desert and climbed from 500 feet below sea level to 5,000 feet above sea level as we crossed the Tian Shan Mountains through a 54-mile gorge. The new road was completed only in 1999, and cuts through a desolate scene that looks more like a moonscape than anything terrestrial. It was beautiful in a terrifying way. Emerging into the plains we passed the entrance to the Hoshot Mongolian Prefecture, largely peopled by descendants of the armies of Genghis Khan, and finally reached more fertile land as we approached the oasis city of Korla, the largest and most developed industrial city in southern Xinjiang.

After an overnight stop in the polluted atmosphere of Korla we pressed on along the northern rim of the Taklamakan desert towards Kucha. Along the way we stopped to view apricot farmers drying and smoking the last of their crop. On the opposite side of the road, two Han Chinese men, immigrants from Henan province, were operating a small sawmill.

Kucha: After arriving at Kucha, we had another cave experience, traveling by mule cart to visit the Kumtura (Sand Castle) Caves. We were only the second group given authorization to see them in 2001 — again the joys of connections. About 100 caves were carved along the Muzart River between the 4th and 11th centuries. Our guide for the visit was Miss Su, an extremely knowledgeable young archaeologist whose ambition is to undertake graduate studies at Harvard! Her English was excellent. The people in this area were devout followers of Hinayana Buddhism (the small vehicle) versus the rest of China, which followed the Mahayana sect. The Indian influence was more in evidence here than at Mogao. Most of the caves have suffered natural and manmade damage but their historic and cultural significance is important to scholars of early Chinese development.

Next day we drove 45 miles to the Kizil (red) Caves, the most extensive cave complex in the region. Carved between the 4th and 9th centuries, they provide researchers with wonderful insights into the customs and traditions of the Quici culture that supported them. The art here was heavily influenced by the ancient Hellenistic/Indian cultures from whence Buddhism came.

This being July 4th we celebrated in the Uyghur way in a fruit orchard with a feast of local delicacies, accompanied by singers, dancers, and traditional music. One male dancer could have been Greek!

On the road from Korla to Aksu (170 miles), we passed through stark desert country into a well-watered oasis. At the town of Shaiya we happened on a market day, with people from nearby rural areas congregating to socialize, and to buy and sell goods of all kinds — livestock, fruits and vegetables, clothing, and a variety of other utilitarian goods.

Aksu: Aksu is a flourishing oasis city on the northern edge of the Taklamakan desert with a population of over 300,000: 57% Han Chinese, with the rest being Uyghur and Hui Moslem people. After dinner at our hotel in Aksu, Julie and I went for a walk past a neighboring college. Individual students studying along the sidewalk said "hello," or smiled shyly. From a group of students, a smiling young Han Chinese girl asked us in English where we were from. They were most excited to learn we were from America and wanted desperately to communicate, but unfortunately their English was pretty much on a par with our Chinese and Uyghur. Julie caused considerable excitement by taking one of the student's notebooks and writing her name in Arabic characters, the same script used by the Uyghur people. Bingo, we made a hit!

The 300-mile drive from Aksu to Kashgar, our final destination city, took us along the narrow strip between the Tian Shan Mountains to the north and the Taklamakan Desert to the south. The landscape was dusty plains with tufts of camel thorn and tamarisk bushes unfolding in all directions. En route we passed a major PLA (People's Liberation Army) cemetery where demobilized troops, sent to the region as settlers in the 1950s and 1960s, are buried. Away from the villages and towns the land is empty. Everywhere wires carried electricity to supply light and power to mud-brick houses in the villages. Tiny buildings often carried a satellite dish on their roofs.

Kashgar: Kashgar was another astonishing revelation. Instead of the dusty town we had expected, it was a flourishing and rapidly modernizing city. Historically, it is extremely important as the junction of the web of caravan routes that made up the Silk Road. Through its gates passed the peoples, the riches, and the ideas of East and West. Through it, Buddhist monks took the road eastward carrying images that artists later painted on the walls of caves near Kucha, Dunhuang, and elsewhere. Islam's missionaries also traveled the Road with the caravans and their fervent converts then defaced the earlier Buddha images. Much later, in the 19th century, Kashgar was also a key center in the Great Game, the competition between Russia and the British Raj for influence and control in Central Asia.

Another surprise awaited us this evening when we dined at the Caravan Café, a restaurant opened by three young Americans who had lived in the city for the past several years. Would you believe sandwiches, pizza, and American coffee in Chinese Turkestan!

Before exploring the city we took our final bus ride, 125 miles along the Karakorum Highway to Lake Karakol (Black Lake) just 60 miles from the borders of Pakistan and Afghanistan. We would have loved to continue along the road to Pakistan but were persuaded that this was unwise given the unstable political climate in Kashmir. The road, completed in 1986, is an engineering triumph. It is open only from May 1 through October 31 each year because the snow on the high passes (the highest is 15,700 feet) makes it impassable during the winter months. Maintenance activity is continuous to clear slides and repair washouts. The scenery was breathtaking as we climbed steadily up a valley along the course of a rushing, glacier-fed river, reaching an elevation of 13,500 feet at the lake, above which towers two of China's highest peaks, the spectacular, snow-covered Mount Kongur (25,318 feet) and

Mount Muztagata (24,750 feet). Along the road we saw the yurts of the summer encampments of the nomads with their flocks. It is easy to capture the romantic appeal of this last leg in China of the Silk Road. We knew our adventure was drawing to a close as we climbed back into our bus for the return journey to Kashgar. Finally we were traveling east after the long trek west.

Sunday July 9, 2001 was spent exploring Kashgar. We began with a visit to the mausoleum of Abakh Hoja and five generations of his family in a wooded setting just outside the city, and one of the most venerated Moslem holy sites in the region. Abakh Hoja was a powerful local lord, said to be a descendant of the prophet Mohammed. Among the descendents of Abakh Hoja interred in the mausoleum is that of his granddaughter, the "Fragrant Concubine," who lived in the Forbidden City in Beijing for 25 years. Castiglione, a Jesuit priest who served at the court, painted her portrait, which is now on view at the National Palace Museum in Taipei.

Next stop was the justly famed Kashgar Sunday Market, the largest weekly bazaar in Xinjiang. The market draws thousands of buyers and sellers from the oasis villages around Kashgar, many making it their most important outing of the year. The bazaar is a vivid celebration of Uyghur life — crowds, colors, and chaos. The livestock market was a whirling confusion of animals and people, with middlemen selling sheep, donkeys, cattle, and horses.

We continued on through the spice and hat markets, where vendors sell all manners of traditional caps — scholars' caps, prayer caps, unmarried ladies' caps, married ladies' caps, and so on — all important indicators of one's status in Uyghur society. We also passed stalls selling musical instruments and spices before ending up in the handicraft and carpet market. Ubiquitously present were the food stalls. We could not resist the bread that sold for pennies. The baker kneels on a platform by the open-topped oven, forms the bread into a disk, sprinkles it with onion, sesame seeds and water, then slaps the circle of dough onto the inside wall of the oven. In minutes he dips into the oven again and removes the delicious loaf. We feasted contentedly. Bagel-like loaves were also very much in evidence. Barbers offer an unappealing haircut, basically leaving their customers with shaven heads, but without benefit of water, soap or much in the way of hygiene. I passed on this opportunity. We will not easily forget this buzzing, blooming confusion.

We could not leave Xinjiang without a visit to a home, to gain some insight into the traditions of the Uyghur in an upper-middle class household setting. Passing through a door in a plain brick wall we entered a spacious vine-covered courtyard opening onto a carpeted verandah. After the ceremonial hand washing, we were invited into the house where, with typically warm Uyghur hospitality, we were greeted by tables laden with nan bread, delicious apricots, peaches and melons, and cookies, cakes, nuts, and dried fruit. It is central to the tradition to provide guests with a sumptuous spread of foods washed down with tea. We were not disappointed.

Our final stop was at the Id Kah Mosque, the largest mosque in China and a substitute place of pilgrimage for devout Chinese Moslems who are unable to find a place in the limited quota allowed to travel to Saudi Arabia to visit Mecca. Today there are some 20 million Moslems in China; overwhelmingly they are minority people like the Uyghur, the Hui, the Kirgiz, the Kazakh, and the Tatar (among many groups). We learned that the Imam of the mosque is a government employee, and that the local people do not respect the current Imam, who is said not to be a religious man. Indeed, we heard that he must use bodyguards as several attempts have been made to assassinate him. If true this may be interpreted as a symptom of the difficulty China faces in dealing successfully with its minority populations in sensitive border areas.

But now, 19 days after we began, it was time to begin the

long domestic flights back to Urumqi and then to Beijing en route to our comparatively humdrum lives back home. We carried rich memories and several hundred photographs with us.

Along China's Ancient Silk Road

Part II: Changing China

First, a disclaimer. I did not meet with any dissidents, and nor have I made a formal study of human rights violations in China. I begin with the presumption that the Chinese people deserve and will get a better, more open government than in the past. I also believe that many Americans fail to appreciate that China's society is vastly freer than the China of 20 year's ago, and that the liberating process is continuing. What follows are my observations based upon visits over a period of years. You may disagree with what I report, and I will be happy to debate, but I have a positive, optimistic view that will be hard to shake.

Before embarking on our 19-day journey along China's ancient Silk Road to the border of Pakistan and Afghanistan, Julie and I spent three days in the latter part of June 2001 revisiting Beijing after a four-year absence. Those four years have witnessed a remarkable sprucing up of the city, much of it I am sure done recently to enhance its prospects of selection as host for the 2008 Olympic Games-and why not? New areas of greenery have appeared at many points along the divided toll highway into the city from the sparkling new international airport. The streets were as clean as Singapore everywhere we went! On a pedestrian mall just a block from our hotel, we saw a wonderfully creative set of entries to the city's Olympics sculpture competition, part of Beijing's celebration of World Olympics Day on June 23. Along the same walkway we saw a number of performances by dancers and musicians. Not coincidentally, there was an obvious security presence, police in gray uniforms and military in olive greens, presumably to deter any unauthorized activity. The star attraction for the celebration was a sell-out concert by the three tenors (Pavarotti, Domingo, Carreras) at the Forbidden City (also much cleaned up). The top ticket price was US$2,000, the cheapest $70!

Personally, we were delighted when Beijing's bid prevailed. The spontaneous jubilation of the city's people and the country's leadership when the announcement was made showed clearly how much it means to them. Billions of dollars will be invested in preparations for the games and there is good reason to believe that they will be a resounding success. I have read the New York Time's sour editorials on the terrible things that are happening and will happen that are cited as reasons why China should not have been awarded the games, and I could not disagree more.

Today, central Beijing is clean, modern, and prosperous. Regrettably, urban redevelopment has resulted in the demolition of some wonderful traditional buildings — a process not unique to China. Capitalism was on full display in a department store we visited, where the volume and choice of clothing and other consumer goods were bewildering. The prices were very reasonable. American brands are widely available, ranging from McDonalds (near Tiananmen Square) to the world's largest KFC restaurant, to Popeye's and Starbucks. By far the most ubiquitous US brand throughout China, though, is Kodak.

In the shopping arcade of our hotel (the Palace Hotel, owned by the People's Liberation Army!) was a remarkable collection of upscale shops representing Europe's greatest luxury brands — Gucci, Ferragamo, Bally, Dior, Channel, Luis Vuitton, Versace, and so on. The shoppers were Chinese, the prices international. Elsewhere, in the arcades of the New China World Hotel and office complex, we found a carbon copy of the Palace Hotel collection. San Diego, America's fifth-largest city, certainly has nothing to match this ostentatious display.

Out on the streets, pollution sheltered us from direct sunlight, but Beijing has made a commitment to clean this up in time for the Olympics. Actions will include moving polluting factories from the center to the fringes of the city and changing their energy source from coal to natural gas. More and more service roads have been built to move bicycles away from vehicular traffic, and the proportion of cars on the roads has risen dramatically over the past several years.

Ironically, while we were in China we were able to observe, at a number of levels, the July 1 celebration of the 80th anniversary of the founding of the Chinese Communist Party. Yet, I believe that Marxism-Leninism has been thoroughly displaced by market Leninism with the emphasis on the former. Communist ideology is increasingly irrelevant. Although orthodox Party leaders still cling to power, as in Russia the Party and its ideology are exhausted and it is just a matter of time before the house of cards collapses. Today there is huge and growing disparity between the demands of a highly centralized government and those of a modern market economy. It is in the interests of the West, and indeed of the entire world, to keep an open mind and open door and to try and support replacement of communism with a kindlier philosophy of government. In his new book, *Does America Need a Foreign Policy* Henry Kissinger argued, as he has before, that the United States must accommodate a rising China, until or unless it poses a direct and unmistakable threat to the United States. As I see it, this implies a form of benevolent strategic competition, not strategic cooperation.

Unquestionably, change is taking place at an incredible

rate. We find this easy to see as we have continued to make frequent visits over the past ten years, some on business and more recently as friendly observers and tourists. One of our local guides in western China commented that he reads Time magazine on the Internet. He said, "The government says we are not to access foreign publications, but how can they stop us?" As the people are increasingly exposed to information about the outside world, I believe that the impetus for change and openness will gather an unstoppable momentum.

As part of the succession struggle going on at the highest levels of the government as President Jiang Zemin prepares to step down in the latter part of 2002 the government has adopted a "strike hard" approach to dissent but this, I believe, is temporary. I also believe that too strong a reaction from US and other Western leaders could prove counterproductive. I may be naive, but I am quite optimistic about the likelihood of China becoming a more open society within my lifetime-and I am no longer a youngster. Remember too that Chinese history is very long, and a generation is nothing.

Some of the factors that support my optimism are:

- The potential positive impact of Beijing hosting the 2008 Olympic games. China will have to learn to deal with an invading media army that will poke its nose into things that the government would prefer to leave unexamined. How it deals with this situation will tell us a lot about the impact the games will make on social and political structures.

- The opportunities for opening coming from China's entry to the World Trade Organization. For the first time in its history, China will be obliged to conform to international norms governing contracts, requiring it to put together more open and formal legal and financial structures. This will not sweep away corruption overnight; after all, we see plenty of corruption in our own Western industrial countries, but it will put limits on how blatantly it can be carried out. In this opening, there will also be difficulties and negatives, as China will have to learn to cope with new international competition, and to deal with an army of displaced former employees of no longer viable state enterprises. These latter could pose huge social threats to political stability if a way is not found to meet their basic needs.

– The energy and entrepreneurial talents of the people. I was told that in Shanghai there are several US-dollar billionaires, while even in relatively poor and underdeveloped Kasha there are at least half-a-dozen dollar millionaires. Opportunities exist and are being exploited. The other side of this coin, of course, is that a widening gap between rich and poor could well lead to resentment and unrest. At least in coastal China, though, enough people are profiting from new economic opportunities that most boats are rising with the tide. Everywhere we saw commerce being conducted at a retail level with great good humor and apparent success. Problems may also arise from the growing gap between the cities and the rural areas.

– China has vast natural resources-oil and natural gas, gold, nickel, and other minerals — that only now are beginning to be exploited. The oil and gas fields in the Taklamakan desert in western Xinjiang Province, for example, are reported to have the third largest reserves of any field in the world — I have seen reports that it has three times the US's known reserves. While traveling in the area we saw oil wells pumping and refineries flaring gas — something I last saw in New Jersey in 1957. This, along with gold and other minerals, is one reason for the strategic importance of Xinjiang province to the Chinese.

– Huge investments are being made in infrastructure. Yes, there is corruption and sometimes shoddy construction, but money is being spent and projects are being completed that will foster growth. It is not just the Three Gorges Dam. In Xinjiang province, for example, China is spending a $2-billion World Bank loan for road construction. A splendid $200 million four-lane divided toll superhighway was completed last year from Urumqi to Turfan, headquarters for the Tarim Petroleum Company that is starting to develop the oil and gas fields in the region. Optical fiber cables are being laid in remote areas. A new train track has been completed all the way to Kashgar in China's far west. In Xinjiang we saw high-tension electric power lines everywhere-quite unlike our experience last year in Yunnan and Tibet. Everywhere we have traveled in China we have passed through new, modern airports or those in advanced stages of construction. In every city, the most impressive buildings belong to the China National Petroleum Company, to China Telecom, and to its new competitor, China Unicom. As a result of huge investments, China is one of the world's largest telecommunications markets, with 120 million phone lines and 70 million mobile phone users.

– For years, the world's largest information technology event has been the annual CeBit show in Hanover, Germany. In August 2001,CeBit Asia was launched. The city chosen is Shanghai.

– All over China, cities are modernizing and becoming wealthier. We were astonished by Urumqi, in Xinjiang Province-now a vibrant and prosperous modern city of two million that essentially was developed only yesterday. Julie counted 26 buildings of more than 20 floors that she could see from the 23rd floor window of our modern and thoroughly satisfactory hotel. All were constructed in the 1990s. Similarly with Korla, which has many high-rise buildings, and Aksu. Have you ever heard of them? Even Kashgar's old city has almost disappeared, replaced by wide roads and modern buildings. Elsewhere in Asia, in Manila, Kuala Lumpur, Jakarta, and Bangkok, it is common to see half-completed buildings abandoned as a result of the Asian economic crisis of 1998. We saw nothing like that in China.

But all is not rosy. Historical attitudes, new problems, and how China deals with change and tries to mould it could all lead to difficulties. For example:

– China has a very justifiable chip on its shoulder about foreigners because of the shabby treatment it received during the late 19th and early 20th centuries when the Ching dynasty was weak and in decline. Using gunboat diplomacy, Europeans, primarily the British and French, forced the Chinese to import and pay for opium, resulting in the addiction of many Chinese and leading to the Opium Wars. Treaty ports such as Shanghai were established, with foreign legations having great power and privileges that were denied to the Chinese. Even the ceding of Hong Kong as a colony and the imposition of a 99-year lease of the New Territories was a lasting indignity. Within this context some more recent incidents, like the "accidental" US bombing of the Chinese embassy in Belgrade, the spy plane incident, and Taiwan arms sales all reinforce an ingrained xenophobic nationalism. As China reemerges as a world power, it is not surprising to see it react strongly to what it views as foreign attempts to wall it in and to contain any expansionary thoughts it might entertain. Outsiders, especially the USA, must keep in mind the historical context in which their actions are viewed by the Chinese leadership. At the same time, they must also be firm in setting limits as China begins to flex its muscles.

– To strengthen its control in minority areas, China is moving in large numbers of ethnic Han Chinese, changing the population balance especially in the cities, and creating a new set of tensions that must be coped with.

Many formerly minority cities now have a majority immigrant Han Chinese population. The situation in the surrounding rural areas has not been affected, and these remain predominantly minority, e.g., Tibetan or Uyghur. One impact is to widen the gap between the modernizing cities and the still traditional rural areas. Delicate policy issues are at stake here, and it is easy to argue with the morality of the decisions taken, but it is realpolitik at work. After all, America's West was not won by being kind to minorities, and I have nothing to boast about in the way the aboriginal people were treated in Australia. I am sure it is no accident that in Xinjiang Province the Communist Party appears to have a stronger grip than in the coastal provinces. There is even a huge statue of Chairman Mao in the main square, something we did not see anywhere else.

– Continuing corruption, especially at high levels in government. For example, we were told by one of our local guides that "big potatoes" in the government protect smugglers. One example is that Lexus cars are smuggled into the country in pieces through Afghanistan, then reassembled, thus avoiding punitive taxes. These cars are then driven publicly by high officials and big wheels in the private sector. Another smuggling example is the "goat in the water" — smuggled goods are packed in large plastic waterproof covers, then tied by rope to the underside of the smuggler's boat to avoid detection by government monitors. Finally, and neatly, the import of a shipment of left-hand gloves, on which little tax is paid, because who wants only a left-hand glove. Separate shipments of right-hand gloves receive similar light customs treatment. Then the pairs are reunited by local cheap labor! Still there is some evidence beginning to emerge that the government is at last beginning to tackle the problem of high-level corruption.

– Political unrest among the many minorities — e.g., Tibetans and Uyghurs. Kashgar, a city of 350,000, with a county population of 3.5 million, is the religious and cultural center for Xinjiang's Moslem population who are not ethnic Chinese. It is only 170 miles to the (now nuclear-armed) Pakistan border, and a similar distance to the (Taliban-controlled) Afghanistan border. Kirgistan, an unstable Central Asian country, is a mere 40 miles distant, while a couple of other countries with minority populations in Xinjiang but with no common borders are also within a hundred miles. They include Tajikistan, which has been in a state of civil war for ten years and Uzbekistan, which is fighting an insurgency supported by the Taliban in its Fergana Valley. As an interesting aside, we were told by a young Uyghur tour guide that, although he has been to Pakistan with tour groups around 100 times, he has not taken the opportunities presented to him to visit Afghanistan. The reason he gave is that there are Uyghur terrorists training with the Taliban in Afghanistan and having an Afghan stamp in his passport would put his name on a Chinese list that he didn't want to be on. On one hand the Chinese are working hard to increase the economic well-being of minority areas to win the allegiance of the people while, on the other hand, guerillas in neighboring countries are interested in fomenting turmoil and independence movements. How will it all come out? Augurs in the West say there are three major issues fueling the desire for independence — the massive Han migration into the province, the use of the province for testing nuclear weapons (at Lop Nor), and the exploitation of Inking oil, which local residents view as their property.

– A political solution must be found to the problem of Taiwan. The world, including the US, has always recognized that there is only one China, even though the players have never agreed on the details. It is notable that Taiwanese investors continue to make huge bets on China's economy, most recently through substantial investments in high technology. The corridor between Shanghai and Scow is a sort of Taiwan-funded silicon alley. There is a basis for hope that, as China's central-ized communist government weakens or collapses, the Taiwanese will see an advantage in rejoining the family on some equitable basis. It is to be hoped that narrow-minded US government policies do not make this re-union more difficult than it needs to be.

– The increasing incidence of AIDS. In June 2001, at the UN summit on AIDS, the Chinese minister of health made the astonishing announcement that 600,000 people in China have AIDS or are infected with HIV. From journalists' reports from different prov-inces, this estimate is probably low. Experts project a major explosion of HIV to occur. China's one-party politics is a barrier to its facing up to AIDS. After long labeling the disease as a Western problem, the government will not easily switch to an attitude of openness about this epidemic. Confronting it would require acknowledging problems, like rural poverty, drug abuse, prostitution, and unsanitary blood col-lection that defensive local and national leaders would rather underplay or keep hidden. Even if the will to fight AIDS realistically can be found, China won't have an easy job doing it. Social and economic change has caused new dislocations. People move around the country much more freely than they once did, making more rapid spread of the disease possible, and intravenous drug use, prostitution, premarital sex, and histories of multiple sex partners are all on the rise in China. Because two-thirds of Chinese HIV carriers are poor and poorly educated peasants and farmers, awareness of the disease is severely limited.

Some general items that don't fit neatly into my other categories are:

- In Xian we saw day workers waiting at streetcorners for work. They included carpenters, painters, and so on, who are paid $6.25 per day. The average salaried worker receives about $125 per month, of which about one-third goes to rent.
- Long-time government employees receive full personal medical insurance coverage, but newer hires have only partial coverage that they must supplement by co-payments, very much like the system in place in US industry today. There is no family coverage. One long-time government tourism employee told us that her husband has his own work coverage, but they must buy medical insurance for their one son. The iron rice bowl has been broken.
- In an English language newspaper we saw bank advertisements offering mortgages — this in a communist country.
- While in Beijing, walking in Tiananmen Square, we got into a conversation with a young man from Xian. He was a recent graduate in art (calligraphy) who had come to the capital to take an examination for certification as a teacher, but he was not at all sure that, even if he passed, he would be able to find a job. Just a few minutes later two young women asked us to take their photographs (with their cameras) with the large picture of Chairman Mao as background. Their American accents quickly led us to the information that they were from Los Angeles. One had just completed a year's study of Mandarin in Beijing. The other was visiting her friend for a few days after her graduation with a mechanical engineering degree from MIT and before starting her new job in Los Angeles.
- Population control. The well-known one-child policy applies in the cities of Eastern China, while two are per-

mitted in rural areas, but a spacing of three years between births is encouraged. In minority areas like
Xinjiang, two children are permitted in the cities and 3-
4 in rural areas. In the cities, if a mother has more than
her quota, she is subject to a fine of Y20,000 ($2,500),
an enormous sum. In addition, all members of her work
group are fined Y1,000 ($125). This applies enormous
social pressure to conform.

- Transportation prices. A good used bicycle can be ob-
tained for Y110 ($14), a Chinese motorcycle costs
Y2,000-10,000 ($250-1,250), a Chinese-made VW costs
Y100,000 ($12,500), and a Chinese-made Buick costs
Y310,000 ($38,700).

- The law says that students must complete nine years of
compulsory education. In rural areas, poverty means
that many children are required by their families to work
to supplement the family's meager income. Even though,
in some cases, there is a fine for not attending school,
the child's contribution is deemed to be greater than the
cost of the fine. In Xinjiang, Uyghur students are taught
in their native Uyghur language with Chinese as a second language. For Chinese students in the province,
the language of instruction is Chinese, with English as
the second language.

- At the Labrang Monastery in Xiahe in Southern Gansu
Province, we met a Buddhist monk who spoke English
which he learned at the Tibetan government-in-exile
center. He returned to China illegally and has no papers. Our local guide there, a native of Xiahe, had also
fled to India at age 12 and was tutored in Buddhism and
English there before returning illegally to China two
years ago. An undocumented immigrant, he is hired
(off the books) by the Xiahe Hotel as a favor because
he has a family connection. He receives $37 a month
plus a room for his work. He is an only child and told
us that he wants to join his father who now has a

restaurant in Lhasa. The problems of journeying to Tibet through many close border security checks without papers boggles the imagination. We were unable to learn how he would be able to make the journey without the proper papers.

I hope I have provided more than a series of scattered impressions. It is difficult to tell a clear story about a subject as fluid and complex as changing China. Indeed, one of the country's major problems may be that the rate of change is too fast to be digestible, especially for traditional rural people. By contrast, in the cities the pace of change by people with access to the Internet may be too fast to be digestible by their leaders.

I also hope that I have managed to convey my basic optimism about China's ability to overcome its problems and to become a more open member of the family of nations.

A Journey to the Mahgreb: Romans and Berbers

Julie and I have just returned from a two-week visit to Tunisia and Morocco, our first visit to this part of the world. One immediate impression was that we felt completely safe in these Muslim Arab nations only a couple of months after the terrorist attacks of September 11 on the World Trade Center and the Pentagon. Perhaps because the local tourist industry has been so significantly impacted by these events, we were especially welcomed as brave souls who did not cancel. Indeed, one intrepid salesman in Morocco, learning that Julie spoke both French and Arabic, boldly told me that she was worth 6,000 camels — a goodly sum since a camel sells there for between $500 and $5,000!

Tunisia: We first spent our first four days in Tunisia, a small country sandwiched between two rather nasty neighbors, Libya and Algeria. Its capital, Tunis, is a low-rise city of two million people (out of a nationwide total of about ten million). On the city outskirts a new, fortress-like American embassy is under construction. Modern buildings line the broad avenues of the city center, which is clean and orderly and seemingly quite prosperous. The people — particularly the women — were dressed in a more Western fashion than we had expected. We never once saw a Tunisian woman with a veil over her face, and many of the younger women were modishly dressed in Western skirts, while others sported jeans. Nor did we see a single beggar. Polygamy is illegal in Tunisia, and divorce is allowed.

One intriguing aspect of the sprawling city was the forest of satellite dishes that sprouted on the roofs of most of the buildings. We learned that an investment of $200 would purchase a satellite dish and a decoder, and no subsequent charges were incurred. Viewers can receive channels in Arabic, French, Italian, Spanish, and English. There are only two local broadcast Arabic channels, government owned, one targeted at adults and one at children. No McDonalds or other US franchised fast food outlets is to be found in Tunisia! The old walled medina contains the souk and the fortified casbah.

The day before our arrival was the country's national day, and there were flags everywhere, along with pictures of President Ben Ali. Since gaining independence from France in 1956, Tunisia has had only two presidents. The first, President Bourgiba, ruled from 1956 until his death in 1987. Ben Ali, who became president in 1987, changed the Constitution so that the president was elected for five years, with a limit of three terms, and won election to his first term in 1989. It will be interesting to see what happens when his third term expires in 2004.

The primary focus of our visit to Tunisia was to see the best-preserved Roman ruins in North Africa. We also saw the few remains of the city of Carthage, capital of the Phoenician Empire from the 8th century BC until its overthrow and almost total destruction by the Romans in the 2nd century AD. The Romans built a city on the same site but this, in turn, was destroyed by the succeeding Vandals and Byzantines. Nearby were the nine-acre remains of the famous Roman Antonine baths.

The Romans paved their homes and courtyards with splendid, colorful mosaics, a tradition followed by their successors especially the Christian Byzantines. The content of the mosaics changes from scenes of classical mythology to Christian and rural scenes during this period. During the first half of the 20th century, while Tunisia was a French colony, many of these mosaics were moved to the Bardo Museum in Tunis, making it a relatively unknown treasure house of beautiful art. Since independence in 1956, new discoveries have been left *in situ*.

Accompanied by our excellent Tunisian guide, a former professor of American Studies at the University of Tunis, we visited two splendid Roman cities in northern Tunisia: Bulla Regia and Dougga. The three-hour drive through the countryside to the first of these took us back in time. We passed through prosperous olive groves, some centuries old. We even passed a semi-nomadic encampment complete with camels and goats. A significant police presence was to be seen at every roundabout, perhaps reflecting that this was the main road to the Algerian border. We were told that they were checking on speeding, drugs, and illegal immigrants. We also saw a number of military posts and our guide told us that the military plays an important role in helping to harvest the economically important olive crop, planting trees at the edge of the Sahara to prevent its northward spread, and in large construction projects.

In Bulla Regia, unlike in any other Roman colonial town, the homes were built underground to provide protection from the intense heat of summer. Consequently, on entering the site through the ancient baths, we came out on a relatively bare field with little sign of ruins. Only on approaching closer could we see the steps leading down to the well-preserved rooms below, complete with magnificent mosaics which came alive with vibrant color when water was sprinkled on them to remove the layer of dust. Most memorable was an exquisite portrayal of Venus, with nearby Amor astride a dolphin.

Dougga, too, is unusual. Built on the site of an earlier city, it stands in a commanding position on the steep slopes of a hill, whereas most Roman towns were built on flat lands with wide level approaches. As a result, some of the main areas of the city do not bear the usual relationships to each other, the forum lying to the side of the capitol, rather than directly in front, for example. The temple of Saturn was impressive, but the heavily restored theater, now used for the Dougga Drama Festival each June is quite oppressive. Elsewhere on the site we saw the elaborate Roman baths and the latrines, a U-shaped bench with a dozen closely spaced holes, making for a very social rendezvous for relief.

For a change of pace we visited the cliff-top village of Sidi Bou Said, which takes its name from a 13th-century holy man. It has a stunning location commanding the Gulf of Tunis. It could well have been Greek with its whitewashed walls and blue doors and grilled windows. On closer inspection, though, the delicately decorated doors were unlike anything we have seen in Greece.

Morocco: Our first stop in Morocco was the large industrial city of Casablanca. Ingrid Bergman, where are you? There has never been a Rick's. Described by some as Morocco's most sophisticated city, Casablanca, with three million inhabitants, has little to offer the tourist other than the new Hassan II mosque, third largest in the world after Mecca and Medina. Completed in 1993 at a cost of $750 million, it is an imposing building on reclaimed land. Closer inspection reveals shoddy workmanship when compared with the magnificent mosaics of the Romans in Tunisia. When the late King announced it was to be built in 1987 he volunteered to foot the bill from his own purse with the help of donations from grateful citizens and abroad. As the costs mounted and the donations lagged, he encouraged the participation of all his subjects via the imposition of a tax. Everyone indeed contributed, including us as visitors, as the entry fee for tourists is $10.

Morocco, with three times the population of Tunisia, is a far more conservative society. Its population is both Arab and Berber. In fact our very well informed local guide told us he was the 16th child of an Arab father and a Berber mother. We saw many veiled women, especially in the city of Marrakech, and many more of them wore traditional dress than in Tunisia. A man is still allowed to take four wives, but only with the agreement of his first wife. If she objects she can go to court and seek to be divorced. Women cannot divorce, but they can "be divorced." Even so, women do have the vote, and are educated — more than half of the students at Morocco's universities are women.

Wherever we looked in the big cities we saw McDonalds, Pizza Hut, and KFC outlets.

Rabat, the capital, is a far more attractive city. The new young king was out of town when we stopped by his palace and the colorfully dressed guards seemed quite relaxed as they lounged about and chatted outside the palace entrance, quite unlike the rigid formality of British palace guards. In a museum in Sale, Rabat's twin city across the river, we were fascinated by the surprising collection of Moroccan Jewish relics, many containing the Star of David.

Flying south beyond the High Atlas Mountains, we arrived in the much different city of Ouarzazate. This is the center of the Moroccan movie industry, and our hotel lobby and patio were filled with Hebrew, Greek, and Roman statues, chariots and other pieces which have appeared in movies such as *Lawrence of Arabia*, *Kundun*, *The Mummy*, and *Solomon*, all of which were filmed here. I suspect that a pretty, but rather bulimic young French woman in the hotel restaurant was the star of yet another epic. We were now away from westernized Morocco and on the old slave route through Timbuktu in Mali. A large signboard in town advertised a 52-day camel trek to Timbuktu but we decided to pass up this great opportunity, at least for now. During the French colonial period, the city was home to Pasha Glaoui, warlord of the region, who died in mysterious circumstances immediately after independence. His Kasbah Tuourirt has been restored with the help of UNESCO and is well worth a visit.

From Ouarzazate we drove east between the snow-covered High Atlas Mountains to the north and the Anti-Atlas Mountains to the south along the Dades Valley, known as the Valley of 1,000 Kasbahs (fortresses). At the end of the valley we arrived at the town of Kalaat M'gouna, where a weekly Berber market was in progress. As usual we were thoroughly entertained by the colorful, lively action in progress.

That evening, to cap a memorable day, we had dinner in a tent at the Fint Oasis Camp, reached after a bumpy, 4WD ride over the desert. Upon arrival, our group of nine intrepid travelers was greeted by 32 Berber performers and assorted assistants. The 16 women dancers and singers were dressed in brightly colored traditional robes and wore bright red scarves on their heads. The 16 male musicians — beating drums and tambourines — were dressed mainly in white robes (a couple wore Yankee pinstripe robes) and either white turbans or white skullcaps. They played a lively piece to which the woman swayed, clapped, and chanted, occasionally breaking it up with a strange ululating sound. One of the men also chanted in a high, almost falsetto voice. The effect was hypnotic. They kept up the music and dance with virtually no break for rest for the next two-and-a-half to three hours. Julie joined in the swaying and clapping and talked with the lead dancer, who spoke very good French. This attractive young woman told Julie that she was a widow and had lost two children, both before they reached their first birthday. She said that the group worked together regularly. We were the smallest group that they had ever entertained. Sometimes they performed for up to 300 conventioneers, and they had appeared in several movies produced in the area.

Bright lights powered by a portable generator lighted the area. Moroccan carpets covered the sand, and the tent in which we dined was made from traditional camelhair cloth. In it were a table with white linen tablecloths, good china, silverware and glasses, and cloth-covered folding chairs! Dinner consisted of a number of tasty (and safe) Moroccan salads, a *tagine* (a traditional Moroccan casserole with chicken, seven vegetables and prunes), a beef couscous, and Moroccan sweets — all washed down with numerous bottles of Moroccan wines. It was truly a feast to remember, and let's not forget the camel, the open fire, and the stars in the night sky.

The next day we drove south through Zagora and towards the Sahara on the old slave route. After passing a barren wasteland of stark, treeless hills we reached an area with many oasis villages where date palms grew. The area is suffering a multiyear drought, and in the northern sections a disease is affecting and killing the palms. As we descended into a river valley we saw a long, dense stretch of date palms. Some landowners here are quite wealthy as a single date palm can yield a crop worth $500. In this remote area we visited a library that is the repository for an important collection of Islamic documents, including an 11th-century Koran. Even though the dry desert air is helpful in preventing mildew and mould, there is an urgent need for proper preservation of these rare documents. We had a picnic lunch at the first sand dunes of the Sahara before returning to our hotel.

Marrakech, our next and last destination, can be reached by air or via the well-paved national highway. Instead we traveled by 4WD vehicles along the ancient slave route across the High Atlas Mountains. But first we stopped at the Ait Benhaddou Kasbah in the Draa Valley. After walking across a wide dry riverbed we climbed up into the UNESCO Heritage ruined fortress — a warren of narrow streets, and location for many films, including *Gladiator*. From the top we commanded a magnificent view of the desolate scenery. It was a natural spot for control of the traditional route from sub-Saharan Africa. Soon after that stop the blacktop disappeared and our bumpy ride began. It was breathtaking because of the spectacular views, but mainly because of the hair-raising bends and precipitous drops from the rocky road with no guardrails. Fortunately there was virtually no oncoming traffic, and when it did appear it became a matter of negotiation as to who would back up to the occasional place where two 4WD vehicles could pass. The ride is certainly not for the faint of heart.

But the sky was blue, the sun shone bright, and in places the snow came down from the mountain peaks all the way to the road on which we were riding. This was the area in which Kipling's *The Man Who Would Be King* was filmed. It is a filmmaker's paradise. The scenery along this wild route is spectacular, with many different hues in the steep rocky slopes — pink, green, red, and black. No trees were to be seen except in the valley floors where water supported some limited agriculture and a number of small villages. A few had electricity, and these sported satellite dishes on the roofs of the more prosperous. Finally we reached Telouet, power seat of the Glaoui Vizier, self-styled lord of the south. Beyond that we rejoined the National Highway, and crested the pass at 7,415 feet before beginning our descent into the fabled city of Marrakech and our stay at the near legendary, but in our view overrated, La Mamounia Hotel.

Marrakech is a pink city. Capital of an earlier dynasty, it contains palaces in varying stages of repair, ranging from the El Bahia (meaning "beautiful" after the vizier's favorite wife) Palace, where the king still stays during his visits to the city, to the ruined Badaia Palace. Only one-third of the Bahia Palace is open to visitors, but this includes the vizier's own quarters, those of his four wives, and the harem where 24 concubines lived with their children. The Badaia Palace was left in ruins when a later ruler stripped it of everything worthwhile to incorporate it in his new palaces in the city of Meknes.

A highlight of our visit was the huge, mesmerizing Marrakech souk or market. Thousands of small (and some large) shops line the intricate network of narrow alleys, a labyrinth of streets displaying the arts and crafts of Morocco. They sell everything you can imagine, and some things you cannot — carpets, leather goods, furniture, clothing and fabrics, all kinds of craft works, silver, jewelry, and food. It was a joy to explore. As dusk fell on this first day of Ramadan, we arrived at Jemaa El Fna Square, the lively center of Marrakech, full of people, acrobats, snake charmers, and other street performers — a chaotic scene with a feeling of expectancy as sunset neared and the day's fast could be broken.

On two evenings in Marrakech we dined in the wonderful Moroccan restaurants that have appeared in formerly private homes in the old medina, reached down narrow alleys and hidden behind blank walls. Behind these walls are wonders. Open candlelit courtyards, fountains, mosaics, musicians, and superb food. We were fortunate to be able to dine on successive nights at the two best known of these restaurants, Le Tobsil and Yacout.

On our last day in Morocco we took a leisurely *calesa* ride through town to the Majorelle gardens, initially created by the French painter of that name in the 1920s. Now owned by Yves St. Laurent, the gardens are open to the public and contain an interesting small museum of Berber arts and crafts. On our last afternoon in Morocco we revisited the souk. Here we saw the excellent Dar Si Said Museum, housed in a particularly impressive small palace or riad, built in the middle of the 19th century by the brother of the Grand Vizier Ba Hmad who was responsible for the El Bahia Palace.

Finally, it was time for us to leave our traveling companions to return home in time for Thanksgiving. We have much to be thankful for.

Southeast Asia:
1. Thailand

A Nostalgic Return to an Almost-Lost Paradise

Julie and I first visited Bangkok in January 1961 en route to my first post-doctoral teaching job at the University of Melbourne. That was 41 years ago! We found it magical and mystical. Over the next three years we spent many hours in the library learning more about this fascinating part of the world. In December 1963, en route to my second teaching job at the University of Texas in Austin, we stopped over in Bangkok again to check out whether our reactions were the same. They were. We/I resolved that somehow I would find a way to live and work in Thailand. Less than three years later, in September 1966, that resolution was accomplished when we returned to Bangkok where I had an assignment as manager of a Ford Foundation-funded research project. We spent two wonderful, educational years in Thailand.

After our departure in 1968 we moved to the Philippines where I represented the Ford Foundation, reporting to the regional office in Bangkok. So visits to Thailand continued on a frequent basis. Then in 1973 I paid what turned out to be my last visit there until January 2002. Julie was in Bangkok on business on a few occasions in the mid-1990s.

So what were my first impressions after such a long absence?

–   The airport is large, modern, air conditioned and efficient.
–   The road into the city is an elevated highway that flies above the crowded streets and dense local traffic below. When we lived there, a divided road from the airport was opened, but it was common to find traffic coming toward you on the wrong side of the divide. No more. In Thailand, traffic drives on the left side of the road. That remains unchanged.
–   There are many, many new high-rise buildings. A number remain unfinished because of the impact of the Asian economic crisis of 1997 and the more recent global recession, accelerated by the events of 9/11. What a contrast with our time, when the Daimaru department store installed the first-ever escalator in Thailand and people came from far and near to see it and to venture fearfully onto it.
–   The Thai people remain as friendly, warm, and open as we remember them, ever ready to greet you with a smile. It is worth noting that Chinese New Year demonstrates the hold that Chinese businesses have on the local economy. Every business closes to celebrate. Only Thai government offices remain open.
–   The Chao Phraya River still wends its muddy way past the Oriental Hotel, where we stayed, and still teems with commercial traffic.
–   The food and service at the Oriental remain at the lofty levels of the past — one of the truly great hotels of the world.
–   January is mid-winter, so the temperature barely made it past 90 on the hottest day of our stay — no rain,

and humidity was relatively low. Just what we had come for.

– A modest, efficient, clean elevated railroad serves two lines, with more planned. There clearly is no "Thais with Disabilities" Act, as you have to climb numerous stairs to reach the platform and there are no elevators or escalators. While riding on the train, seats were given up to us by two Thai men who wanted their daughter/sister (I believe) to have a chance to practice her English. She had just completed her degree in finance from a small provincial university in the south and had come to the capital to take the entrance exam for a master's degree at Kasetsart University, the nation's number two educational institution.

One of our nostalgic visits was to Jim Thompson's house/museum. Thompson is the American businessman who revived the dying Thai silk industry and made it into the thriving business it is today. In March 1967, during our time in Bangkok, Thompson was vacationing in the Cameron Highlands of Malaysia, when he went for an afternoon walk in the jungle and was never seen again. Just two weeks after his disappearance we spent a few days in the Cameron Highlands, and the small community there was still rife with rumor and speculation about his fate. The mystery of his disappearance was never solved, and created the second great story of his life. Thompson's house on the *khlong* (canal), now a well-tended museum, is a must-see for any visitor to Thailand.

Another nostalgic visit was to our favorite Buddhist Temple, Wat Benjamabopitr or the Marble Temple. Fortunately, it still is not on most tourist itineraries, so was relatively free of visitors. Around the inner courtyard of the temple is a gallery of 53 bronze Buddhas — exactly as cherished in our memories. There is a remarkable degree of subtlety in the seemingly stylized faces, which range from the almost peasant simplicity of the earliest periods to the haughty elegance of Sukhothai and

Ayutthaya. All have been increased or reduced in size to give them a common dimension. Our favorite is a copy of a really gaunt fasting Buddha; the smaller stone original is in Pakistan's Lahore Museum, Kipling's House of Wonders. We were in Lahore in the mid-1970s and were really looking forward to seeing the original. Imagine our horror on arriving at the museum to be told that it closed in 20 minutes and that it was too late to admit any more visitors. A small well-placed contribution soon had an attendant hurrying us through the corridors of the museum to our target, which we were able to stare for fifteen minutes before being ushered out.

Breakfast on the hotel terrace on the riverbank was a tremendous way to start each day. Barge trains, rafts of teak logs with what looked to be teenaged boys tending them — moving precariously around — rafts of bamboo, and people movers of all kinds. There were commuter boats, elegant hotel boats from the Peninsula Hotel immediately across the river from the Oriental, and the *Oriental Queen*, which later brought us back down river from a visit to the old Siamese capital of Ayutthaya. One day for lunch there I had a truly astounding delicacy of steamed sea bass with lemon grass and chilis (on the side) called Pla Kapong Nueng Manao. The subtle nuanced flavors still linger lovingly in my memory. That, however, was because I asked the waiter to have the chef go light on Thai peppers, which otherwise heat it to an intolerable level.

The tropical fruit of Thailand are also joys to behold and to taste. Mangos, papayas, pineapples, mangosteens, guava, and pomelo were readily available. Durian was an ever-present aroma in the food markets, but never once offered in the dining rooms we frequented. For those unfamiliar with it, durian is the king of fruits in Southeast Asia. Its foul-smelling spiky exterior encloses large seeds covered with a buttery flesh that tastes, to the initiated at least, like heaven. Sir James George Scott, who wrote *The Burman, His Life and Notions*, said: "Some Englishmen will tell you that the flavour and odour of the fruit may be realized by eating a 'garlic custard' over a London sewer; others will be no less positive in their perception of blendings of sherry, delicious custards and the nectar of the gods . . . ." Personally, I like to eat it with sticky rice!

One real disappointment was a visit to Wat Po, the temple of the reclining Buddha. Just as fantastic in every way as we remembered it, admission is now charged and the grounds were flooded with tourists — thousands upon thousands of them. After this, we decided to skip the palace grounds and the temple of the Emerald Buddha, and to keep in our memory what it was like before the days of mass tourism. Getting to and from Wat Po did get us onto the city streets, where the traffic is hell. Passing through Chinatown, at least here was a part of the city that appears unchanged. If I were a young man visiting Bangkok today, I doubt that the magic that captured me forty years ago would work today. Pollution, traffic, crowds, but most importantly, the dilution of the Thai culture by the intrusion of the modern and secular, all say no.

One day we traveled by bus up to Ayutthaya, last visited in 1966. Much reconstruction has been done, and you now pay admission to the grounds, which are securely guarded. When the Burmese captured the great city in 1767, they not only sacked and burned but also, in search of treasure, decapitated and mutilated most of the numerous Buddha images in the old city. Country folk still retain a visceral anti-Burmese feeling because of this vandalism. I was told that a much-traveled, well-educated Thai businessman suggested to a Western friend that Burma's current economic and political problems may be delayed vengeance for their desecration of the Ayutthaya Buddhist images. The return to Bangkok along the Chao Phraya River aboard the *Oriental Queen* was a respite from cities and traffic.

In Bangkok, there are wats (temples) everywhere, but virtually no monks in evidence today, in sharp contrast to the situation 35 years ago. Outside Bangkok we saw more monks, but instead of spending three months or longer as a monk, a young person today is likely to spend only three days. In Bangkok, too, there are a sprinkling of mosques (five percent of the population is Moslem, mostly in the south near the border with Malaysia), and Christian churches. We were told that the rich want their children to attend Christian schools because there they learn much better spoken English from American and British teachers. Two fellow-passengers on the *Oriental Queen* told us that that they had been in the south and had seen T-shirts with large pictures of Osama bin Laden, but we did not see them on our travels.

Another memorable visit that we recommend to visitors to Bangkok is to the private Prasart Museum, a treasure house collection in wonderful original buildings in a five-acre tropical garden in the suburb of Bangkapi. Because it is an eclectic mixture of originals and copies, it is not for purists, but is a joy for the rest of us. We met and chatted with Mr. Prasart, who made his money in construction and sees his collection as his heritage to the state since he has no children.

Leaving Bangkok, we flew north to Chiangmai, last visited in 1966. Now a city of 1.7 million, it is an hour and a world away from the hectic pace of Bangkok. Here, at least, traces of the Thailand we remembered still exist, mixed in with progress. It is clean, and there are better roads and bigger buildings. At the airport we were met by a representative of the Four Seasons resort and whisked away to a magic world of great service, good food, smiling faces, and rice paddies between the luxurious villas. While I relaxed with a book, Julie retreated to the Lanna Spa, from which she returned glowing with reports of the heavenly encounter with "magic fingers" and aromatic lotions which were nothing short of divine. Most of our fellow guests were French and German. Only very few were American.

Venturing forth from the resort, we visited a magnificent orchid farm where literally thousands of all kinds of orchids are cultivated, and then an active night market. Far more oriented to tourists than Bangkok's weekend market, it was jammed with foreigners speaking a babel of mostly European tongues — French, German, Russian, British, and Australian English — but again very few Americans. As I visit markets all over the world I continue to marvel at the quantity of inventory of tourist trinkets in the pipelines. If manufacturing suddenly ceased, it would still take years to clear the supply backlog!

Next morning, after a leisurely breakfast, we set forth with a car, driver and guide to visit a few temples. First we climbed the mountain (from 300 feet altitude in town to 3,000 feet) to visit Wat Phratat Doi Suthep, riding the final 300 steps in a small tramcar. Glittering with gold, the temple is clearly a highlight of our entire Thailand visit. The king of Chiangmai, 700 years ago, obtained a true relic of the body of Buddha, which was then split apart. One part was placed in a wat near the palace, while the second was placed on the back of a sacred white elephant, which was then turned loose and followed to determine where Buddha wanted his remains to rest. First the elephant climbed the mountain, then circled it three times before kneeling down and dying. This was the spot on which the new wat was built. It is magnificent, and commands a dominating view of the city and the plain beneath. Returning to the city, we visited a small sample of the more than 300 wats within the old city walls.

From Chiangmai we flew north again to Mae Hong Son, no more than a village only 12 miles from the border of Myanmar (Burma). At last we have regained paradise! This is the Thailand we remember so well; smiling people and a relaxed pace of life. Our first visit was to the Karen "long-neck village," almost on the border. To get there we drove along a newly constructed concrete road, but in the process had to ford thirteen small streams, which in the rainy season are deep torrents. To visit the Karen village foreigners must pay a government fee of Baht 250 ($6), the money going to the village and its people. In return you are allowed to take as many pictures as you please. The houses are of woven reeds with leaf roofs — said to be good for four years. And the long necks. As children, the women of this tribe begin to put on layers of golden bands on their necks to stretch them, considered a sign of beauty. With increasing age, the number of bands is increased, so that the older women's necks are may be twice as long as nature intended. The people here weave interesting textiles and make purses and garments as well as woodcarvings for sale to visitors. The people came here from Myanmar to this village about nine years ago, and the number continues to grow. Each year, most return to their villages in Myanmar to see their relatives and to take home money from their relative lucrative cash earnings. On our return trip to town we passed a working elephant being led by its keeper, and three other elephants returning from giving rides to visitors.

Our next adventure was a boat ride for some five miles up the Pai River in a long, narrow, shallow-draft boat with a "long-tail" outboard motor. As we raced upstream against gentle rapids we saw mostly jungle on the banks. In the river itself, there were many small boats into which local people were loading stones and mud from the river bed for use as construction material. At one point we passed a half-dozen or so bamboo rafts carrying tourists downstream. Our trip was about half-an-hour, theirs more like an hour-and-a-half.

The wats we visited around Mae Hong Son were architecturally very different from others in Thailand. Here they are wooden and silvery, unlike the gilded cement structures of the south. On our last morning in Mae Hong Son we were up early to visit the local market — definitely not for tourists. Here we saw all sorts of fresh vegetables and chilis. Food stalls sold a kind of fried pancake, some folded around an egg — even waffles! Most curious to me was the flower market, where locals were buying. I don't have any idea of the cost of a large bunch of roses or daisies, but I am sure it would be a very small fraction of what we pay to our local florist or supermarket. After this we spent the rest of the day at leisure as we girded our loins for a strenuous attack on our next destination, Myanmar.

Southeast Asia:
2. Myanmar

The Golden Land

Like all of today's potential travelers to Myanmar (formerly known as Burma), we were aware that it is regarded as an international pariah by a large section of the global community because of the human rights abuses perpetrated by the ruling military junta. The question is: Does visiting Myanmar endorse the regime or, in a small way, reduce the country's isolation from the outside world and constrain the junta's actions? For right or wrong, we decided on the latter and made our plans to proceed.

We arrived in Yangon (formerly Rangoon) after dark. Waiting to greet us as we entered the international terminal building was a lovely young lady from the Myanmar Tourist Authority. She took our passports and other documents (the complicated and expensive visas had been issued at the Myanmar embassy in Washington, DC) and skirted the long lines being slowly processed by the immigration inspectors. In no time at all she was back and ushering us around the lines to where we were required to change $200 each into Foreign Exchange Certificates (FECs) — funny money. The legal exchange rate of dollars or FECs is 6 kyat (pronounced chat), but the black-market rate varies from 650 to 740 to the dollar/FEC. Truly we were entering wonderland. Most of the charges we incurred in country were billed and paid in dollars or FECs. We spent only $35 in kyat (obtained from our guide at 650 to the FEC) in total during our entire visit.

The drive into the city from the airport was on an excellent wide road, well lit and with light, orderly traffic. Later we were to find that it was a rare example of its kind in the entire country. Under British colonial rule, the Burmese drove on the left but switched to the right on regaining independence — a somewhat odd choice given that their neighbors to the east (Thailand) and west (Bangladesh) drive on the left. Most of the cars on the road have the steering wheel on the right hand side of the car. Very strange. As we entered the city, we saw the brightly illuminated Schwedagon pagoda gleaming in golden majesty. More on this later.

Our hotel, the Strand, on the banks of the Yangon River, was built about 100 years ago and was completely refurbished in the mid-1990s. With only 32 suites, large air-conditioned rooms with high (16-18 foot) ceilings and revolving overhead fans, it was truly a gem. The attentive staff welcomed us and whisked us directly up to our room where an almost completed registration form awaited a signature. Our room had a huge balcony overlooking the river. The teak hardwood floor of our room positively sparkled. It seemed a shame to walk on it.

Our stay this time was to be short — just long enough to reduce our luggage to one suitcase for travel within Myanmar, the other to stay at the Strand until our return. After an excellent 4:30 a.m. room service breakfast we repaired to the lobby where we met our guide for the next week, a cheerful, pleasant woman named Yee Yee, and headed back to the airport, and to our first destination, Bagan. The international airport, no paragon of efficiency, appeared so by comparison with the chaos of the domestic terminal. Luggage is handled manually through the entire process that gets it to the plane. There is security screening for hand luggage. As part of our consolidation of our luggage, we were carrying our toilet kits in our hand carries. The X-ray machine picked up nail scissors and we were required to remove them and hand them over. After passing through the remaining formalities (including immigration, which we encountered at every step of every domestic flight) we reached the "tourist" departure lounge where Yee Yee produced our scissors and returned them to us! So much for security!

Yes, tourists are segregated from the locals. Most of the few tourists were French, German or Japanese. Very few were American. The air-conditioned departure lounge had swinging glass doors onto the apron and I was amused to see staff stepping in and out through one of the closed doors — the glass was missing. The whole process is computer-free. There are no screens showing arrivals and departures. When a flight is due to board, a uniformed employee appears with a hand-carried sign (like a page in a hotel lobby) announcing the flight. As we waited our eyes stung from the smoke of smokers in the area.

As we came in to land at Bagan airport we got a brief overview of the marvels that awaited us. How do you respond to some 2,200 pagodas, temples and cave temples scattered seemingly randomly across a honey-brown, arid landscape — all that remain of 13,000 more than 700 years ago? They date from the 11th through the 19th centuries, but most were built at the height of the powerful Mon Kingdom in the 11th through 13th centuries. What a contrast with the Europe of that time, and what a sad contrast with the broken, poor country of Myanmar today.

So many stupas. The effect is stupendous, stupefying, it defies description. Superlatives really cannot capture the impact as you bump past them along the narrow roads, passing cyclists, pedestrians, horse-drawn vehicles, and even the occasional oxcart. The ravages of time, earthquakes, war, looting and general theft and vandalism have taken their toll. Despite this, what remains is overwhelming. Only a few of the more notable pagodas and temples have yet been reconstructed. For most ruins, that is what they are.

Although Bagan's glory days are long past, what remains is a treasure trove, the most memorable of all the sights we saw in this golden land. The stupas (also known as pagodas, chedis, or zedis) contain sacred relics, sometimes of the Buddha, but more often the ashes of rulers and important monks. Temples have four entrances and contain Buddha images and statuary showing the life of the Buddha. Cave temples have only a single entrance and contain both Buddha images and frescoes and wall paintings. Most of the latter are in seriously deteriorated shape today, although the government, with the help of UNESCO, is beginning some restoration and preservation. The cave temples are reminiscent in a small way of the Magao caves at Dunhuang in western China which we were privileged to visit in July 2001.

The Bagan Hotel far exceeded our admittedly modest expectations. There was television in our room, but nothing in English — no CNN, no BBC World! We truly were out of this world. There are no computers, either, so all billing is done manually. On one of our two evenings in Bagan we had dinner with our local driver, Win Swee, who spoke quite good English, picked up simply by listening to tourists talking with their guides as he drove them around. What would such a young man accomplish in an opportunity culture? We learned that a schoolteacher earns $10 per month. We also learned that there are only two TV channels available, both government controlled. Only the rich can afford TV — our driver had one — and in villages, set owners charge their neighbors a small fee to come and watch! From Yee Yee we also learned that if a Myanmar (Burmese) wants to travel abroad, he/she must apply for a passport specifying where, and how it will be paid for. The process, when successful, takes at least a month. After the journey is completed, immigration authorities collect the passport at the point of international reentry. Next trip requires a repeat of the process. It is not easy.

We began our second day in Bagan with a visit to the market. We are market/bazaar/souk freaks and always enjoy browsing, whether in a Paris food market, an Arab or Turkish souk, or an Asian market. Bagan's was a good choice — interesting people and interesting goods. The gentle, serene people, both men and women, wear traditional *longyis* (a wrap-around long skirt, which seems well fitted to the climate and life style). Many of the wide variety of fruits and vegetables in the market were unfamiliar to us. A one stall a woman was selling "cheroots" — foul-smelling local, hand-made small cigars. From there we went for a boat ride on the Ayeyarwady (formerly Irrawaddy) River. It was a tranquil episode on a busy day. We saw workers removing large glazed pots from a raft on which they had been floated down river from where they were made, now to be sold in Bagan; overloaded ferries; fishermen; women washing clothes on the river bank; and everywhere chedis.

Back on land, we continued our visits to pagodas and temples. We quickly learned that, like many religions far from the centers of orthodoxy (Catholicism in the Philippines and Mexico, Islam in Indonesia) Buddhism in Myanmar contains important elements of animistic beliefs. Here it is evidenced by the *nats* or animal spirits, which play an important part in religious expression. Although we saw a few very beautiful nat figures, most were quite crude in appearance. There are 36 nats, plus a 37th, Indra, king of the nats who was introduced by one of the Mon kings. By now we are at the end of our Bagan visit, and return to our hotel hot, dusty, but feeling very much in awe of Bagan and at peace with ourselves.

Next morning it was on to Mandalay. The flight from Bagan is a continuation of the flight we took from Yangon. Because of the absence of computers, there is no way to know which seats are free, so it is free seating (shades of Southwest Airlines) from here on. Our first stop in Mandalay (en route from the airport) is at the Maha Muni Pagoda, which houses Mandalay's holiest Buddha statue, the wish-fulfilling Buddha. Tradition says that this is one of only five made during the lifetime of the Buddha. Two others are in India and two are in paradise! By now, the Buddha is coated with some five inches of gold leaf, and believers were busily adding more. Repeated everywhere in Myanmar, the skeptical secularist (namely me) wonders how this treasure can be redeemed and put to work to develop the country economically. Oh well, I didn't expect an answer.

When we were at the Maha Muni a novitiate ceremony was in progress for children who were to become monks the next day. We were fortunate to be able to photograph the elaborately dressed children. A purple-robed monk led me (no women allowed) around to an area where steps led up to the base on which the huge Buddha image is seated. We climbed up all the way and I was able to see one young boy going through the ritual of making an offering before he became a novice. The whole area was crowded with worshipers. I found myself wondering if the military government does not encourage this reverence as a way to channel emotions away from dissatisfaction with their rulers.

Mandalay was the capital of independent Burma at the time it was captured by the British and made a British colony on January 1, 1886. It finally regained its independence in 1948. The palace area, a walled square two kilometers by two kilometers surrounded by a wide moat, today is a military compound closed to the public. The city, situated just 300 feet above sea level is flat, making it an ideal bicycle city — and that is exactly what it is. The number of bicycles is reminiscent of what we saw in Beijing and Shanghai in the early 1990s before they were overwhelmed by motor vehicles. Such a fate seems highly unlikely in this poor, Third-World country, one of the failed states.

Another visit on the way to our hotel check-in was to the Kuthodaw Pagoda, which houses the world's largest book! Around the central pagoda are 729 smaller zedis, built in 1872 during the Fifth Buddhist Synod, each containing one page of the Buddhist scriptures carved in Pali script on a marble tablet.

It was the first time the entire Tipitaka was recorded in Pali script. The final morning visit was to an ancient teak wood building in which King Mindon (founder of Mandalay as the capital) died in 1878. After his death, the next king had the building moved outside the palace grounds to its present location, where he used it as a place to meditate until he was sent into exile in India by his British conquerors.

Finally, we checked into our modern international hotel, the Sedona, where our room rate was $130 (for our Burmese guide, we paid just 10% of that, or $13 for a similar room!). We found CNBC here, but no CNN or BBC World! Our afternoon outing was a drive up Mandalay Hill, a killing field for the British during World War II when they fought their way back up it to defeat the entrenched Japanese troops. At the top we saw a glass-studded temple, including riding barefooted up three escalators (a first) and descending, still barefoot, by elevator (also a first). Throughout Myanmar, one must be barefoot (no shoes, no socks) to visit temples and other sacred sites. The Buddhist Burmese were deeply offended by the British troops who wore boots in their temples during the colonial period.

On our second day in Mandalay we began joyfully with a visit to the main market, then on to Sagaing, briefly a Shan capital in the fourteenth century after the fall of the Mon kingdom of Bagan. Centered on a hill just 30 minutes drive from present-day Mandalay City, Sagaing still has some 900 monasteries and many temples and stupas. It is regarded by some as the living center of the Buddhist faith in Myanmar today. Four hundred years later, in the 19th century, the capital was moved back to the area, first to Ava, on an island in Ayeyerwady river, then to Amarapura, both of which we visited. Mandalay is a center for cottage industry, and we were able to see artisans making silverware, embroideries and puppets, as well as drive through the stone carving district where Buddhas images are made to order for donors to present to their favorite temple. Our evening was enlivened by a visit to a puppet the-

ater where traditional performances are presented to the rau-
cous accompaniment of local instruments. A real treat!

Next morning we flew to Heho (you don't close your lips!)
airport on the way to Inle Lake, at an elevation of almost 3,000
feet. At Heho the military bureaucracy has run wild. No vehicles are allowed within a quarter of a mile of the terminal, so
we had to hike to our waiting car. Our luggage followed on a
hand-truck some ten minutes later. When we were all together,
we set out on a 22-mile, one-hour drive along a narrow, bumpy
road with only a rutted muddy shoulder, complete with bicycles, motorcycles, and a little vehicular traffic. The ride was
very slow as two vehicles cannot pass without one moving
over into the mud. If we had an impression of a desperately
poor country before, it was thoroughly reinforced by what we
saw here, although the countryside itself is lovely. At the end
of the road, we transferred to a boat for the last 20-minute ride
to our hotel, the Inle Princess Resort. We had a lovely villa,
mosquito nets on the beds, and a hot water bottle provided at
night to supplement the two heavy woolen blankets. There
was no TV in the room, and the phone instrument was crank-
operated!

Inle Lake has a unique culture. The lake people (Intha)
live in simple huts on stilts above the water and derive their
entire livelihood from the bounties of the lake. Large sections
of floating weed are laced together, covered with mud from
the lake bottom, then anchored by driving long bamboo poles
through them and into the lakebed. Vegetables (cauliflower,
tomato, cucumber, peas, beans, and eggplants) are cultivated
in the floating fields and shipped to markets across the country by truck. The Intha men are fishermen. They use conical
nets and propel their long, narrow, flat-bottomed boats by standing and using one leg to push the oar to propel their boats
through the water. The lake is ringed with mist-shrouded
mountains, and the setting is serene, splendid, and relaxing.

A boat ride takes us across the lake to visit a famous pagoda which house five small Buddha images that have been

covered so thoroughly by gold leaf that they have totally lost any human shape. I contributed by chance as our guide wished to add gold leaf as a petition for her great niece's health — the child was born with a hole in her heart. Women are not permitted to climb the stand on which the Buddha images rest. It was a privilege to oblige. I think I could even become a Buddhist! As an interesting aside, Yee Yee, our guide, told us that she had been raised a Christian (Seventh Day Adventist) but had converted to Buddhism as she learned more about it after becoming a guide.

Each year, the five Buddha images are carried around the lake on a golden barge in the shape of a mythical bird, spending a day or two in various monasteries on the fringe of the lake. In the first year this was done (it is said) the smallest Buddha fell overboard and to the bed of the lake. Miraculously, on the return of the remaining Buddhas to their home pagoda, the lost Buddha had reappeared in his normal place. Obviously, he did not like water, so today, only four Buddha images make the ceremonial circuit, while one remains home. Other visits around the lake included a monastery famous for its jumping cats (they were sleeping when we were there); an interesting lakeside market (the famous floating market only happens every five days and was not scheduled during our visit); a workshop where girls were weaving on wooden looms, and a blacksmith shop where they make knives, scissors, and other useful items not to have in hand luggage when traveling today. We were fortunate, also, to see a water-borne novitiate ceremony, accompanied by lots of highly amplified music.

An early morning departure took us away from the unique sights and dreadful food of the past two days. It was so cold that the Inle Princess Hotel provided us with blankets to keep us warm in the boat as we proceeded to unwind the complicate arrival process — boat, taxi, propeller plane to Yangon, hotel car — and brought us back to the luxury of the Strand Hotel. Our stored bag was waiting for us in our suite, and we were warmly greeted personally by the general manager, Sally

Baughan, a New Zealander. It was wonderful to be back with good Western food. That evening in the dining room we were entertained by a Myanmar guitarist who had studied in Strasbourg with the teacher of Pepe Romero, one of the great modern classic Spanish guitarists, now resident in Del Mar only about three miles from our home in Rancho Santa Fe! Our waiter told us that he was the leading musician of Myanmar. He certainly was a master of his instrument, and I believe I am in a position to judge as I regard myself as a connoisseur of this genre. We were made somewhat uncomfortable when we realized that the inflated rate we were paying for the Strand each night represented almost four years' salary for a Burmese elementary schoolteacher. With tourism at a low ebb, the hotel was practically empty. I believe there may have only been one other couple on the second night we were there.

Yangon is a sprawling, distressingly poor city of five million. It reminded us a little bit of the Bangkok we first visited more than 40 years ago, but Yangon is neither as developed nor as prosperous. We struggled to answer the question of how you bootstrap a society with so little going for it. Unemployment and underemployment are obvious and endemic. Indeed, a major industry seems to be cooking and selling food on the sidewalks of the city. As a former development professional, an obvious first step in the enormous task is to get rid of the military government and replace it with a more representative government that can win the support of the international community. As already mentioned, the gold locked up in Buddhist temples would be more usefully employed in bettering the lot of the people, but I fear that idea is totally unrealistic.

Our tourist visits in Yangon began with the National Museum to see the Lion Throne of the last king of Burma, which was taken to India by the British and finally returned by Lord Mountbatten in 1948 when Burma regained its independence. A model of the royal palace in the museum showed the regal splendors of the kingdom before its overthrow. From there we proceeded to Schwedagon Pagoda, Myanmar's pride and joy. Schwedagon defies the ability of superlatives to capture its sheer immensity and beauty. Holy ground to the Buddhists of Myanmar, at the time of our visit it was crowded with people praying, making donations, and offering their devotions. We spent a couple of hours at Schwedagon, which is like visiting 60 wealthy major temples joined together. It is impossible for a visitor really to comprehend the enormous religious vitality of this great temple complex.

On our final morning in Myanmar we spent the time walking along broken sidewalks and taking our lives into our hands crossing the streets filled with undisciplined traffic. Bicycles, trishaws, motorcycles, cars, trucks, and buses defied safe passage. Interestingly, none of the cyclists wore helmets, while all of the motorcyclists did. If they do not, they are subject to a healthy fine! At the riverbank, one small boat after another discharged commuting passengers from across or up and down the river. Most carried small lunch pails! These were the workers. The independence monument, a 150-foot high tower, is situated in the middle of a garden. Admission was 10 kyat (about one-and-a-half cents). It reminded us, many years ago, of paying one millieme to cross the Suez Canal from Port Said to Port Fuad. The aim clearly is to keep out the street urchins and the poor, who would otherwise find this an amusing and pleasant place to escape from the crowded streets. We ventured into the duty-free store, where people with dollars can purchase imported basic Western goods, such as canned food, wines, and sodas. And we passed through local shopping districts where people buy books, plumbing and hardware supplies, batteries, Italian pumps, and even one selling television sets and other electronic goods.

A car from the hotel took us to the Elephant Company, where superb handicrafts are made and sold at modest prices. Some are exported to the US, Europe, and Japan. Right now, tourism, limited though it is, and cottage industries, are major income sources for the country. But without tourism, there really is little market for the handicrafts produced by the cottage industries. In our view there is no way that Myanmar could cope with mass tourism without huge damage to its culture and to the fragile ecology of destinations like Bagan and Inle Lake. It is a dilemma.

Departing from Myanmar was yet another adventure. The airport, as before, was totally chaotic. Operations are almost completely manual. While we were in line at the immigration counter, an official went down the line collecting our passports, placing the passports of the people at the end of the line at the top of his pile. They were then turned over to the people at the desk, who dealt with them as they stood, meaning that the people at the end of the line were processed first, those at the front last. When the passports were stamped the officials held them up until someone came forward to claim them! Nevertheless, we made it through into the arms of Thai International, which welcomed us into its warm embrace and carried us safely back to Bangkok, en route to our next destination, Cambodia.

Southeast Asia:
3. Cambodia

Hope in a Ravaged Land

After Myanmar, arriving in Cambodia was like finding the light at the end of the tunnel. Visas were issued at the airport for only a modest fee. Although still desperately poor and devastated by the brutality of the Khmer Rouge during the years of the killing fields, we detected a palpable feeling of optimism about the future of the country. The contrast was stark as we moved from the almost empty, splendor of Yangon's Strand Hotel to the bustle of the equally historic grandeur of Phnom Penh's Le Royale hotel, refurbished in the 1990s by Raffles of Singapore. The tourists were mostly French, but also Germans, Japanese, Italians, even Greeks. Very few were Americans. The hotel television carried CNN, CNBC and BBC World, as well as French, German, Italian and Japanese programs. All tourist transactions were in US dollars. We neither saw nor handled any of the local currency during our stay.

The streets of Phnom Penh, Cambodia's capital, were relatively clean and in a reasonable state of repair. The sidewalks, unlike Yangon, are not broken or jammed with food vendors cooking and selling their wares. People ride motorcycles rather than bicycles — often three or four people to a motorbike, usually family groups. For $1-2 you can ride all over town on the pillion seat of a motorcycle. We saw a number of foreigners, both men and women, doing just that, including one woman tightly clutching a quite large suitcase. The people are poor, but they seem busy, and involved in many small entrepreneurial activities. There is a sense that they are all pulling in the same direction.

There is the beginning of democratic government. On the day of our departure from the country an election was held for local government offices, and reports indicate that it was conducted reasonably cleanly and openly. One of the opposition parties received enough support to suggest that it could become a force in the national elections to be held in 2003. We will watch with interest as the future unfolds.

One tragic reminder of the horrors of the recent past is the number of men with no legs, with just one leg, or missing an arm, presumably the result of encounters with land mines, which still are a huge problem in many parts of the country, especially near the borders. Several foreign governments and international organizations are providing assistance to clear mines, but this will continue to be a problem for a long time to come. The amputees beg, but you cannot give to all, so you end up feeling guilty. Elsewhere in the country we saw small groups of blind musicians playing traditional instruments at archaeological sites, and were able to make contributions to them.

For $35 we rented a car with a (sort of) English-speaking driver for the day. Our first visit was to the National Museum that houses a fine collection of Hindu and Buddhist statuary from Cambodia's long, rich, and powerful past. It is sad that they could not remain *in situ*, but so many were stolen and channeled onto the international art market during the late 1970s and the 1980s that we felt grateful that those remaining have found a safe haven in their own country. It was a joy to see the many groups of local high school students at the museum listening attentively to the explanations of their teachers or guides. As a parenthetical aside, the very best of Cambodia's art treasures are to be seen at the recently reopened Musée Guimet in Paris, a treasure house of Asian art collected by French colonials.

King Norodom Sihanouk had returned to his palace from a trip abroad on the previous day. Fortunately, the public rooms and the grounds of the palace remained opened to visitors. Like the Royal Palace in Bangkok, it is splendidly exotic. We were able to visit the grand reception room and the silver pagoda with its own "emerald Buddha". Across the road from the palace, the Tonle Sap River feeds into the mighty Mekong.

After the palace visit we stopped by the Foreign Correspondents Club, a hangout for the expatriate community, and visited the other major sights, the Russian Market, the Central Market, the Independence Monument, and Wat Phnom, the signature temple of the city. In the markets we saw the early markers of a consumer society: television sets, boom boxes, cell phones, and watches. It was intriguing to see people buying flowers.

Phnom Penh was cleaner than either Bangkok or Yangon. We noted with interest the number of Internet cafes, and the presence of FedEx, DHL, Motorola, and Telstra (the Australian telecommunications company). We chose not to visit the museums housing relics (including huge numbers of skulls) of the Khmer Rouge's mad killing spree.

Next morning we were up early for a short flight to Siem Reap, to visit the vast monuments of Angkor. Phnom Penh was new to us, but Angkor was a return visit. We spent Christmas 1963 at the Grand Hotel d'Angkor and were looking forward to staying there again. Like Le Royale in Phnom Penh, Raffles refurbished the Grand Hotel D'Angkor in the mid-1990s. It is again a grand hotel in every sense of the word, with new wings and a huge swimming pool.

Our flight was in a large modern propeller plane. We still

have vivid memories of the flight in 1963, in a DC-3. It was the custom then to offer candy on take-off and landing, in the belief that swallowing would lower any ear pain resulting from changes in pressure. On this occasion, the candy offered to me had somehow been soaked in gasoline! I was closer to being airsick (while still on the ground) than at any other point in my many flights. For those of you old enough to have flown in a DC-3, one of the great planes of history, you will recall that it was an uphill walk from the doorway to your seat. In this one, luggage had been loaded in the rear of the passenger compartment and a rope mesh thrown over it to keep it in place. There was no air conditioning, and small electric fans mounted on the edge of the open overhead storage compartments kept the air moving a little. We noticed one of the other passengers counting. When we met him later at the hotel, we found he was an El Al official. He told us that the international treaty governing the number of passengers in a DC-3 had been exceeded by four! Our pilot, a Frenchman, had one wooden leg, and smoked a pipe! How times have changed.

Siem Reap has moved from being a quaint village backwater to a bustling tourist town with cookie-cutter hotels and guesthouses springing up like weeds. The new hotels mostly belong to military officers who were able to profit from their positions during the past two decades.

A pass (complete with a passport-size picture) to visit the monuments costs $20 for one day, $40 for three days, or $60 for a week. It must be shown at the entrance to each site. We had allotted two-and-a-half days to visit and revisit the great archaeological treasures of Angkor. These are scattered over a wide area, so we arranged for a car with a driver and a guide to take care of us. Although the ancient Khmer people were Buddhist, most of their rulers were Hindu, so most of the temples deify Hindu gods.

Our guide, Beuk, took us first to Ta Prom, built from the 6th through the 13th centuries, where jungle trees are so entangled with the half-ruined structures that removing them would lead to the collapse of the structures. The thick roots snake down and over the ruins, devouring the portals and archways at will, flowing from crevices like streams of water, reaching down to seize a bas relief as if choosing one that pleases. On the walls, carved dancers maintain their dignity and their 1,000-year-old balance, even as the stones tumble about them. As we had anticipated, our return to Angkor is quickly becoming the highlight of our 2002 Southeast Asian trip.

The last two hours of the day were spent at Angkor Wat, the central complex of this entire group of temples. At the height of its power, the Khmer capital was home to more than a million people. It suddenly declined around 1430 as large numbers of people left, but still there is no satisfactory explanation of why. Angkor Wat's outer wall, surrounded by a moat, is about three-and-a-half miles long. Passing through the west gate, the visitor walks about a quarter of a mile along a causeway to an inner wall in which the main structures are to be found. They are awe-inspiring in their beauty and majesty. The walls contain relief carvings of the Ramayana epic in magnificent detail, and the beautiful relief carvings of apsaras (celestial dancers) possess a fluid motion. The experience is magical.

Fortunately, during the evil days of the Khmer Rouge, the monuments were not destroyed, as was the case with schools, hospitals, and modern temples. But security was removed and many culturally important images were looted.

It was with a feeling of deep spiritual satisfaction that we return to our hotel at the end of our first marvelous half-day in Siem Reap. Angkor is certainly one of the real wonders of the world. At one level, the scale of the ruins and monuments conveys the enormous power and wealth of the Khmer civilizations of the tenth through thirteenth centuries, leaving us humbled before its grandeur. At the opposite end of the scale, the subtlety, harmony, delicacy and beauty of the bas reliefs — Hindu and Buddhist — help to convey the richness and complexity of the culture. There is myth, the Ramayana story, and tales of war with the Cham kings of Vietnam and the many details of the life of the courts and the common people: chariots and cockfights, fishermen, festivals, and market scenes. And everywhere we could see the graceful figures and movement of the beautiful apsaras, the celestial dancers.

We began our second day by visiting Angkor Thom, the capital of the Khmer nation at the height of its power. A causeway flanked by 108 large stone statues, 54 gods on the left and 54 demons on the right, leads to the south gate of the city. Beyond it we drive past Bayon — to which we will soon return — to visit the terraces of the elephants and of the leper king. The relief carvings are so many and so impressive, covering a sunlit wall some twenty feet high and a quarter-of-a-mile long that they challenge anyone to capture their effect in words. Here was a truly regal kingdom, brought to its height by the prodigious output of its greatest king, the Buddhist Jayavarman VII, who ruled for 39 years from 1181 to 1220.

Although not as celebrated as Angkor Wat, Bayon, built by Jayavarman VII, was our clear favorite, containing some of the most remarkable bas reliefs. Above them are the towers with large mysterious stone faces in relief looking out in all four directions with sublime smiles. A glorious morning indeed, enhanced by the cloudless blue sky smiling down on us.

Rest and lunch, then back on the sightseeing trail, this time on the "great circuit," taking in Phra Khan, Neak Pean, Ta Som, and East Mabon. Although relatively minor sites in Angkor terms, anywhere else in the world each would be a cherished gem. All are in poor repair, but the first two are undergoing significant repair and preservation by the New York based National Monuments Fund. Phra Khan, the temple of the sacred sword, still has trees and roots tangled with the broken structure. Neak Pean, the temple of the coiled serpents, is small and quite unlike the others. Ta Som is a tranquil and charming Buddhist temple. It was at these monuments that we encountered police security guards who offered to sell us their police badges for $1!

On our final day we drove 25 minutes along a blacktop road through the jungle to Banteay Srei, a delicately carved jewel of a Hindu temple. Despite the fact that we left our hotel at 7:30 a.m., we found Banteay Srei already crowded with tourists — what a disappointment. In 1963, when we rattled over a dirt road in a jeep for almost three hours to reach the temple, we were two of a total of six visitors. There were no stalls nearby selling trinkets, no security, no entry fee, and no area that was off-limits. Today the entire center section of the complex is roped off. Returning to Angkor Wat, we spent a couple more hours reveling in the bas reliefs. On our final afternoon we occupied our time with visits to two local markets and a government handicraft training center where young people are being trained in stone and woodcarving, lacquer work, and various construction skills. Our 2002 visit to Southeast has drawn to a close.

Beuk's Story (as he told it to us)

Our guide, Beuk, was just a five-year-old when the Vietnam War was expanded to Cambodia. Lon Nol became the US puppet leader. He ousted the king, Norodom Sihanouk, who sought refuge first in Hanoi, then China. Ho Chi Minh promised the king that Vietnam would return a number of southern Cambodian provinces in return for support for the North in its war with the South. These provinces had been transferred to Vietnam by the French colonial administration. Of course, the king was betrayed and the border never changed. Older Cambodians still revere the king, but the younger generation is very dissatisfied by his return to power in the mid-1990s.

With the end of the Vietnam War, a far greater catastrophe overtook the country when Pol Pot and his Khmer Rouge began their savage, almost four-year rule in which more than two million people, twenty percent of the population, were slaughtered in the killing fields. Anyone with education, knowledge of a foreign language, or any Westernization was targeted for death. Only a few of the elite survived by fleeing abroad or successfully hiding their background. People with no education were appointed as leaders.

The towns were emptied. All cash was declared illegal. Education and medical care stopped. All children were required to address their parents as "comrade". Children seven to ten years old were put to work in the fields to pick up animal dung for fuel and to do light clearing. Children ten to seventeen (including Beuk) became agricultural laborers, toiling for eight hours daily except in harvest season when an additional three hours evening period of labor was enforced. A big gong was struck to announce the times to start and stop. In return, they received very little food, served by communal kitchens. Men 18 to 35 became "mobile workers", serving wherever they were sent, while those over 35 were put to work weaving. There was never enough to eat — just a small ration of rice twice a day, rarely vegetables or meat. Buek told us that the only visitors to the monuments at that time were a few Chinese. He could hear the buses carrying them pass on road six near the fields where he worked.

Rice and gold were the basis of a barter economy. One small can of rice would pay for a movie ticket. Twenty kilos of rice would buy one kilo of pork. (Today, a worker hired by the government to clean around the Angkor temples, is paid $2 per day plus a small ration of rice and cooking oil. A government clerk earns $20 per month. A middle manager in the tourist industry earns $70-80 per month, while a hotel general manager might make $300.)

With the fall of the Pol Pot regime, the country remained in a state of anarchy and civil war through the 1980s. It was only in the 1990s that recovery began, and in the last half-dozen years that tourism has taken off. Although the people are still poor, health services and education have been restarted, and many foreign governments are helping to build roads and other infrastructure and to preserve and reconstruct damaged tourist sites. Malaria remains a problem, and Beuk told us that his own 17-month-old daughter has recently contracted a mild case of the disease.

Beuk himself is a fine example of the entrepreneurial spirit of the country. Somehow he has learned sufficient English to become a guide, and now he is attending a night class in Japanese to increase his earning ability.

Vietnam: Changing Winds

(by Julie Hill)

*B*etween November 10 and November 27, 2002, I was privileged to visit Vietnam, covering over 1,000 miles from the Mekong Delta to Hai Long Bay in the North.

A group of 14 redoubtable travelers journeyed under the leadership, guidance and tutelage of one of the best guides of Abercrombie and Kent — Eugen Koenitz. Eugen is an old Asia hand, born in Malaysia where his family from the 18th century was involved in trade, tea planting, and government administration. The family heritage has served him well. His expertise allowed him to be the chosen guide for the former Prime Minister of Canada Pierre Trudeau, US government officials, and many people involved in the arts. But let's stop the commercial on Eugen and proceed with my impressions.

I wanted to go to Vietnam, as it is one of the few Asian countries I have not explored with Arthur, a new place with no memories. It worked most of the times. It can be an easy place to love Vietnam when you are roaming undisturbed through thousand-year-old palace ruins in the Imperial City of Hue, when you are meandering through the picturesque market of Hoi An, when you are walking on the sandy beaches of Da Nang, when you are eating another of those giant grilled prawns, when you are fussed over in a tailor's shop in the ancient fish port of Hoi An being fitted for custom-made silk clothing that will be delivered at the hotel within 24 hours, when you experience your first ever ride in a military helicopter.

We started in Ho Chi Minh City (HCM), formerly known as Saigon, a city of eight million people; it is an exciting place to visit, but at times a tiresome one. Nowhere the activity is more intense as HCM the country's largest commercial and industrial hub and a fascination mix of Eastern and Western cultures. There are no glittering skyscrapers, still a low-level architecture with the exception of the new Caravelle Hotel where we stayed. Outside shops sell electronics, jewelry, clothes, dryers, scooters ($1,200 for a Honda, $800 for a Korean-made, and $500 for a Chinese-made scooter) while noodle vendors squat on the sidewalk, serving meals all day from their portable kitchen. The streets were crowded with taxis, small trucks, and motorbikes. We were told that two million motorbikes are registered in HCM. They travel six to eight abreast. There seem to be no lanes, few traffic lights and only one rule: do not hit any one. Crossing the street takes courage. I walked alone towards the Saigon River, crossing a couple of busy streets. I simply took a deep breath, walked slowly and deliberately, keeping an eye on the traffic, to ensure I was seen, and miraculously the scooters swerved around me every time.

HCM may not have the high-rise buildings of Bangkok or Makati, but the investors are coming fast and the highly entrepreneurial Vietnamese seem concentrated in developing capitalism to its limit. All those millions of motor scooters in the streets are a good measure of a strongly rising middle class.

We did the usual sights of a tour: the old Cathedral, the post office, a temple in Cholon. I had a drink with fellow travelers at the old Continental and Majestic hotels, so well described by Graham Greene in *The Quiet American*. Parenthetically the film had just been released and was brilliantly reviewed. We all reread the book during the trip.

Tourists were mostly from Europe (France) and elsewhere in Asia (China), while very few tourists were from the United States. Vietnam hosts two million tourists a year (by comparison, 10 million visit Thailand and only 80,000 visit Myanmar a year). Shops, hotels, restaurants and tourist offices were everywhere. Every one offers a smile or a "hello" and has something to sell. Every one wants a piece of this new economic boom. Vietnam has the air of a place just about to explode. Trying to walk to a nearby market I could not take two steps without being asked to buy something Postcards? Cyclo ride? Taxi? Chewing gum? Stamps? Spring rolls? Cigarettes? Beer? Hotel? Guidebook? Guide? Hot and frustrated I retreated back to the comfort of the air-conditioned tourist bus provided by A&K.

The Americans in our group wanted to see the Cu Chi tunnels, some 40 kilometers (four hours on a bus) from HCM and barely six miles from the Cambodian border. It was here that the Viet Cong constructed an amazing underground base that extended beneath the boundaries of the American base from which they were able to launch surprise attacks within the base itself. It is a fantastic network 200 kilometers long, a network of command posts, hospitals, living quarters, weapon factories, several stories deep in places. The place is invisible from the outside, so cleverly concealed. We started with a short propaganda movie and then proceeded to the tunnels. I spent only few minutes on the first level. I felt so claustrophobic even if it was one of the enlarged tunnels. I was crouched suffocating from heat and dust; I decided I did not need further experience of the conditions in which the Viet Cong lived.

We proceeded to Tay Ninh, just six miles from the Cambodian border to witness a Cao Dai ceremony. I had never heard of the Cao Dai sect with its two million followers. It is a synthesis of Buddhism, Hinduism, Islam, Christianity, and Taoism. It was very colorful ceremony with all those participants wearing white supposedly communicating with spirits through séances, ancestor worship and meditation. The cathedral was full of tourists, mostly French.

Another day we proceeded to the Mekong Delta. Fortunately they were no remnants of "war" to visit. We had seen the Mekong source a couple of years earlier in the high mountains of the province of Yunnan, from where it impetuously precipitates. We crossed the Mekong from Thailand to Laos on our way to Vientiane in the mid-'60s and we took a boat ride in Phnom Penh earlier this year, but here I was alone at the Mekong's delta. A great, splendid, noble, majestic, mighty river, the Mekong has not managed to attract the same level of interest as the Nile or the Amazon, although French scholars have written a few books about it. Today faceless scientists, mostly Chinese, accumulate raw data and calculate the acre-feet of impounded water, the kilowatt-hours of wired light and power to be produced. For me it was exhilarating to stand wide-eyed in the middle of the river. Sixty million people live on or are conveniently near its more navigable portion. It is possible to travel only certain portions of the river; there are a great variety of small power craft that carry passengers between various destinations. Rates, fares schedules, and accommodations remain very flexible. It is difficult to cover the river along its length. I took a pirogue, a gondola–like canoe of great elegance and durability, and my boatman bounced with grace, daring, and skill. My other traveling companions stayed on land, taking photographs of the flotillas of small boats moored together, buying lychees and bananas from boat to boat, buying conical hats, and photographing my adventure in the middle of the river.

We stopped at a French plantation for the evening. It was a rubber plantation. The destructive Agent Orange had damaged the whole area. The trees, although tall, looked very anemic, the bush very thin. It will be years before the trees attain the majesty of their counterparts in Malaysia and produce rubber of quality. There were abundant cashew nuts but the plantation and its accommodation was a poor image of its past glory.

From HCM we flew in a Russian plane to Hue and stayed at a charming little hotel, the Morin. It was raining most of the time and I had to buy one of those inexpensive plastic raincoats. Hue is an old historical city. We visited royal tombs, pagodas, a mausoleum, the museums, the citadel, and markets. The Thien Mu pagoda is the symbol of Hue; it was a Buddhist sanctuary laced with so many legends, which our local tour guide recited faithfully.

Local guides speak good English, but as soon as their English improves they get better jobs in commercial enterprises. They are all provided by the government and our US-based tour operator has very little to say. Hi, our guide in HCM, was very open, and spoke of the corruption and challenges of the country. However, our guide in Hanoi, Tyin, recited the party line; he was very courteous, very well trained. I suppose you have to be a Party member to be an English-speaking guide for a major tourist operator. Fortunately we had Eugen in the evening answering our questions. Why Hi was so open? Did the driver understand English? Did he report the conversation?

The ride to Da Nang is considered one of the must-see's. The morning was hazy and foggy, and we drove through long stretches of small faded buildings with their metal security doors rolled shut, advertising restaurants, *hot toc* (bridal shops), *bia hai* (fresh beer), and karaoke (no translation necessary). Da Nang was reached by crossing the Hay Van Pass (Pass of the Clouds). We went through a couple of fishing villages, and then the road followed the coastline. This route, formerly known as the Mandarin road, was strictly for the use of mandarin bureaucrats at that time. It is a pretty ride but nothing spectacular. Our home for a couple of nights was the Furama Resort, a Japanese modern resort. You could be anywhere else in the world, with its Four Seasons quality and service with plush accommodations, great views, impeccable service, and superb Vietnamese food.

We spent a day in Hoi An, one of those gems that you often come across in Southeast Asia. It is only 15 miles (a one-hour drive) from Da Nang and we spent a delightful day there. It is an ancient trading port that has been frequented by the Chinese, Japanese, Dutch, and Portuguese traders. The Bon River, which connected Hoi An to the sea, silted up and became unnavigable in the 19th century; at this time Da Nang took over as the main port of the Central Region,

The most famous place in Hoi An is the Japanese covered bridge which was built in the 16th century by the Japanese community to connect their neighborhood with the Chinese quarter. There is a small pagoda in the entrance of the bridge with a pair of dogs at one end and a pair of monkeys in another. For most tourists, it is a shopper's paradise, with tailors willing to make anything "en measure" for no more than $10 and to deliver it your hotel by next morning! As most of the shoppers were French and were paying in euros, we found ourselves becoming international bankers willing to purchase the euros for dollars at a favorable exchange rate! The market was a gem and many films use the little town as a background. We visited a couple of homes, the entrance regulated by the government. You clearly feel even in this small town that your movements are controlled.

We learned during our trip that, by the mid-'80s, the government had relaxed its land tenure program. Communes divide the land to families, giving an equal proportion of good land to every one. A small amount of tax is paid yearly. Land can be inherited or sold. But if the government wants it back for whatever reason, as for widening a road, they can take it and recompense the owner at a fraction of its value.

We hopped on a flight to Hanoi, the northern capital. The center of the country's Communist Party, Hanoi with its three million people has a reputation as a gracious reserved city, older and quieter than HCM, retaining a bit more of its French colonial heritage and architecture. Also, it is roughly a thousand miles to the north and it was cooler, so that we all needed our sweaters. Hanoi proved to be my favorite place. I could have stayed longer; three days was not enough. What a gem of a city, with the remnants of French colonial architecture. We stayed at the old wing of the Metropole Hotel, which was at full occupancy, as the cruise lines, tour operators, and international business people opt to stay there. The hotel is centrally located, well run, and charming, though exorbitantly expensive by Vietnamese standards. The restaurants were superb, with baguettes and croissants being baked every hour; the variety of French cheeses was staggering and some meals would rival a two-star restaurant in Paris.

The opera house is a smaller version of the Palais Garnier, the Paris opera house. There is a new hall built for a conference of Francophone people, inaugurated few years ago by President Mitterand. The presidential palace could be any *grande maison* in France. The Fine Arts museum contained a diverse collection of artifacts, sculpture, paintings, woodcarvings, and lacquerware, as well as many modern Vietnamese painters. However the paintings were all propaganda, all brave soldiers, Uncle Ho, and victories at Dien Bien Phu. Still it was an impressive museum, with well-displayed items. Its museum shop was one of the best galleries in town, with prices not yet of international standards.

We were told that government is not issuing any more scooter licenses. You can only trade your old license. Hanoi is jammed with traditional tourist sites including ancient temples and pagodas, French cathedrals, scenic lakes and parks and buildings dedicated to the late Vietnamese ruler Ho Chi Minh, including a museum, the stilt house where he lived in the '60s, and the outside of the mausoleum where his remains are displayed. The mausoleum was closed for repairs. The city is compact, walkable, and beautiful. The old quarter has been the city's commercial center for more than 1,000 years. We took a cyclo ride to reach it, and then walked back to our hotel loaded with our shopping. The district begins at the edge of Hoan Kiem Lake, edged by weeping willows and a small park where young and old gather to exercise at dawn. At one time each of the narrow twisted streets in the quarter was named for the type of goods you could buy there — silk, bamboo, copper. Today, the old names are still used but the streets have become less specialized. Stores sell merchandise of all sorts from traditional water puppets, carved wooden boxes, and silk clothing, to two-dollar T-shirts printed with the image of Ho Chi Minh. The exception is the meat and produce market with sections still dedicated exclusively to astoundingly fresh fish, flowers, live chickens, vegetables, herbs, and fruits. It became a favorite place.

I decided to skip the army museum and war museum but I had to see the famous Hanoi Hilton. Part of it was reconstructed: a real guillotine from French times was on display, as well as the solitary cell where John McCain spent more than five years, gruesome torture instruments, and mannequins of American soldiers, so real, so gruesome that I had hard time getting over them.

We spent an enchanting evening at a water puppet show; the whole theater was closed to outsiders and the performance was reserved exclusively for us. Water puppetry has a prestigious place in traditional Vietnamese culture; its gracefulness has to be seen to be believed and you ask yourself how it can be done. The show, just 30 minutes long, was followed by entertainment of traditional Vietnamese musical instruments. It was splendid and brilliant. Dinner was served at the Puppet Theater under the trees, catered by the Metropole Hotel and another triumph of French cuisine.

We went to Haiphong by bus, a good six hours' drive on a bumpy road. Haiphong is an industrial city that has preserved its colonial architecture with a French opera house and several Catholic churches. From there we proceeded for another two hours to Ha Long Bay where we spent the night. It proved for many of us to be the highlight of the trip. Ha Long Bay, meaning the Bay of Descending Dragons, has been designated a UNESCO World Heritage site. It is a 3,000-island archipelago that looks like a mountain range, with limestone rocks rising up from the sea. The islands consist of dolomite and limestone, which have eroded into exotic shapes. We took a small boat and cruised among them. The ride was more beautiful than anything I have seen in China in Guilin. There were a number of red-sail junks gliding gently as we made our way through the islands and we stopped to visit one of the caves. The views from the entrance of Thien Cing cave with its cascading torrents of water was spectacular. No one warned us, however, of the more than 300 steps needed to reach the cave and another 300 steps to get back. By the time we finished exploring, we were all exhausted. Fortunately we did not have to face an eight-hour bus ride. We were treated with a helicopter ride back to Hanoi, just 30 minutes away. It was my first helicopter ride in a military aircraft and the view of the bay as the helicopter hovered over it was nothing but spectacular.

What can I say about Vietnam? It stood the ultimate test of a nation. China occupied it for more than a thousand years. It was conquered, it was divided, it was wrecked by a sorrowful war and it was locked out in the wilderness. Yet, today it is again a nation on the move. The Vietnamese Zen Master Thich Nhat Hanh says: "Life is filled with suffering but . . . to suffer is not enough. We must be in touch with the wonders of life." For Vietnam that moment may have finally arrived.

G